MANY A FAR COUNTRY

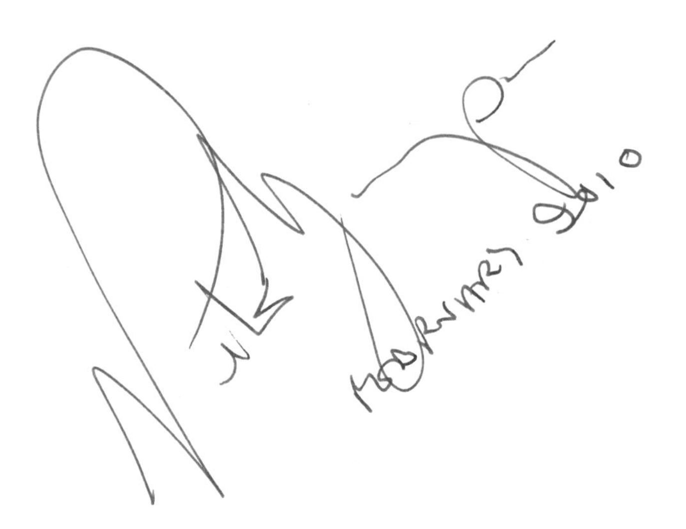

Also by Peter Youngson:

The Long Road – A Driver's Guide to Jura

Jura – Island of Deer

Ancient Hebridean Tales of Jura

MANY A FAR COUNTRY

PETER YOUNGSON

Illustrated by Lyn Youngson

Astute Scotland Limited
www.astute.uk.com

2009

First published in Great Britain in 2009 by
Astute Scotland Limited, Caxton House, Silvie Way,
Orchardbank Business Park, Forfar Angus DD8 1BF

ISBN 978-1-897950-03-6

Typeset in 11/14 point Constantia

Printed by Astute of Forfar, Angus, Scotland

For Margaret – who longed to see

this little book published,

and who I miss more than I could

ever have imagined

Contents

List of Illustrations

Acknowledgements

When the text of this book was first completed I asked five close friends if they would agree to read it, and give me an honest appraisal of it. All of them encouraged me to publish, at the same time making a number of constructive suggestions as to how the text might be improved. These folk know themselves who they are and how grateful I am to them.

My daughter Lyn has produced the attractive illustrations at the beginning of each chapter. She has illustrated books of mine before, but never more felicitously than now. I am happy to express my thanks to her here.

I am also indebted to my cousin, Alan Robiette, for his patient and painstaking copy-editing of the text and for his advice throughout on questions of typography and book design, all of which have contributed greatly to the final state of the book. I myself have learned a great deal during this process, and now feel more confident about possible future projects.

In addition I am most grateful for all the assistance I have had from Alastair Donald and his colleagues at Astute in Forfar in bringing the book to printed form.

Preface

I'm not sure when I first encountered the Bible story known as 'The Prodigal Son'. Since I was taken to church every Sunday as a child, I suppose I heard Jesus' parables either there or in Sunday School. The one that had a great fascination for me was the one about the boy who ran away from home, and had a high old time, and then was sorry and came back again. When I grew up and decided that I wanted to become a minister in the Church of Scotland, this story became a kind of personal theme. I made it in a way my 'Trade Mark'. It had a high priority in my early preaching and teaching in every new church I went to. I adopted it as part of my adult thinking, and as part of that process I gave it a new hero and began to think of it more as the story of 'The Forgiving Father', rather than of the younger son, and to see the point of the story in the fact that his father accepted him back after he had upset him so much by going away.

None of this comes anywhere near to explaining why the story gripped me so firmly as a child, and looking back as far as I can, I think the key to my interest lay in the place the younger son went to. In St. Luke's words from the Authorised Version of the Bible:

'He gathered all together, and took his journey to a far country.'

It was the 'far country' that caught my imagination. Where was it? What was it like? How did you get there? Where would be my "far country"?

There were 'far countries' in my childhood. My father went to one called Egypt throughout the Second World War, leaving my mother and me at home.

There was a special one where, seated at my desk at the window of my tiny bedroom, my mind's eye could take me anywhere I wanted to go, and my dreams were infinitely more attractive than the painful reality of having my father back in my house, and home from the War.

Later I escaped from home to do my National Service, and I was posted to the 'far country' of Hamburg in North Germany for a year and a half.

Other 'far countries' followed; I went to London to make my fortune, but found little at the end of that rainbow.

My church ministry took me to a Glasgow housing scheme called Easterhouse, a 'far country' as different from my upbringing as could be imagined.

Later still, my wife and children and I spent many years in the Hebridean Island of Jura – truly a 'far country' to end all 'far countries'.

And there were others!

All this is why, now that I have written down something of my experiences and of the people and places I have known in my life, the account which follows can be given only one title: 'Many A Far Country'.

Peter Youngson
Kirriemuir, 2009

Chapter One: The Far Country of a Wartime Childhood

It was a War all right. Of that I was quite sure. I didn't know quite what a War was, but I knew it was the explanation of all kinds of funny things that were happening.

It was why Mummy and Daddy and I left our nice house in Aberdeen and went to stay in a nasty furnished room in a village called Scone, and later to a similar room in the town of Perth. This was so that Daddy could do what was called his training.

It was also why, when he came to stay with us at the week-ends, Daddy wore his khaki uniform with lots of shiny brown leather belts, and a very special broad one that went diagonally across his chest which was called his Sam Browne. I thought the belts were wonderful, and I thought he looked terrific. He was very slender and elegant with his smooth shiny black hair, and his slightly olive complexion. He looked so different from me, that I sometimes wondered if we could really be part of the same family – I with my bright red hair, and chubby round face – but Mum and Dad seemed to assume that I definitely belonged to them, so I supposed everything was all right.

I started school in Scone and in Perth, and began to do reading and writing and sums. Sometimes there were friends of Dad's who visited at the week-end. Angus Liddle, a friend from Aberdeen, was a young officer in the Air Force and wore a different uniform from Dad, who I knew was in the Army. Angus took time to play with me, and on one memorable occasion brought me a model aeroplane. It came as a kit in a cardboard box, and was made by Frog. The kit could be put together very simply, and when the elastic was fully wound up the plane flew beautifully, even landing without crashing. The model was of course a Spitfire. I can still see a sunny grassy meadow with my father and Angus Liddle flying the plane to and fro across it. There was a lot of shouting and laughing, and this remains my happiest recollection of my early childhood.

When father finished his training he went away, and mother and I went home to Aberdeen by train. The flat in Aberdeen was just as we had left it a year before, and I think we simply went on as if nothing had happened.

I don't think I really remember much about what happened before we went to Perth. My ideas of my first five years are probably reinforced by what mother told me. We had been away for a whole year and I had to go to school in Aberdeen. In fact it was actually a going back, because I had been to Gordon's College before.

Although I didn't know it, there was never any doubt about where I would be going to school. My grandfather had been ambitious about his children, and he had managed to pay the fees so that my father and his twin brother Lex could both attend the prestigious Robert Gordon's College. This imposed a consequent responsibility on my father, and my name was put down for Gordon's College the moment it was known that I was a boy.

I was five years old on 14th May 1939, so I was ready to go to school at the beginning of the autumn term, and I apparently duly attended Robert Gordon's Kindergarten One. Mother often said later that the date was 1st September, and that I was issued with my gas mask on that day. I don't remember my first day; however, I do recall falling in the playground while pretending to be a railway train. Both my knees were skinned by the rough tarmac, and Miss Clark, my teacher, applied chunks of cotton wool to the scraped patches. The cotton wool stuck fast and had to be pulled off later at home. This resulted in quite conspicuous scars which re-surfaced as identification marks on my army passbook, eighteen years later, as 'scars on both knees'!

I think I was only at Gordon's for a few days. War was declared with Germany on 3rd September 1939, and family tradition said that my father volunteered for military service the next day, and was accepted. As a fully qualified Chartered Accountant it was decided that he would be of most use in the Royal Army Pay Corps, and he was posted to Perth to begin his training. Mother always said that he left for Perth on his thirty-fifth birthday on 13th September. When my father left Perth it was to go to a Pay Corps appointment in London. He was there during the blitz. Later he was promoted and sent out to Cairo. When the war came to an end he was still there, with the rank of Major. He took many leaves locally, but he never came home.

My Own Arrival

With my father now absent, I would live the next five years in the closest possible contact with two people other than mother. These were my grandfather and my grandmother, called Granda and Granny.

Granda Youngson was called Peter and was born in 1877, one of the seven children of Alexander Youngson and Jane Anne Warrender. He became a flesher to trade, and in 1902 he married my Granny, Maggie Ann Donaldson. She was one of the seven children of James Donaldson, who had a draper's shop in Aberdeen. It was always said within the family that she had married beneath herself.

Granda was always known as P.Y. He worked hard and got together enough money to buy a new granite house in Mile-End Avenue in Aberdeen about 1904. The city was expanding west through streets of terraced houses like Mile-End Avenue. It was there in number 91 that my father James Donaldson Youngson – or Don as he was known – and his twin brother Lex were born in 1904. Their sister Kath arrived in 1907. The family home was the ground floor flat in a two storey house. In 1918, Granda managed to buy the upstairs flat as well, and the family moved up to a larger apartment, number 93, which had its own lined attic. He rented out number 91.

Don fell in love with my mother when she was a young nurse from Huntly, who looked after him when he had his appendix out in hospital in Inverurie. Jean MacDonald was an only child, whose mother had died of cancer when she was eighteen, and whose father remarried and stayed in Huntly. My father qualified as a CA, and they married in 1933 in a 'quiet wedding'. The need for the wedding to be a quiet one remains a family mystery, as I was not born until nine months later, and there would seem to have been no urgency.

Father's health broke down during their first year of marriage, and he was forced to give up his ambition to have his own accountancy business in London, to retreat to Aberdeen to be nursed at home until well, and then to find a job.

During her pregnancy, my mother had been working at a local nursing home, and it was there, at The Osborne, that I was born at twenty minutes past two in the morning of 14th May 1934.

There is a family story about my father's first visit to my mother and me. It comes from Mrs Morrison, who was not only the matron of the nursing home, but also a personal friend. I was apparently wrapped up and handed to my father.

My father's assessment was immediate. 'What an ugly looking owlet' (he pronounced the word 'oolet').

Mrs Morrison was outraged and snatched me away from him as if he was unworthy to handle the child.

My mother told me she had wanted to call me David, but the Youngson family insisted that I had to be named after my grandfather, and I was baptised Peter by Rev. W.W. Gauld, of Queen's Cross Church, who had conducted my parents' wedding.

When I was born we started off in Granda's attic, but when I was a year old he re-possessed the downstairs flat, and we moved in. No.91 became our home, and I would live there for the next eighteen years until I went into the Army.

I have no recollections of my first few years in Mile-End Avenue, although the family album has numerous photographs of me with my father and grandfather. Many of them are taken in Granda's beloved greenhouse. I have a very faint memory of a teddy I had when I was two, who appears in several snaps. I have a clear memory of a pram cover with a fringe, which is also in photos. In July 1939, when I was four, we had a holiday at Cullen, on the Banffshire coast. My father and I played cricket on the sand, and I clearly remember the wooden bat I used, which survived in our cellar for some years. I have good photos. War came in September, and we had our year away.

In Aberdeen with my Mother

My mother and I went back to live in a house I can still picture vividly. It had a fine front room, called the lounge and seldom used. At the back, looking out on to the garden, were the living room and my mother's bedroom. There was a tiny kitchen at the back door which led into the garden. There were two other rooms with special significance for me.

First, the bathroom. This was long and narrow with the washhand basin on the left, with the bath beyond, and the toilet at the far end, straight ahead as you went in. The bathroom was concerned in an incident which occurred about 1937, when I was three years old. Mother had become pregnant again. It seems that the new street was plagued with rats finding their way in from the farmland, then very near. Mother heard a noise coming from the bathroom. When she opened the door, she saw that the sound was coming from the toilet roll holder, rotating, apparently on its own. Toilet paper was streaming up over the edge of the bath, and when she went closer to see, there was a rat pulling the paper down the bath waste hole. She apparently collapsed, and immediately miscarried. Family lore said that my mother gave up all thought of having another baby after this.

This bathroom had been a place of fear for me as far back as I can remember. This may be because it was I who found my mother lying there, unconscious after the rat incident, as I was later told, although I have no recollection of this. Apparently I was the one who ran upstairs to tell Granny.

There may be another reason for my fear of the room. Mother couldn't ever keep any bad experiences she had to herself, and she probably established our bathroom as a dangerous and frightening place by telling me all about it.

The terror of the bathroom was located precisely, and I knew where it came from. It came from the cistern. The cast-iron water cistern was overhead and was flushed by pulling down on the round handle which dangled down at the bottom of its chain. As I now know, but didn't then, this chain was attached to a crank which when pulled down allowed the contents of the cistern to rush down into the bowl. It was this rushing sound which I found most alarming, and I literally could not bear to stand and listen to it, or watch it happening. I was never able to give a clear shape to what it was that I thought was going to get me, in connection with the cistern, but I was absolutely convinced that something was. To deal with this problem, I would complete my toilet, and do up my trousers and wash my hands. Then I would prop the door open with something. It had to be propped open as it would swing shut if allowed to. I then approached the chain, reached up, and pulled it firmly down. The split second I had done that, I sprinted for the door and slammed the door shut behind me. If I got everything just right, I could be outside the door and into the hall before the water arrived in the bowl. If I got anything even slightly wrong, I wouldn't make it, and I was faced with complete disaster. I can't remember the exact shape of the disaster, but I know that it was very awful.

Only my own little room is left. Standing at my open door you looked at my window which looked out through the gable wall of the entire block into our lane. On the right was my bed. There was enough room to take a normal single bed, and it must have been about five feet long, as I was still sleeping in it right up until I went off to do my National Service. To the left of my bedroom door there was a shallow hanging wardrobe and beyond it a chest of drawers.

My room was directly under the staircase of the upstairs flat and the ceiling sloped sharply down from above the right hand edge of my floor passage. By the time it reached the far edge of my bed it was only three feet high, and it continued on down into our Glory Hole. This was where our suitcases lived.

After mother and I returned to Aberdeen I went back to Gordon's College. Mother suffered from lumbago at this time. She always put it down to having to lift heavy patients during her nursing days in London, which on reflection may very well have been true. At any rate she was in bed for nine months, with a housekeeper in attendance called Miss Burns. Miss Burns was a Roman Catholic. Mother was brought up with little or no contact with Catholics, and was suspicious of her. Miss Burns went off to Mass early on Sunday mornings, and went out every evening. Our neighbour in the house just across the lane, one Mrs Campbell, was another one, and could also be seen setting off for church at what mother called an ungodly hour. Mother later told me that one Sunday, Miss

Burns was fed up with me larking about in my bath, and held my head under the water to punish me. Mother said that I tottered into her bedroom, black in the face, and she kept me there all night with her. She sacked Miss Burns when she came in. The doctor visited and she told him she had arranged for an invalid chair. She said he was angry, and told her she wouldn't be able to manage on her own. She used the chair for six or seven months, but eventually got herself back on her feet. I have a dim recollection of the wheelchair, and of fetching and carrying lots of stuff for mother while she was using it.

I Encounter Music

It was in the winter of 1941, once I had re-started at Gordon's College, that on one of our regular visits to Queen's Cross Church I first heard a piece of serious music. My grandfather was singing a solo. I later learned that he had a renowned tenor voice, and sang solos in oratorios, not only in his church choir, but with the University Choir. On this occasion he was singing 'Comfort ye my people', from the opening of Handel's *Messiah*. He was sixty-four at the time, and I was seven. I remember as if it was yesterday. His appearance, his immense poise, and the wonderful sound he made, moved me profoundly, and I dimly remember resolving to make similar exciting noises myself.

About the same time mother and I went to hear her friend Lily singing in church. I remember this event too, and her solo, which was 'Alleluia' from Mozart's *Exultate Jubilate*. This was another magical experience, but with a different kind of identity, for I felt I could hear and feel this music in my head. Lily came for lunch after the service, and in the afternoon I presented myself, and with no warning or permission launched into my own remembered version of the opening passage of the 'Alleluia'. I don't know now how accurate it would have been, or how much of it I remembered, but it seemed effortless to me, and it completely bewildered Lily. My mother of course knew perfectly well that I had a boy-soprano voice, as I was forever singing around the house, but I don't suppose Lily had known. She was insistent that I should sing, and that I should have lessons, and she remained a firm supporter of my efforts for many years. I think from that time on I began to sing more and more on my own, and mother, who could play the family piano quite well, taught me a lot of songs which I sang in front of family and friends. I think I enjoyed this, which fell into the category of showing off, and I certainly wasn't anxious about it.

The Air Raids

Up until the air raids, I suppose the war was just the thing that had taken Daddy away, but with visits from German bombers it became more personal.

During those early war years P.Y. enlisted in the ARP, and was frequently out on patrol duty at nights. There were more air raids in Aberdeen than is generally realised, and some involved a considerable amount of damage. One night, probably in January or February 1942, my mother was entertaining old friends – Lily Liddle, and Deeny and John Low – when the air-raid warning went. John was Lily's boy friend, and he and his sister Deeny were frequent visitors. In an air raid everyone crowded into my tiny bedroom under the stairs. 'If everything else fell down in a direct hit, the stairs would survive,' we were told, so my room was the safest place.

Mother, Granny and our three guests all crowded in, and stories were told to keep our spirits up as distant thunder spoke of the bombs dropping nearby. Several explosions which we could clearly hear actually rattled the glass in the window, and Granny was obviously worried about P.Y. who was out on his rounds. He was by then in his sixties. In due course the all-clear sounded, and shortly after, Granda appeared at the bedroom door. He appeared to be covered from head to toe in some greenish substance – glutinous in texture, and smelling most foul. He always stammered a little when excited, and I can still hear him: 'There's n-n-nothing l-l-l-left of Westburn Road.'

Granny told him not to be silly, and to calm down, and she shepherded him away to get washed and changed. I think his clothes later were disposed of. Our visitors set off for home in the early light, only to return in a few minutes to confirm excitedly that the old man had been right. Westburn Road had received several direct hits. One bomb had landed on a fully occupied concrete Anderson shelter which had withstood the impact and successfully protected the lives of its fourteen or so inhabitants. It later became clear that P.Y. had shown a rash degree of curiosity, and was still intently watching an approaching bomber, until the moment when he could see its stick of bombs slowly fall. The blast of the nearest explosion lifted him bodily over a nearby privet hedge and dumped him into a front garden. This garden unfortunately belonged to the house of a curious and eccentric old lady at the corner of Argyll Place, who gave refuge to stray cats and dogs, and whose garden was always deep in animal excrement. The state of my returning Granda was explained, and his stories were taken more seriously from then on.

We had several major air raids. I remember being told about the cork factory in Constitution Street. It was apparently vital to the war effort: presumably this had more to do with life jackets than with wine bottles. On one such raid, a high explosive bomb fell in my school playground and resulted in a whole week's holiday.

The memory of the air raids with everyone packed into my tiny room brings the room itself back to mind. When air-raid refugees crowded into it they had to sit all along my bed, and I got pushed back to the point at which I almost fell under the curtain into the low dark corner where the suitcases lived. The wee room became very cramped and crowded. The atmosphere was tense, and I remember the air raids as quite enormous fun.

A Flight of Darts

Although the wheel chair had been pensioned off, and was no longer in use, it still lived in a corner in the front room, and mother continued to have treatment for her back. This consisted of weekly sessions of massage. Masseurs would come to the house by appointment. The first I remember was called Mr Ackerberg. He was a tall thin man with a heavy continental accent. I know I used to think he might be a German spy. After he stopped coming, his place was taken by a Mr Smith.

Mr Smith provides the setting for one of my most vivid memories of this period. It seems likely that I had just had my ninth birthday. Mother always tried to give me splendid birthdays and Christmasses. I know that she felt that I shouldn't be penalised by the war and by Dad being away.

On this occasion one of my presents was a set of darts and a dartboard. This was a pretty daring gift for a cosseted boy like me, and I doubt if mother actually bought it herself. Perhaps Uncle Jack next door got it. There was nowhere inside the house which would be considered suitable for the darts, so the dart-board was hung on a nail on the inside of the coal cellar door, which could be opened back against the wall. Granda put the nail in the door, and had a few goes with the darts himself.

No doubt the excitement of the game began to pall when played alone, and I was always an immensely solitary little boy. Alan Ross and Hamish Martin were the two boys in my class who gave me most grief. They were rough and physical, and quite undeterred by getting the strap. (Corporal punishment was a fact of life in Gordon's Primary, and the belt was administered daily, although not to me.) They called me a mummy's boy, which I was, and a teacher's pet, which I certainly did my best to be. Their bullying stopped short of punching and hitting, and mainly took the form of name-calling, and pinching of books and pencils, and especially of articles of clothing. I am certain that it would have been with the motive of ingratiating myself with Alan and Hamish that I would have told them about my darts set. They announced that they would come to see them after school. This was an unheard of event, as any friends I had were not invited home with me, for I knew that mother would not admit them to the house. In this case the darts were outside in the garden, and with Mr Smith at work on mother's back she would hardly know anything about it. I imagine I ran in to get the darts, and announced that Alan and Hamish had come to the garden to see them. There wouldn't have been a lot that mother could do about it at the time, and no doubt Mr Smith would have reassured her that all would be well. I remember that we had a happy time throwing the darts until the fun began to pall on Alan and Hamish. They knew a variant game which related to air raids and bombers. In this game the dart board was laid on the ground and the darts were thrown high in the air to loop over and hurtle down, and hopefully land on the target.

The game was as exciting as it had appeared likely to be and discretion was thrown to the wind. I must have been kneeling to collect up fallen darts when a dart, thrown high in the air by one of the boys came down unseen from a considerable height and hit me on my right knee. At that time short trousers were the rule, and the knee in question was bare. The dart buried itself deeply in my knee, and remained there, sticking out. I don't remember any pain, but there was certainly an element of shock, mixed with excitement that something truly dramatic had happened to me. I ran into the house where mother, surprisingly didn't panic, and Mr Smith pulled the dart out of my knee. There was hardly any blood, and an elastoplast was applied. The incident was over with hardly any fuss.

I didn't even get a day off school. However, the episode of the dart made a deep impression on me, as the dart itself had, and it came back to haunt me in all kinds of situations over the years. I think I dimly realised that there was often a price to be paid for showing off, and certainly that it was dangerous to go along with more powerful friends in the hope of impressing them. The situation had got out of my own control. I was aware, as mother later endlessly told me, that the dart in my knee could as easily have been in one of my eyes. Many years later, when doing my army service, I recognised similar dangerous situations, and warning bells rang, set off by the childhood encounter with the dart.

Gifts from Cairo

During these years I think I found father's absence difficult to understand, but there were various reminders of what was happening. There were letters. These were air mail, and the ones from him had exotic Egyptian stamps. I wasn't allowed to have these because they would have had to be cut off the corners, and mother didn't want her precious letters destroyed.

There was also the question of the packets of stamps. Father was evidently well placed in his position in the pay office in Cairo to collect any number of used stamps from the neighbouring states and countries. From time to time he sent home packages with stamps 'for me!'. These were collections of unused stamps which he must have bought from a dealer in Cairo. They were all very beautiful, and mostly of bizarre and unusual shapes. There were triangular stamps and lozenge shaped ones. Some were enormous, and there were many strange patterns. They came from countries with exotic names like Eritrea and Somaliland and often portrayed wild animals and birds and insects. They were wonderful!

I think I was well aware what these packages were really all about. I knew in my heart that he expected their contents to be waiting for him when he came home. Oh! They could be carefully stuck into my own album, but they would be there, and safe. So when I started taking them to school and using them to bolster my weak image there, I knew perfectly well I was doing wrong, and that some day there would be a reckoning. Some day, but not for a long time, and perhaps never. Dad's special stamps became my treasure – they could not only be drooled over by other boys in my class, but they could even be swopped for exciting things like Dinky Toys. I never told my mother what was going on, and she was pretty vague about things like stamps anyway. I think I started with the view that there were lots and lots of them, and that if I only swopped a few there would still be plenty left and no one would ever know the difference. In fact that idea is always a slippery slope, and the time came when there were only a few stamps left, and then there didn't seem much point in keeping the rest. Finally there were none! The long term result was exactly as I had feared, but not feared sufficiently.

When my father finally came home and found that all his precious stamps had disappeared he flew into one of the very few rages I ever saw, but much worse than that, he was bitterly disappointed by what I had done, and told me so in no uncertain manner. I think the stamp incident was one of the big ingredients in the dreadful atmosphere which developed between us in the years after the war; and even in later life, when we had established a much better and more adult relationship, neither of us ever, ever, referred to the matter of the stamps again.

Books and Toys

For some unknown but somewhat perverted reason I seem to have portrayed my childhood as deprived, when speaking of it to other people in my early adulthood. I recall telling my own children that on one birthday I was given a tennis ball, and on the following year I was allowed to bounce it against the wall. This aberration may have its roots in my feeling of loss during the years when father was away in Cairo, and confirmed when things were not always as I had hoped when he returned. However, the reality is that I was more spoilt than deprived, and mother made great efforts to ensure that I would not suffer as a result of the war. My birthday in May meant I always had two separate times of present giving, and there were always presents from my father as well as my mother. In addition there was an annual Christmas gift from Great-Aunt Frances. This was not sent, but had to be collected. I had to get dressed in my Sunday best on Christmas morning and walk all the way round to her big house to be given it. It was always a book, and always an enriching one. I remember one entitled *A Child's Garland of Verses*. Her gifts were seldom even opened, far less read, but Aunt Frances had to be kept sweet, as she could easily make life unpleasant for my mother.

My favourite toy was Meccano. I think I started with a small set like No.3, and went on with accessory sets, some of which I think I bought with my own money. I quickly mastered the necessary skills and built every model in the manual. When I reached No.6 I dropped hints to mother about the next Christmas present, and was confident of what would arrive. On the day I opened my present and found that my mother had gone one better, and instead of 6A had bought me another set number six. She had thought that I would now have twice as much Meccano as before, and ought to be completely overjoyed. She would never have understood that the longed for accessory 6A, which would have turned my number six into a number seven, had all the new parts like gear wheels that number six did not have, and opened doors to wonderful new models. Since I never had any talent for inventing new designs of my own, the second number six was utterly wasted on me, and remained for ever unused. I may have acquired some spiritual merit from the fact that I never, ever told her how bitterly disappointed I was!

Keeping such secrets must have run in the family for my mother also did it with me. I always found buying her presents was a nightmare of confusion and indecision, until one year I spotted something I knew she would love. It was a small glass frame containing a design of flowers and some text such as 'Easte; Weste; Hame is Beste'. I thought it was beautiful and it used up all the money I had. She was suitably enchanted, and the whole thing passed off satisfactorily. It was shortly before I left home, when I was perhaps seventeen, that I was rummaging in forbidden drawers while mother was out, probably looking for her nursing handbooks which had drawings of genital organs. I encountered, carefully wrapped in tissue paper at the bottom of a drawer, the original motto gift. But it was not alone! Under it also in tissue paper were two other very similar gifts. In my childhood years I had evidently decided I had stumbled on a winning formula, but remembered only the satisfaction and feeling of success, and not the more basic fact that I had chosen this gift once already; and even twice. Mother never told me, or let me feel that she was disappointed although by the third one she must have been near screaming. I think this was real love!

I was an early and inveterate reader. Mother bought me a lot of the original Beatrix Potter books when I was very small, and I read them constantly. They have survived with my original scribbles and now belong to Lyn our daughter, who has read them to our grandchildren. I devoured all the Arthur Ransome series, and the Dr Doolittle books which I loved. Romany, Muriel and Doris and Raq probably started my love of the countryside. I read all the classics like *Treasure Island* and *Alice*. I also had a complete set of Arthur Mee's *Children's Encyclopedia.*

P.Y. and his Garden

As I have said, Granda was a skilled and enthusiastic gardener with a beautiful garden and greenhouse in which my father co-operated to the full. The greenhouse was his special joy. He was immensely proud of his chrysanthemums and dahlias, and did well with them at various shows. The enemy of the chrysanths were the earwigs in the garden – called forkytails in Aberdeen – and these were the subject of all-out warfare. Each plant was tied to a bamboo cane, and inverted on each cane was an empty shot-gun cartridge case. Every morning each cartridge case was tapped firmly in a small metal pan with a wooden handle, and the forkytails which fell out were squashed; either with an inverted cane, or with Granda's thumbnail, kept specially long for the purpose. He was interested in the comparative success of the various colours of cartridge cases, and I think he kept notes about which colours were most deadly.

It was the great chrysanthemums which produced the occasion for one of the few times when I was in trouble with my Granda. I had been playing in the garden, and whirling a cane around my head to hear the whistling sound it made. It struck a prize bronze chrysanthemum just below the head and knocked it clean off. Not knowing about such things, I decided it would be all right if I mended it. So I got some sticky stamp paper and made a little collar to surround and support the broken stem. I got some crayons or paints and coloured the paper green, and after I had finished it looked so good you couldn't see where the accident had happened. I went to bed happy. Unfortunately the next day the flower head had withered, and I was immediately in serious difficulty. It was suggested that I would have been all right if I hadn't tried to conceal the crime, but I knew then and still know now that this was a lie. I'd have been in trouble anyway!

The House Upstairs

Granny and Granda's house upstairs was a wonderland where I was allowed to go and play under Granny's eye. In my early years she used to lie on the settee in the best room, the front room, while I would play happily out of sight behind the sofa.

Through in the main sitting room there was a huge sideboard with some wonderful toys. These had been played with by my father and his brother and sister, and were still there for me. There was the yellow clockwork biplane that ran along the floor and looped-the-loop, and a round cardboard box with a picture of a cow's head on the side and holes in its lid, which mooed like a cow when it was inverted. Best of all there was a small bagatelle set, with pins and balls and a wooden pusher which could keep me occupied for hours. There was also a red cardboard box containing the set of dominoes. I was dependent on Granda playing this game with me, which I remember was something of a rare privilege which happened only when he had time, or perhaps when he could be bothered. The game was played according to normal rules, but Granda had a vocabulary of his own. When he couldn't go he was 'aye chappin' and he had several names for the double tiles. The double five was George Street, and the double six was Lang Hutcheon Street. There may have been other names which I no longer remember, but these always delighted me.

Everything about '93' was pure magic for me, and I never tired of exploring. The front staircase was splendid, with a beautiful stained glass window overlooking the bend in the stairs. On the wall at the head of the stair hung a picture. At the time I didn't know it was a famous etching by D.Y. Cameron. All I knew was that the subject was a strange figure with a lion's head and a man's body. His face had a kind of smile on it and he fascinated me and terrified me at the same time. I watched him carefully all the way up the stairs, and then scuttled past him to safety as fast as I could go. The etching has since come down to me, but has now become an old friend.

The sitting room had a long horizontal framed picture of *Widdicombe Fair*, which told the story in a series of individual coloured pictures. Each picture had the appropriate verse of the song underneath, and the chorus, with the wonderful list of names, ran along the bottom of the whole picture. The final picture showed the skeletons dancing and riding on the back of the old grey mare, which was also skeletal. 'And all the night long were heard skirlin' and groans, of Tom Pearce's old mare and her rattling bones.' I learned the song by heart, and still remember it, and loved to look at it, but was very frightened of the last picture, and tried not to see it.

In the famous blizzard of 1942 when the snow came to the top of our windows downstairs, Granny's window looked out to a snowfield which reached to only a few feet short of the windowsill. I remember longing to jump down into the snow, possibly with a parachute made out of the bedspread, but the dream died still-born. Fear of the unimaginable consequences stifled the exciting venture.

Granny and Granda at Home

Several domestic events in Granny and Granda's life created family stories. During the war, when meat was hard to come by, Granda could always come home with something from Murray's meat market, where he worked. The specialty used to be ox-tongue which was washed salted, cured and pressed. The pressing was done under a large rounded boulder which lived on top of the brander, or drain, at the back door. This big beach pebble was called The Stone of Destiny and was there for years. It was still there in the 1970s, when I went back to visit the house.

There was also the saga of the cheese. Granda had a passion for Stilton, and the stronger the better. A complete round was purchased in the autumn each year, and then wrapped in many layers of newspaper and buried with due ceremony at a chosen spot in the back garden. After the snows had gone it was dug up again, and carefully unwrapped. The outer layers were discarded, but the central portion was put beneath the cover of the cheese dish. This was a very special delicacy for Granda. There was one famous occasion when guests came to eat upstairs. This didn't happen very often, and I never knew if it was some kind of business dinner. It certainly wasn't family. It seems a shame that they did so little entertaining when I knew them, because my Granny was a wonderful cook, and some of her specialties, like her 'stovies', remain as a kind of benchmark of excellence in my memory. On this occasion the meal was concluded, and something possessed Granny to bring in the cheese. P.Y. blenched, and took the article from his wife. He held it momentarily before his guests:

'Cheese, cheese, cheese, cheese, nobody wants cheese, take it away, Minnie,' and, faster than the eye could follow it was gone. The emergency was over, but it had been a narrow escape and Granny never heard the last of it.

During those years when my father was away in Cairo, I had a lot to do with my Granda. I would often beg to go with him on various ploys especially on Sunday afternoons after church. He certainly carried his gardening activities to St Peter's Cemetery, off King Street, where he planted neat bedding plants around the plots of his parents' and other family gravestones. In those days there was a granite coping stone which enclosed each entire plot. He would load the plants and his tools on his wheelbarrow, and set off on foot. It was a really long walk to King Street. I should think it took nearly an hour. Granda would start on the flowers, and I would wander round the cemetery. It was absolute magic. I read all the names and the dates and tried to imagine what the people had been like. Finally he would tidy everything up, and we would set off for home, arriving tired but happy.

Our other favourite place was to go to Rubislaw granite quarry off Queen's Road. There we would walk to the edge of what was then the deepest hole in the northern hemisphere. Granda knew relatives who had actually worked there. Holding tight to Granda's hand I would peer down into the depths and see the tiny shapes of huts and cranes, and the crazy ladders that zig-zagged their way up the sheer walls.

Granda would step back, and looking around at great grey Aberdeen, he would spread his arms in a broad sweep:

'See now, Petery Boy,' he would say, 'Aa' this, came oot o' aa' that!' (All this came out of all that.) Late at nights when I couldn't sleep, I would lie in bed and try to drop all the buildings in the whole of Aberdeen back into the great quarry, one by one, and see if they all would fit in. Long before the hole was filled up, I'd be asleep.

Granny seemed to me always to be very hard on Granda. As he got older he began to suffer from loss of memory, and Granny would send him out to settle accounts for things like electricity, with a note pinned to his lapel saying who he was and where he lived.

In the year before he died I was in my last year at school. I was in the garden one day doing something at the door of the garden shed. Granda came past. He looked up at the shed and scratched his head.

'Aye, Petery Boy, I think that sheddie roof needs a spot of pint' (meaning paint).

'I think father has that in hand, Granda: I think he'll take care of it', I replied.

Granda took in the answer, nodded, and made his way up the garden. Before he reached the drying green he turned and came back.

'Aye, Petery Boy, I think that sheddie roof needs a spot of pint'.

I made the same rejoinder as before, and satisfied, he set off again. He never did get as far as the grass, and the shuttling conversation could have gone on all day, but suddenly the lower sash of Granny's sitting room window shot up with a bang.

'Come out of there you stupid old fool,' she screamed, and that put an end to it.

I best remember our weekly visits to Queen's Cross Church in the nineteen-forties, while dad was away. Granda would set off to walk just after half-past ten. My mother and I would leave some minutes later, but Granny would depart last of all, her hat pinned on securely, a dead fox round her neck. As we marched down Blenheim Place towards the distant kirk we would see P.Y. in front of us, and a glance over our

This is my grandfather, Peter Youngson.
He was always known as P.Y.

This is the only picture of my granny
in which she doesn't look grim.

My father, James Donaldson Youngson,
known as Don – here as a Lieutenant
in the Pay Corps during the war.

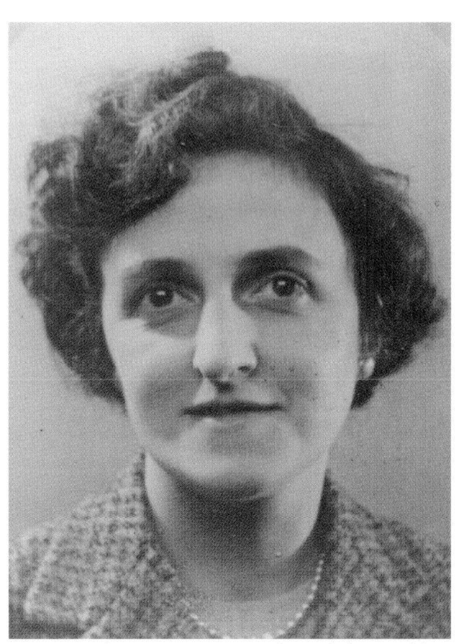

My mother, Jean Macdonald, as I like
to remember her from the war years.

Plate 2

Granda always seemed happy
to be with me.

My father and I on holiday in 1937.
I appear to have been very content
with him before the war.

Mother and I in the garden in 1941.

Having a good time in the snow in 1944
when I was ten.

Private 22720464, Youngson, P.
at Depot Seaforth Highlanders,
Fort George, in 1952.

Spey Barracks, Buxtehude,
near Hamburg: 1st Bn Seaforth
Highlanders in 1953.

Preparing to go on a border patrol
to check on crossings from
East to West Germany

Mounting guard, seen through the
window of the RSM's office.

Plate 4

Margaret in 1955, when we got engaged. The brooch is still a family treasure.

Queen's Cross Church, Aberdeen– my family kirk. Father and grandfather were elders here. I was singing here in the choir when Margaret and I met.

We were married in St Chad's Church, Poulton-le-Fylde on 10th September, 1956.

shoulders would show Granny bearing down on us. If the timing was right, and it often was, she would overtake us first, and in the last yards would pass P.Y., snapping out a warning: 'You'll be late!!' We would come abreast of him as we approached the door of the church, and I remember on one occasion seeing his head slowly shaking from side to side, and hearing him mutter to himself, in tones of mixed awe and admiration: 'My God! What a woman!'

My Illness

It was during 1944 that I became ill. The symptoms of my illness were simple. I ran a very high temperature with shivering and teeth chattering and lots of sweat. I fancy this started near the end of the summer term for I remember being taken home in a taxi from school one afternoon and being put to bed.

Mother's GP was in charge of my case, although I do remember 'consultations' in which other doctors, presumably specialists, came to the house. It was decided that I would have to stay in bed, although I was allowed up to go to the bathroom. I was moved out of my own little bedroom, and took up residence in a bed which occupied the alcove in the sitting room.

My illness was never given a name within my hearing, and I never knew what I was ill with. It was not until many years later that my mother whispered to me the dreaded letters TB, and I learned that I had had tuberculosis. However, it appears that I had the uncommon form in which the primary infection was not centred on the lungs, but on various abdominal glands.

As far as I can calculate I had completed my recovery shortly before my father returned from the army in May 1945, although it was not considered practical for me to go back to school for the remaining few weeks of the summer term. I must have been ill from about August 1944 to April 1945. This amounts to about eight months.

My routine during these long months, which stretched through a whole winter, followed a well-established daily cycle. I would wake early, feeling bright and cheerful, and full of energy. I would get my dressing gown on and get up and wash before having my breakfast in bed. My temperature would be taken, and was always found to be normal. In the mornings I would read and do school homework. There were regular visits from a lady who came in to help me, although I don't remember anything about her. This was also the time for such toys as I was allowed to have in bed with me, and the morning would pass happily with my mother doing housework around me, and often having neighbours in to see us both. After lunch everything would begin to change, and I would become tired and hot and flustered. During the afternoon I would get steadily more miserable, until by the late afternoon I would be very hot, and being bathed to cool me down. My temperature by then would be high enough to cause anxiety, and the doctor would often come in. I think I was often confused and delirious at this time of day, and remember still how wretched I used to feel. Mother ran the whole business like a hospital with a temperature chart at the foot of the bed. Of course she may have been under instructions to do this from the doctor. I know that she became very panicky as I got very hot, and would sponge me down with cold water. Years later she often spoke of my temperature as being dangerously high. Sometime during every evening the fever would break, and I would pour with sweat, soaking the sheets, and forcing me to sit huddled under a blanket in front of the fire while the bed was changed. In the late evening I would be much brighter, and would want to read, much against mother's wishes. It was often difficult to sleep, and later I would read with a small torch under the blankets. It was this practice which was later blamed for the problems with my eyes which resulted in my spectacles. In reality the problem with my eyes was diagnosed much later as severe astigmatism, which I couldn't have caused by any kind of naughtiness.

This daily cycle was profoundly wearisome for me, and during the bad times I remember crying a lot. The treatment for my condition seemed to include a number of intensely uncomfortable procedures.

I suppose there must have been some involvement of my chest as well, because I had several kinds of things applied to it. The worst of these was the kaolin poultice. This was a white chalky powder which was mixed to a firm paste with water, then wrapped in a cloth and put into very hot water to get warm. The hot paste was smeared over a piece of cloth with a knife and then laid against my chest and kept in place with a broad bandage until it cooled. I remember endless tearful protests against this treatment, which was horribly painful, but was supposed not to be of benefit if the paste wasn't hot enough to burn the skin.

There was also a kind of impregnated cotton wool called Antiphlogistine which was applied to my chest. This was less traumatic, but itched a lot. I also remember the trade name Thermogene, which may have been another version.

I remember quite a variety of mixtures which had to be taken. These varied in degrees of unpleasantness. There were also endless pills. I seemed to be quite unable to swallow pills with a glass of water, and my mother had to go through all kinds of complicated procedures to get pills into me. The routine I remember best was that they were crushed into a powder and the powder was mixed into a spoonful of raspberry jam and taken off a teaspoon.

During the winter of 1944 our house was invaded by a mouse. Food in the pantry was nibbled, and droppings appeared. I think mother tried cheese in a trap, but for some reason was not successful. She fell back on a technique she had seen in her own childhood in Huntly. This consisted of a china bowl inverted on the carpet in front of the fire and held up at an angle by a pencil propped under its rim. A length of string was tied to the pencil and led across the floor to my sickbed, which was for this purpose occupied by both my mother and me. A large piece of cheese was put under the bowl. The lights were put out and mother and I settled down to wait.

In due course the mouse could be heard coming along the linoleum, and after a suitable time it was deemed to be eating the cheese. Mother pulled the string. The bowl came down. The lights went on and there was the bowl with the mouse under it and able to be heard scrabbling about. A piece of cardboard was slid under bowl and mouse and they were all put on the floor inside the back door. Mother went back to her own bed, and in the morning Granda was left to dispose of the mouse. I thought my mother was both clever and brave.

My kind of TB was probably *M. bovis*, contracted from unpasteurised milk. On a hospital visit about April or early May 1945, a gland appeared on an X-ray. I was told that this meant that it had calcified, and that meant I was then completely recovered.

The War is Over

The end of my illness and the end of the Second World War seem to have occurred quite close together in time. At any rate, it was before I was able to go back to school that the news arrived that my dad was shortly to be coming home from Egypt.

This was a hugely exciting prospect, and I think was probably unclouded by apprehension. After all, the days of my embezzlement of postage stamps lay back in the past, before my months of illness. I suppose I told myself that these episodes could no longer be held against me.

My father was to arrive back in the south of England, and would have to pass through London. It was arranged that mother would take the train to London and that she and my father would meet there and spend a few days together, having a second honeymoon. A taxi was sent to the station in Aberdeen to collect them off the train, and I was allowed to go to the station in the taxi.

The black-haired darkly-tanned soldier in the splendid uniform, with polished belt and Sam Browne, was almost too glamorous to be spoken to, and I think I probably had nothing to say. A strange and unfortunate incident took place at this point, which boded ill for the future.

On arrival at Mile-End Avenue, I begged the door key from my mother, and ran up the path to get the door open while my father paid off the taxi. I remember thrusting the Yale key into the lock and twisting hard, only to have the key snap off in my hand, leaving the door still locked. My father came up the path, took in the scene, and probably uttered some mild expletive indicating annoyance along the lines of 'Stupid boy'. I was mortified, and dissolved into tears.

I think I saw this small incident as presaging a future in which all would not be well between my returned father and me, and this premonition was certainly borne out in full during the following seven years until I went into the Army. Looking back over those years I often used to say: 'The Second World War came to an end at that time, but the Third War was declared between my father and me.'

I have no clear recollection of what actually happened when he found out about the postage stamps collection. I think it was probably too upsetting for me to have retained it in my memory. I remember clearly how strange it felt having this quiet and remote man living in my house, with my mother. He went back to the Town House and resumed his duties in the City Chamberlain's department. All was far from well at work, and I learned later that the colleagues he had had there before the war who had not gone into the Forces had moved up various rungs of the promotion ladder, whereas he was forced to start again where he had left off. I remember in those days listening to what seemed like endless arguments in the sitting room between my mother and my father. My mother would be complaining that he was too acquiescent in the situation.

'You should stand up to D.R.B.,' she would shout.

'Yes, and get the sack,' he would reply.

The arguments would end with mother storming out. I was an inveterate eavesdropper on these rows from inside my bedroom door. Very often they would be about me.

Having been sick so long, I presented myself again at Robert Gordon's College on the first day of the new year. I went into my classroom and encountered my familiar set of classmates. I don't remember any kind of fuss being made, or any welcome as we all sat there. A teacher came in who I didn't know.

'All right! Everyone stand! Not you Youngson! Now, off you go next door.'

The entire class stood up and filed out of the classroom leaving me sitting there completely alone. A few minutes later a new set of boys filed in and sat down around me. They were none of them known to me, and they looked to my eye to be too young to be my pals. Miss Reid came back in and took down the roll. She was to be my teacher in my repeat of Primary Four, and this was to be my new class.

The whole experience stands out in my mind as one of complete desolation. Everyone I knew and was friendly with in the world had just walked out on me and I was left alone with a group of complete strangers. No one even took the time to say good-bye.

There was a bonus, however, as Miss Reid was as good a teacher as Miss Mitchell had been a horrid one. She had no favourites. She was very efficient, with a great sense of humour, and if you worked well there was plenty of fun and a great sense of security which at that time I really needed. I did very well academically in my new class, although I quickly discovered that I had been joined by two boys called Murray Copland and Richard Wallis who were very clever indeed, and who could consistently get higher marks than I could in everything except English. Murray would be first in the class at the end of the year, and Richard was second. Murray would later become dux of the primary school. I was third in the class, which in those days did not rate even a bronze medal. I think that mother and father were aware of the situation and that I was doing as well as I could.

Amongst my new classmates there were a number who became close friends. Ferrier Raitt and Stewart Mitchell and I became close, and remained so throughout Secondary School. Ferrier and I joined the Scottish Youth Hostels, and went off together on our bikes in later years.

After the summer holidays of 1946 I and my new classmates moved up into Primary Five and encountered our first male teacher. Mr Cardno was tall and rather quiet. He had served during the war in the Air Force, and although he never spoke of his own experiences I have a feeling that he was a member of a bomber's crew. Mr Cardno was a good teacher and a kind and fair man, and I did well in his class. I took it for granted that I would remain in slot number three, and that turned out to be the case. Although he did not give personal reminiscences, Mr Cardno was a sucker for war topics. When things were getting really boring, for example in long sessions of arithmetic, someone would ask a war question:

'Please Sir, is it true that the Messerschmidt 109 was faster than the Spitfire?'

This would bring a standard reply.

'Now boy, don't think that you can divert me from the subject in hand; we're not here to talk about the war.'

He would then turn back to the blackboard and add a few more lines to the arithmetic problem in question, before:

'As far as the Messerschmidt 109 is concerned ...'

And he was off. There would be no more mathematics for the next half hour, but a fascinating exposition on the merits of some aircraft or weapon.

We learned that Primary Five ended with The Qualifying exams. On these results we would be 'streamed' for the secondary school intake, into A, B, C, D and E. I came out third, so was securely in 'A'.

After the summer I moved up into the secondary school to join class 1A. I and my friends from Gordon's Primary were joined by a lot of common boys from lesser primaries in town and country. Surprisingly they all turned out to be as bright as we were.

We now had a form room, with a form teacher called Mr Fraser. Davie Fraser, as he was universally known, also took us for my worst subject, Mathematics. He had an extraordinary personality, and kept complete control in class without apparently the slightest difficulty. Although we all knew that he kept a leather belt in his desk drawer I can never remember seeing him using it, although corporal punishment was rife throughout the entire school. I think we all admired Mr Fraser so much that we would have been embarrassed beyond belief to know that we had earned his displeasure sufficiently to merit the strap.

Our English teacher was Mr Foster. The 'A' stream studied Latin and French. 'Hooter' Gibson was my first Latin teacher, and under him I encountered: 'Gallia, est omnis divisa in partes tres,' or 'Caesar's Gaul, divided in three parts.' For French we had first a lady called Miss Smith, but later an extraordinary gentleman called Mr Hugelshofer. He was stooped and elderly, with a big nose and bushy eyebrows, and some extraordinary behaviour. I think he was probably born in Scotland, although his name must have been an embarrassment in earlier days. He could snap his fingers like a pistol shot, and preferred to use gestures to convey meaning rather than words. If he asked you to stand to answer a question, and your response was not adequate, he would snap his finger, which snap left the index finger pointing straight at you. This was followed by the open hand, palm down, being moved quickly from side to side with a sinking movement. Transfixed by this performance, you fell silent and sank down into your seat, dismissed. I became very fond of Hugels, and found French easy, getting good marks, and plenty of praise for my spoken attempts which had a naturally good accent. I still enjoy speaking French at any opportunity.

English, Mathematics, Latin and French would all be studied with a view to sitting the Higher Leaving Certificate exam in our fifth year.

The final subject which was also to lead to a Higher qualification was Science. I expected to be in my element in this subject as a result of my wide general knowledge of science subjects gained from intensive home reading, especially during my illness, but I had the misfortune to encounter a particularly hateful teacher in my first and second years. This elderly man was universally known by his nickname, which was Pudner. The man was permanently bad-tempered, and I think should not have been doing the job at all. With us he was dealing with the brightest group in the first year, which most of the other members of staff seemed to find quite rewarding. He was very physical indeed. He employed the belt with little excuse, for inattention or talking. He hit us with anything that came to hand. It was while watching Pudner that I had my first opportunity to define sadism, for he was evidently only happy when causing pain, and usually more relaxed after having done so. I worked hard and generally kept a low profile, assisted by my genuine interest in the subject. However, I ran into trouble more than once, and on one occasion the matter was memorable.

We were in the early stages of chemistry, probably in second year. The lesson was about oxygen and an experiment was set up to manufacture oxygen. There was a reaction between two chemicals which went faster with a catalyst. At the present moment I can't remember what the three chemicals were, of which I am ashamed. I think the catalyst was manganese dioxide.

The oxygen bubbled out under water and was trapped in a series of jars with removable slides which ended up full of oxygen. Various experiments were conducted to demonstrate the properties of oxygen. A wooden splint was lit at the bunsen burner and then blown out. The slightly smouldering splint was popped into one of the jars and burst into excited flame. My turn came, and a lid was slid back and I was told to sniff the oxygen, and say what it smelt like. It was horrible, but I had read all about oxygen and knew what effect it was supposed to have on people who sniffed it. I even had a word for the effect, although I didn't know exactly what the word meant. It was my big moment.

I said: 'It's exhilarating, Sir.'

Pudner grabbed me by the nape of my neck, and slid back the cover of another jar.

'Is it, indeed?' he said, and thrust my nose into the open jar. 'Better have a good few long sniffs of it then.'

I tried to hold my breath, but couldn't, and gulped the stuff in, and was promptly sick all over the floor.

'Exhilarating was it? Well? Now what is it?'

'Awful, Sir.' I groaned.

I learned long afterwards that oxygen made in a classroom by the manganese dioxide method was full of impurities which gave it a particularly bad smell. I ought to have told the truth, but I didn't know that at the time, and telling the truth had often been a poor strategy in the past. Not only was the teacher unnecessarily cruel, but I was aware, even through my discomfort, that he was enjoying himself. It never occurred to anyone to complain to anybody about Pudner's behaviour. It wasn't all that unusual in Gordon's and I suppose the staff would simply have closed ranks. Schoolboys in my time were entirely without any kind of personal rights.

Once I got away from Pudner I found science very satisfying, and could when I wanted to get good marks in the various exams.

More Music

It was when I was half way through my first year that the music department was transformed by the arrival of Norman Hyde. It had been under an elderly and severe man who kept us singing awful songs.

Mr Hyde transformed the school's musical profile instantly. No more singing of 'Bobby Shafto'. Instead there were gramophone records to listen to, of magical content like *Tubby the Tuba* and *Peter and the Wolf*. Music always had a story for Mr Hyde. He immediately formed a School Choir, which practised after school on Wednesdays, and a little later a second choir known as the Small Choir, which practised on Thursdays.

I joined both choirs immediately, and soon became their undisputed leader. There were some good treble voices in the choir, but it was soon clear that my voice was not the same as the others. Mine was completely different. I was a boy soprano, and Mr Hyde always referred to me by this description. My voice was warm in tone, rich and round and powerful, with an absolutely enormous range going right up into the coloratura register. At home, I could easily imitate records like the Queen of the Night's aria from *The Magic Flute*. My voice could reach, very, very high!

By my second year the choir was giving various public performances, and I was the usual soloist. An evening concert in Drum's Aisle, which was part of St Nicholas' Church, was covered by the press and is dated 1949. My mother kept the cutting, which has a photo. The music correspondent says: 'The surprise of the evening was Peter Youngson's singing of "I know that my Redeemer liveth". Here is one of the best trebles Aberdeen has had for quite a time.' So I was still singing soprano solos when I was fourteen and a half. About the same time my mother paid to have two records made in an Aberdeen studio. I still possess these, and can listen to the distant soaring voice from another world.

At some point in the next year or so my singing voice began to deepen. I had been told to expect that one day my soprano voice would suddenly break, and I would then be a bass or a tenor. This never actually happened to me. I joined the bass part in the school choir, but could still be called upon to sing soprano solos. By my fifth year in school this was no longer possible, and I joined the bass part in the church choir at Queen's Cross. It seemed I was not going to be a tenor like P.Y., but that my adult voice would develop into a deep and powerful bass-baritone. I quickly learned a new repertoire of solos, and began to sing alone whenever I got a chance.

Top of the Form

It was in 1948 that Top of the Form came to radio, and I was picked as the youngest member of the general knowledge team, and represented the First Year. We lost in the first round, and although I was by no means the only team member to get something wrong, I was held to account for not knowing the battle which gave rise to the song Johnnie Cope, which was of course The Battle of Prestonpans. My unusual store of general knowledge was widely known, and I probably made myself obnoxious by over-using it, so Prestonpans stayed with me throughout the whole of my school life, like an albatross round my neck, and I grew to resent any mention of it. I was fourteen years old just before the end of my first year.

There was a battery of end of year tests in which I did quite well in most subjects. Some of the incomers were very bright, but no one displaced Murray Copland from gaining the top place in the year. I suppose in numerical rating I was about half way down the class. My report card started to contain comments like careless, and, untidy, and – worst of all – could do better if he would apply himself. From things that happened later I imagine this irritated my father greatly.

I began my second year. It was at this point that I was allowed to cycle to school in reasonable weather. My route took me down Rosemount Viaduct and on past His Majesty's Theatre to Schoolhill and Gordon's College. There was a policeman on point duty at an intersection somewhere short of my destination, and I thought I saw him beckon to me to come on. At the last moment I tried to avoid him as he moved to avoid me. I ran into him and we both went down in a heap. The front wheel buckled. It turned out that the officer's signalling hand had in fact been held firmly up to instruct me to stop, but I hadn't been able to read his signals at that distance. He abandoned his post and picked up my ruined bike in one hand and guided me forward with his other. On arrival at the school he sought admission to the headmaster's office, and, on being sent in, declared, in a broad Aberdeen accent:

'Heidmaister, this loon needs specs!'

I presume this started the procedure which resulted in my having my eyes tested. I have very clear memories of the day that this happened at an optician's in Union Street. I remember being asked to read out the letters on a series of charts and having to admit, somewhat shamefacedly, that I could only manage the big A which occupied one chart on its own. I had the heavy metal frame put on me – the one into which the interchangeable lenses could be put. In due course I went back and was ultimately fitted with my glasses. They were the basic shape with round lenses and metal rims, and I thought they looked horrible. I still remember coming out of the optician's on to Union Street, and with my new glasses on, being able to identify my mother, looking into a shop window on the other side of the street. That was the first time I had ever seen anything clearly at that distance. I still don't know how I managed to cover up for years and years the fact that I couldn't read the blackboard from my seat in class. In fact, if truth be told, I couldn't read it from more than a couple of feet away. Nor could I identify birds in flight, although by hard practice I had taught myself to catch a rubber ball thrown to me. I turned out not to be short-sighted, but to have a severe case of astigmatism.

Founder's Day

One of the highlights of the school year at Robert Gordon's was Founder's Day, when the whole school marched over to West St Nicholas' for a Commemoration of Robert Gordon himself, who died in 1731 and is buried somewhere in Drum's Aisle. The occasion was conducted by the school chaplain, Rev. Anderson Nicol. The highlight of the occasion was an address given from the pulpit by a distinguished former pupil. I attended all these events, but the memorable one came when I was in third year. The guest speaker on this occasion was a man who had become wealthy in business of some kind. I don't know if I ever knew his name, but if I did I have long ago forgotten it. He had a very rough Aberdeen accent, quite unlike that which one would expect from a distinguished former pupil. He may have prided himself on being unchanged by success and remaining one of Jock Tamson's Loons. He spoke, as I recollect, without notes and reminisced about the school in his day, which would have been long before the Second World War. Things were evidently very hard at Gordon's in his time, and he was at pains to point out how grateful we all ought to be that matters had improved so much. He went on:

'I was specially pleased to see on my visit to the school this morning that you have a wee tuck shop where you can buy things to eat during playtime. There was nothing like that in my day. One thing I especially noticed was that the tuck shop was selling pies.' (The man pronounced this word with an Aberdeen stress, like 'pice' to rhyme with spice.)

'Boys, I would give you all a serious warning about pice. You never know what can find its way into a pie. You can find all kinds of things in pice. I've even heard of spaiver buttons being found in pice!'

There was a long stunned silence in the kirk before the uncontrollable explosion of boys of every age in the grip of hysterical laughter. Such pure joy is a rare experience, and the service was brought to an untimely end as order could not be restored. The Dictionary of Scottish Usage says that the spaiver refers to the opening at the front of a boy or a man's trousers, which can be undone to allow him to make use of the toilet. Now a zip, in former times – as in my childhood – it was always buttoned. In the same way that the term flies is considered somewhat indelicate today, the word spaiver was considered completely inappropriate at that time. I myself had never heard it anywhere but on the lips of coarse loons in the school lavatory. I am sure that no boy present would ever have heard it uttered in public before, but heard on that occasion it would never be forgotten.

Back at Home

The church was always important to our family. My father had been ordained as an elder in Queen's Cross Church after the war, and the whole family continued to attend every Sunday. I was sent to Sunday School, which met after the morning service, but somewhere about my twelfth year I began to absent myself from this organisation, which I did not like. Once I was into Secondary School I think this behaviour must have been discovered, and by the time I was fourteen my mother and father had given up the struggle to force me to attend church at all. At sixteen, children qualified to join the church Youth Fellowship, and I attended this on Sunday evenings for a couple of years until I left school.

I return to June 1949 and the end of my Second Year. I think my results and my report card were much the same as before, but I recall a distinctly cooler relationship with my father at this time. This all centred around his disappointment at my lack of achievement at school. He was quite determined that I would be going on to Aberdeen University to take a degree in something, and that only this would produce a fulfilled and productive life. He could see no sign of my being able to achieve this unless I improved in my exams, as I slowly sank down through the ranks of the 'A' stream. He was also incensed that of the Aberdeen grammar schools, he had selected the one that was fee paying and my poor performance was costing him money.

It was probably about this time that he developed a particular repartee with my mother. He would come in from work to have his tea, and begin:

'Well, Mother! I've been!'

'Been where, dear?' my mother would rejoin.

'The Corporation Cleansing Department!'

'What on earth did you go there for, dear?'

'He's starting on Monday as a "scaffie". That's all he's ever going to be good for.' (A scaffie was local Aberdeen dialect for a scavenger or street cleaner: as far as my father was concerned, the lowest of the low.)

In our third year those of us who were still in the top class, 3A, were to specialise and concentrate for the next three sessions on preparing for our Higher Leaving Certificate. As 'A' boys we were expected to gain five subjects at higher level and one at lower. The highers were English, Maths, Science, Latin and French. History would be the solitary lower. I still found English and French reasonably effortless and did well, while the other subjects were more unsatisfactory all the way down to my terrible problems with Maths. I was actually steadily sinking down through the class rankings, and this process was intimately related to my difficulties with my father. It is very difficult for me to sort out why my relationship with him was by this time so bad and getting steadily worse.

What he may have actually felt about me he never, ever let me know, and indeed I never found out, for in later life he would not talk about these post-war years. I suppose he resented my importance in the family, and my close relationship with my mother, but he never made that clear. There was certainly no way in which she ever took my part against my father, indeed my abiding recollection is how completely unanimous they always were in standing against me.

My father openly resented everything he had to spend money on where I was concerned. He resented bills for clothing and school books, and he complained about routine things like haircuts. He said it was my fault that my hair grew so thick and bushy and cost so much to cut. In a better situation this might have been funny, but I didn't see it that way. It all came down to school, where he resented paying the fees for a son who was simply not trying to do well. He never realised that the main reason I wasn't trying was because he wasn't interested in me, and at least my poor results brought some reaction, even if it was a bad one.

Attempts to involve him in my life always came to nothing. I had no real interest in the gardening enthusiasm of my grandfather or my father, but I remember thinking it might be politic to show some interest. I asked Granda if I could have a wee bit of earth, and if he could suggest some seeds which I could collect and plant, and then show to my dad. Granda was surprised and quite keen, and marked out and raked a little patch, about two square feet of soil in an unused bit of border. He suggested lupin seeds, and I collected them and sowed them and watered and weeded the patch. In due course the little seedlings came up and began to grow, and I told my father about the experiment, although I was unable to persuade him to actually go out and see the little plants. One day I went out to see how they were getting on and found they had all been pulled up. I was shocked, and I asked Granda where they were.

'Your dad pulled them up,' he said.

I went to see my father, and he brushed my story aside. 'I wanted the ground ... We've got plenty of lupins ... I didn't know they were yours.'

Later I eavesdropped as usual on the row about the lupins. For once my mother was cross on my behalf. He admitted that he had known they were mine, but that it wasn't my garden, it was his. This jealousy was never absent in my house, and was no doubt responsible for the fact that he never came to hear me sing. To attend the one thing I could really do very well, and of which he might have been proud, was more than he could face.

One story has always stood out in my mind from these days. My father was a complete genius with numbers. Although I was learning that mathematics was to do with far more than arithmetic, we still had to handle numbers, and I still found many of the concepts impossible to grasp. I have watched in sheer bewilderment as my father added up columns of cash figures in a big ledger. They were in pounds, shillings and pence, and he could do them in his head, effortlessly carrying forward the pennies in their twelves and the shillings in their twenties.

One day, at the end of my tether with maths homework which was completely beyond me, I broke an unwritten rule and took my exercise book to my father.

'Excuse me, Dad,' I said, 'I can't do this problem.'

He took the book in silence, and made a few notes on the margin of his paper. He did the problem three different ways in his head, and noted the three answers, which were all the same and all correct.

'No, you can't, can you', he said, and turned back to his paper.

My feelings of alienation from my father would become progressively deeper during the next three years.

At the end of my third year, just after my 16th birthday, my exam results were appreciably worse, and I realised that I would have to be careful not to get displaced out of the 'A' stream, which would mean losing touch with my friends. That had happened when I was ill, and I had never forgotten how painful it was. Although low marks made my father satisfyingly angry, I would have to be careful about what I was doing.

The exams at the end of my fourth year brought me perilously close to losing my place in the 'A' stream, and a grim silence from my father, who was presumably now confronting the possibility that I would not work hard enough in my last year to get my Highers.

My Highers

Shortly it was August 1951 and I went into my final year at school. This was class 5A, and now contained the School Captain and Vice Captain and most of the prefects. Although I had no bad record of misbehaviour I was not selected to be a prefect, presumably because at an academic level I was seen to be not trying!

As I went on through my fifth year things got very much out of control. I think I had become desperate about my relationship with my father, and had become a bit unbalanced about everything. I planned to simply fail my highers and go into the army. This would mean that the fees he had been paying since I was six would be money right down the drain. This was the worst thing I could think of doing to him. I hadn't thought about the Prelims. These were an internal device to allow the school to control sending boys forward for the highers, and allowing them to sit only if they would pass. I treated the Prelims as a kind of dry run for my master plan, and produced very bad results. Not one, even my beloved English, was actually a pass mark. I ought to have passed my prelims to allow me to sit the highers, which I could then have failed. What I did was to blow my cover.

My former form master, Davie Fraser, and my French teacher, Mr Hugelshofer, were, unknown to me, still taking an interest in me. They had smelt a rat about my exams, and suspected, quite correctly, that there was some kind of hidden agenda going on. This resulted in interviews and ultimately a visit to Davie Fraser – in his own house! In no time he wormed out all my secrets. I told him about my life since my father came home from the war. I admitted the entire plan and laid it all out before him. He pointed out to me that what I was trying to do was the very worst possible example of cutting my nose off to spite my face. If I really wanted to get my own back on my father, what I needed was power, not weakness. Success, not failure. Only from a position of power would I be able to force him to see how unfair he had been in all his bad treatment of me. The way to get that power was to *pass* exams, not to fail them. He would then have to admit that he had been wrong about me all along. In addition to that, armed with my University Entrance I could do what I liked and go where I wanted. It was all a complete revelation to me, and fell on me like a thunderclap.

'Do you agree with this assessment?' I was asked.

I said that I did.

'Are you prepared to do something about it?'

'Yes,' I said, 'But it's all too late now anyway!'

But Davie Fraser was sure it wasn't too late, and laid out his plans. I had three months to put right three or four years of idleness. I would have to work long hours and into the nights to stand a chance. He and Mr Hugelshofer would discuss the whole matter with the headmaster, and negotiate permission for me to sit those exams which they thought I should be able to pass. There would be informal coaching available after school to help me catch up.

It was decided to write off Maths and Latin. I had little talent for the first and had done so little work for the second that it seemed unlikely I could come back. English was just waiting in the wings and would be a pass. A Science master called Mr Wilson – Pudner had retired – would coach me in his subject and Mr Hugelshofer would help me with my French which he thought I could manage. I would have to work on my lower History syllabus, and relegate Maths and Latin to the status of lowers as well. If all went well I would emerge with 'three and three' (three highers and three lowers), one better than the minimum University Entrance group of three and two.

I went home from Davie Fraser's in deep shock. I never told anyone what had passed between us. I suppose something of what was going on must have been communicated to my father, but he never referred to it. The three months was very hard, and I worked as I had never worked before. Permission was duly forthcoming for me to sit the planned group of highers and lowers, and I passed them all.

An Entrance Certificate for Aberdeen University was duly issued to me in June 1952, shortly after my eighteenth birthday. At this point – namely July 1952 – I applied for, and obtained, exemption from my statutory two years of National Service. All that was necessary was to send forward the Higher and Lower Leaving Certificates, and deferment, based on University Admission, was automatic.

The day I left Robert Gordon's College, I turned my back on all the fellow pupils who I had kept company with through many years. As far as my class was concerned, my involvement ended there and then, as did my interest in Robert Gordon's College.

Chapter Two: The Far Country of the Seaforth Highlanders

When the highers' results were published, I had passed everything I sat. I had a Higher Leaving Certificate for English, French and Science, and a Lower for Latin, Maths and History. The minimum entrance qualification for University at that time was three highers and two lowers, so I had my necessary group, and made an application to start at Aberdeen University at the beginning of the session of 1952 – 1953. I was also issued by the War Office with a Certificate of Exemption from National Service, which had been obtained by sending my Higher Leaving Certificate papers to the appropriate department. This did not amount to a permanent exemption, but only to a deferment of my military service until I had completed my university degree or degrees.

Father certainly felt that my final results represented complete failure. Nothing less than 'five and one' would have satisfied him, and I don't suppose he ever knew how close I had come to getting nothing at all.

I Decide to Enlist

The fact that I can remember nothing about the summer of 1952 seems to indicate that I was pretty miserable. Certainly the atmosphere was very unpleasant. The prospect of continuing to live at home for the next three or four years while doing a degree course in Aberdeen seemed quite intolerable, and one day in August I went down town and presented myself at the Woolmanhill Army Depot. I evidently had the presence of mind to take with me my documents of exemption from National Service. My arrival at the entrance desk resulted in a series of interviews with progressively higher ranks of soldier until I was taken in to see an officer who I think would have been a major. He had to satisfy himself that I was in my right mind, and knew what I was doing in surrendering my right to have my service deferred. Once he had heard me out, and understood the position, he produced a couple of witnesses and I was given a document to sign which made the decision official. I was sent home to await my call-up papers.

There was hell to pay when I got home, and father certainly made some effort to have the decision reversed. However, I was eighteen years old, and had appended my signature to the necessary documents, and he was told that there was nothing to be done. In due course my posting was confirmed, and I was told to report to Depot Seaforth Highlanders at Fort George. I had no idea what the Seaforth Highlanders were, nor any idea where Fort George was. In my innocence I had always assumed that as a native of Aberdeen, I would do my National Service as a member of the Gordon Highlanders. However, the Gordons were not having an intake of new servicemen near enough the time that I had given in my personal notice that I wanted to enlist. Along with my documents came a rail pass to Inverness, and instructions how to find a truck which would take me to Fort George. I have a dim recollection that mother said a tearful goodbye to me at the house, and that father took me to the station in the car. I think my basic feelings were of relief, and that, whatever I was facing, it couldn't be worse than staying at home. This turned out to be more wrong than I could possibly have imagined!

Fort George

There was a truck at Inverness station, and a uniformed man, to whom I showed my travel warrant, found my name on a list and told me to get on board. In due course we rattled off to Fort George, which turned out to be about fifteen miles away, along the Moray Firth.

I suppose I first stepped out on military soil sometime early in the afternoon, and was herded together with a considerable group of other arrivals to stand in a huddle in a big open space. We were the ones not in uniform, and I was the one who didn't know anyone. It immediately become clear to me that many of the group were on familiar terms with each other, for greetings were being called from one to the other. A uniformed man came and shouted at us, and told us to stop talking and to stand still. We would shortly be individually processed and recorded, and enrolled on 'the strength'. We would give the Army some personal details and the Army would give us our clothing and other personal possessions, our food, somewhere to sleep, and most important of all, our identity – contained in a personal number.

Much of what followed seems very confused, but I suppose it probably took place between, say, two thirty and five o'clock in the afternoon.

First we were told to arrange ourselves in alphabetical order of our surnames. I was well used to this, having lived with the surname Youngson all my life. I moved to the back of the queue, and my position there was never challenged during the next two years.

My medical examination produced no surprises, and I was deemed completely fit. The examiner, like all such, insisted that I read the eye chart without my glasses on. My astigmatism is so bad that I can't really make out anything like that, so I was told to put my spectacles on, and normality returned.

The personal examination involved giving a series of answers to questions asked me by a seated sergeant, who entered them on a form. Name and date of birth were simple, and some physical data like height and weight had already been entered from my medical. I have never forgotten two of the questions.

The dialogue, which I have often recalled and told through the years, went something like this:

'Colour of hair?'

'Auburn, Sergeant!'

'Auburn? We don't have auburn in the Army! Brown.'

'Colour of eyes?'

'Hazel, Sergeant!'

'Hazel? We don't have hazel in the Army! Grey.'

Little was I to know that the colours which my mother had proudly used for my hair and eyes, since my hair darkened from bright red in my early teens, would not be acceptable in the army. He must have thought I was really weird. He was probably right.

'Identifying marks?'

'Like what, Sergeant?'

'Like birthmarks, or tattoos or scars.'

Early school days came back. 'I've got scars on both my knees, Sergeant.'

'Let's see.' So trousers were rolled up, and down it went on the form: 'Scars on both knees.' Robert Gordon's playground had left its mark.

'Religion? C of S, C of E or RC?'

I knew the answer to that one.

'Church of Scotland, Sergeant.'

With that the questions seem to have come to an end.

On the basis of all this information a small brown folded card was made out and given to me, with dire warnings about what would happen if it were to be lost. This was my Pay Book; presumably so named because it had to be produced on Pay Parade in order to get your week's wages. I was rather shocked to discover that I would earn 28/- (twenty-eight shillings) per week in the Army, the equivalent of £1.40 in today's currency.

My Pay Book was also inscribed with my Army Number, which was 22720464 – the fifth digit was pronounced as 'zero' – and I was told to memorise this number. I did so, and if senility finally robs me of my wits, this army number will probably be the last thing I can still remember.

After medical and personal matters had been dealt with we were herded to the stores to draw our clothing and equipment. This had elements of sheer farce. We moved along a long broad counter while a row of soldiers behind it slapped items on an ever-increasing pile of things in front of us. Their names were being shouted out as we went, and most of them were double-dutch to me. At the end, and confronted by a mountain of stuff, a pen was pushed into my hand, and I was told to sign a form. I had undertaken personal responsibility for all of this equipment, and that form would return to haunt me often during the following two years.

The rest of that first day is a blur. We were taken to a barrack room where we dumped our mountain; then to the cookhouse for something to eat; then back to the barrack room where we met our training staff, before stowing our stuff in lockers, spreading up some kind of bed with the bedclothes provided, and falling asleep.

Basic Training

There seems little point in trying to record much of what happened in the first few days of my basic training. I passed most of the time in a state of confusion. Some of the general picture gradually became clear, and I can set some of it down.

Fort George turned out to be a Regimental Depot and training centre. It was the home of the 1st Battalion of the Seaforth Highlanders, which was presently serving in Germany in the British Army of the Rhine (BAOR). Members of other regimental groups were stationed there, and many others were in transit.

The Fort was isolated at the end of a peninsula, sticking out into the Moray Firth. I was one of the intake of National Service recruits, who would, after training, join the regiment in Germany. I think that there were 72 of us altogether, and we were divided into three training platoons of 24 men. Our barrack room had spaces for twelve beds and lockers down each side. Each platoon was commanded by a subaltern; in our case a 2nd Lieutenant, whose name I don't recall. There was a more senior officer, a Captain, I think, in overall charge of the entire intake.

We had our own training Sergeant, Sergeant Kirk; a full Corporal, Corporal Kyle; and two Lance-Corporals whose names I don't remember. We were assigned to a company and had a Company Commander, who was a Major. There were several Company Sergeant Majors (CSMs) and one Regimental Sergeant Major (the RSM), and a whole lot of specialist people through whose hands we passed. Somewhere in a remote and exalted region there was a Commanding Officer. Our basic training would last for six weeks. We were told that we would probably get a week-end pass to go home after the first four weeks – if we were good enough – and we would undergo a passing-out parade at the end of the period. We lived in our own barrack room, with just enough personal space for our beds and the tall narrow lockers which stood beside them. Beyond the door were two small rooms where our corporals had their billets.

At the beginning there was far too much to take in, and my memory is that everything was simply impossible. We were allowed to keep hardly anything at all in the way of personal possessions. Civilian clothing was wrapped up with the paper and string provided, and posted home. Even at that early stage I was aware that I was less well equipped for the army than many of those around me. Some knew enough to retain their own personal underwear, while I of course knew no better than to send mine home, and had to wear the wretched army issue articles, which were named 'cellular drawers.'

Most of our uniforms didn't fit and looked and felt absolutely awful. Other members of the platoon seemed to know various things that could be done about this, but I did not. I remained looking dishevelled from the beginning to almost the end of my service. My issue of boots was the wrong size, and they were replaced after I spoke to the sergeant. One attempt at exchange was all that was allowed, and the replacement boots were too big. This resulted in chafing and discomfort, which became part of normal life. I have never worn any kind of boots since I left the army, and never will.

The food which was served at the cookhouse was simply not edible, and I couldn't manage to eat it at all. I was always hungry, and spent all my money on eating at the NAAFI. Without the NAAFI I would have starved. The only beverage available was tea, which I have never been able to drink. The sole alternative was water.

Sleeping was equally difficult. The beds were unbelievably basic, with thin hard 'biscuits' for mattresses. I, who had never slept with other people, found the noises and the sheer presence of twenty-three other men very disturbing, and I slept only because I was exhausted.

Many of my new experiences must have happened within the first few days, and they merge into a confusion of memories.

There was 'shaving'. I had not shaved before joining up, as I didn't have a beard, just a kind of haze of fair fluff. In 'this man's army' (a phrase which seemed constantly upon our NCOs' lips), everyone shaved, and shaved every day. The water was cold, the lather didn't lather, and the razor blades were either too sharp or too blunt. I wasn't sure which. I emerged with cuts and scratches, and within a day or two I was covered in acne spots, which I had escaped as a schoolboy. These remained with me to some extent throughout the next two years.

There was 'the haircut'. This must have happened either on the first or second day. At least the butchery was uniform and impartial. Very little was left by the time the barber was finished.

Both of the above turned out to be the subject of continual taunts and jibes, employed by the corporal and sergeant on parade, and supposed to be funny. These were all time-honoured. As in shaving: 'Put a blade in the razor next time.'

'Take the paper off the blade when you shave next.'

'Try standing closer to the blade when you're shaving.'

And as in the matter of hair:

'Get a haircut, Laddie!' Said by somebody most days.

'I've just had one, Sergeant.'

'Well, get another one!'

And said on inspection by an NCO standing out of sight just behind one's back.

'Am I hurting you, laddie?'

'No, Sergeant!'

'Well, I should be, I'm standing on your hair. Get it cut!'

My Uniform

The biggest traumas seemed to concern everything which was termed 'your kit'. This was divided into things you normally wore – your uniform, and things which were largely kept for show.

The uniform had to be in perfect condition for daily inspection on parade. As well as the basic shirt and tie, jacket and trousers, there were several articles which came in for particular attention. These were the boots, the web belt and gaiters and the cap badge. These required daily treatment. The cap badge was relatively simple. It was removed from the cap and polished with Brasso. The gaiters were brushed each day with blanco, an opaque khaki substance which was made up with water from a block, and applied with a brush before being left to dry. Each gaiter had two small buckles, which had to be kept clear of blanco and polished.

Blancoing had to be carried out the night before the equipment was to be worn. If attempted too near the time, it simply would not dry.

The belt got special treatment. Each night it was disassembled from its buckle and retaining circlips and blancoed. The two halves of the buckle were polished with Brasso and buffed until they shone. The retaining circlips were a real problem. They were slid as close to the main buckle as they would go, and the visible front surface was highly polished. The trouble was that the procedure involved in their manufacture did not take their future polishing into account. The main front bar was slightly convex, and at the top and bottom, when it turned over and under the belt, the clip bulged out in a way that created hollows in the brass. This shape defied all attempts to bring it to an even high shine. Gradually, and to my mind, magically, the buckle clips of many of my comrades began to take on a smoother shine than mine. This was because, unknown to me, they had gone to the quartermaster, and either exchanged their newly issued clips for older flattened ones, or had the battalion blacksmith hammer them flat. A photograph taken of me in the midst of my basic training, and some weeks after I had arrived at Fort George, plainly shows my buckle clips still to be lumpy, and much less reflective than the desired standard.

My Boots!

I have left the matter of boots to the end. By the time I was eighteen I knew how to polish my shoes, and often did not only my own for going to church on Sundays, but my father's as well. This treatment was quite adequate for the uppers of my new boots, but they had two areas which needed something special. The entire toe-cap of each boot, together with the leather portion which rose up and lapped around the heel, was made of a different kind of leather to the upper. This material was as hard as granite, and the manufacturers had decorated it with a pattern of tiny pits or dimples. These occurred evenly across the surface and were less than half an inch apart. The Army's requirement was that these toe-caps and heel-caps were to be polished to a high gloss. In bright sunlight they should be 'too dazzling to look at!' The dimpled surface would not take such a shine, as, no matter how much polish was applied, the pattern persisted in showing through. The dimples had to be removed, and we were instructed in the procedure by our corporal. The technique was called 'boning', and involved a candle and a spoon. The spoon was heated in the candle flame to something a bit less than red hot. The bowl of the spoon could be used, although many favoured the flattened end of the handle. The hot spoon would then be rubbed vigorously over the surface of the toe-cap. The dimples began to become flatter and flatter, and finally disappeared altogether. The procedure took many hours of work as the spoon cooled rapidly, and a cold spoon did not get rid of dimples. There were four separate areas to be treated, two to each boot. We were told in the sternest terms that there was absolutely no point in attempting to polish the boots until the dimples had been completely eradicated. Various individuals in the squad varied greatly in the success of their boning techniques. Private Sullivan was the champion, and could even be persuaded to help some of his close friends to get better results. I was probably the poorest in the platoon, my efforts no doubt being undermined by a private belief that what we were engaged in doing was the most completely pointless exercise imaginable. The result of all this was that I never did manage to get rid of all my dimples, and this largely nullified all the effort I put into polishing. My boots were always a failure, and often 'a disgrace', and remained so for a long time.

The polishing itself was also an arcane mystery. Not for our boots was the application of polish with one brush, and the rubbing off of it with another. No! A deep bed of polish had to be laid down on the toe caps by applying it with a duster wrapped round the tip of the index finger. This was dipped into the polish to bring up a substantial amount which was gently applied to the leather. Spittle was then applied to the finger, and with small circular movements the polish was brought to a hard even surface to which a shine could easily be imparted. The movements concerned were called 'magic circles', and they went on for hours and hours. Once again, impatience to achieve the result quickly was self-defeating. Sullivan's boots became the pride of the entire depot, while mine attracted serious criticism. I believe I was even told to strip all the polish off and start again, but nothing really made any difference. The production of shining toe and heel caps was really just not one of my talents, and there was nothing I could do about it. In any event, the boots question was evidently intended to have been sorted out within the early weeks, and as the main problem of the entire six weeks was that there was never enough time to meet the staff's requirements, and we were dogged by near exhaustion every night, once you had fallen behind – as with boots – you could never catch up.

My Kit

If it is possible to imagine a greater challenge than that of the boots and brasses, then one's kit would have to be the obvious candidate. After breakfast each morning, and before getting out to the parade ground, we would be required to 'stand by your beds!' We ourselves had to be smartly and cleanly dressed by this time, and have our beds properly and neatly made up. (We had been taught the army way on our first arrival.) However, in addition to all this, on selected mornings there would be a 'kit inspection'. The various articles which we had been issued with at the stores had to be arranged on top of our beds to be examined. This arrangement was not an opportunity for individual artistic expression, for there was absolutely no latitude allowed in the way the kit was laid out. A black and white photograph of the required setting was displayed at the end of the barrack room, and had to be reproduced in the finest detail.

Total uniformity was required throughout the entire barrack room. There was a certain amount of crazy logic to some of this. Our backpacks and front pouches, together with their various web belts, made an arrangement along with our folded greatcoats at the head of the bed above the pillow. This equipment had to be freshly blancoed and with its buckles polished. The desired shape of these articles was neat rectangles, and they were not willing to assume these shapes while empty. Stuffing them with spare possessions was risky, and not very effective. No! Scrap cardboard boxes had to be scrounged and cut to size and shape to distend the packs so that they took up the correct appearance. The supply of cardboard was limited, and I always seemed to be at a disadvantage. Other items of clothing such as pyjamas, spare shirts, vests and the famous cellular drawers had to be neatly folded to the prescribed pattern and laid out on the main area of the mattress. Again, their natural appearance was of soft, rounded edges and corners. These were simply 'not military!' Squared off boxes were required for all these items – even the cellular drawers. More cardboard had to be found, and clothing pinned round it. There were never enough pins. The experienced members, who had managed to continue to be wearing their own underwear, could store squared off vests and pants in their lockers and trot them out quickly, as often as was required. For them a kit inspection was little more than a neat arrangement of pre-packed articles. Not so in my case. I always seemed to be working from scratch.

I should perhaps mention that the assortment of things which were collectively termed kit contained various objects which were previously unknown to me. There was a flat sheet of brass with a slot in it. This was slid along the stem of a brass button so that the button could be polished without getting polish on the cloth.

There was also a small cloth package which was rolled up and tied around its middle with two tapes. This was called a 'hussif', which appeared to be a colloquial form of 'housewife', and was a domestic sewing kit. Little did I know how much time I would spend using this piece of equipment. It contained a darning needle and a hank of wool. After suitable instruction from the sergeant, I learned how to create acceptable darns to fill in the worn areas in the heels of my socks.

In kit inspections as in other military matters, my best efforts attracted nothing but scorn. Not infrequently my kit would be turned out on to the barrack room floor, by the simple method of pulling the blanket off the bed, and I would be told to do it all again.

A Square Peg

I have highlighted the problems with my kit because it surprises even myself that an intelligent and well educated eighteen year old could not do better in this situation than I did. I suppose some of the reasons are easy to understand.

None of my experience was helped by the great gulf which yawned between myself and the rest of the platoon. I was the only one from Aberdeen and the east coast. They were all from the Black Isle and various areas around Inverness. I was the only one who had been to a good secondary school, and the only one with highers. They were mostly agricultural workers who had left school at sixteen. All of this set me apart from them, and they didn't know how to cope with me, or I with them.

My own attitude didn't help. I suppose I wasn't thinking very straight for most of the time. There were various disasters. For example, at some point in our first week we had to sit a set of intelligence tests. One tested your basic knowledge of vocabulary. It started with words like orange and apple and went on to more sophisticated ones. I remember it ended with the words 'esoteric' and 'homunculus'. I completed the entire paper with no difficulty. I was the only one who did! Many of my companions got not much further than 'apple'. The same held true for the more general tests. The staff member in charge of all of this, who I think was a sergeant in the Education Corps, did me the favour of proclaiming my unusual results to all and sundry. I think he said I had the highest score that had ever been achieved. This seemed unlikely to me, and I said so. However, none of this did anything to help me becoming accepted.

I lacked any of the social skills which would have made light of this situation, and consequently was seen as different. My previous social contacts had been with people like myself. The lads in my platoon were what my father would probably have called rough. I found their accents hard to follow, and their humour was beyond me. They swore quite a lot, using the kind of four letter words which I had always found embarrassing. All this probably stopped me getting any help when I was stuck, which I often was. I have to say that our training sergeant was aware of my problems and did everything in his power to help me, but there was obviously a limit to how much attention he could pay me, and that same attention was a bit self-defeating anyway.

Another difficulty I had was that the Army was a new and alien world to me. Many of the lads in my unit had had some previous experience of it. The Seaforth Highlanders had a high profile in their district and many had been cadets, and had been looking forward to their National Service. Many had fathers who had served in the Regiment. They were already familiar with many aspects of the strange things we were continually being asked to do, and found no difficulty in performing many tasks I simply didn't understand. From my point of view they seemed to have a head start, and I resented it all as deeply unfair.

Underlining much of the difficulty I had in getting things right was the early dawning of an awareness of how profoundly stupid and utterly pointless many of the things we were being required to do actually were. I think I also entertained the concept that I was much cleverer than the people who were giving me the orders. This may actually have been true in some cases, but it was certainly not always true, and this attitude did me no favours throughout my two years. In fact, although it took me a long time to find this out, the Army had generations of experience in sorting out 'awkward customers' like me. One of the things which upset me most was the collection of apparently time-honoured verbal games which were designed to make the object of the NCO's or Officer's repartee look and feel foolish. The commands to 'Stand still!' and 'Face the front' and 'Did anyone tell you could speak, laddie?' were all intended to degrade, and were very effective. Worst of all was a game in which you were invited to agree with some unflattering assessment delivered at a range of two inches by an NCO. This went like this:

'You are a horrible little man! What are you?'

The required and expected answer went like:

'I am a horrible little man, Sergeant.'

I found it impossible to play my part in this game, and would reply with some more sensible answer like 'I'm very sorry, Sergeant.' This would result in an escalation of the anger of the NCO and would often produce a punishment exercise like running round the perimeter of the parade ground.

I remember a painful evening session with our sergeant, in which it was pointed out to me that my lack of verbal compliance on the parade ground was covered in King's Regulations by the crime of 'dumb insolence', and this could be a serious matter if I did not mend my ways. As a matter of fact I was never actually charged with dumb insolence in the army, and I later concluded that it was covered by the catch-all charge which was levelled at me a number of times. This was 'Conduct to the Prejudice of Good Order and Military Discipline', or a '252' for short. This one worked very well, and caused much grief not only to me but to many of my comrades.

Strangely enough I think I got on better outside in the open air than I did in the barrack room. I was moderately fit, and reasonably well co-ordinated, and I don't suppose I found the business of doing drill any harder than anyone else. The problem with this, as with everything else, was the pressure. Everything was done in a climate of unreasonably high demand and expectation. Looking back on it, I now think that this was self-defeating. I can understand the point of it if you are dealing with a group of volunteers who want to learn to become jet pilots. You presumably push them to the point at which the less capable ones start to crack, and you end up with the best, having got rid of those who don't make it. But we were not volunteers. We were conscripts. We had nowhere to go, and nothing to do supposing we did reach the point of giving up, as a number did. I suspect that if the administration had been required to give a rationale for its harsh approach to us and our training, it would have been that we were to be turned out ready to obey orders without question. Although this was all happening thirty-five years after the end of the First World War, we still heard the phrase 'over the top' used, as if we would be involved in trench warfare.

We were continually told that we were an *Infantry Regiment* and that 'drill', or 'square-bashing' as it was often called, had to become second nature to us. It finally did! We did drill every single day, often several times. Drill involved us in recognising a whole complicated set of commands, and responding to them with the appropriate movements.

We learned how to *Fall in!* to start things off; to take up positions in a long line according to our height; and how to transform the line into the three ranks in which most drill takes place. We learned endlessly how to respond to the positions of *Attention!* and *Stand at ... Ease!* and the relaxed *Stand Easy!* until the sound of our boots changed from a ragged staccato to a single loud bang. We were lucky that our platoon did not include someone like Corporal Jones of Dad's Army, who was always late in his responses, and no one person got regularly picked on in our drill squad.

As a matter of fact we did lose one recruit. The boy's name was Stornoway, although I think he came from the Black Isle and not from

Lewis. He was a fairly simple sort of fellow, though very good-natured. However, his weak spot became apparent on the drill square. As we began to march it became apparent very quickly that Stornoway couldn't march straight. Placed in the left hand column he would edge to his right, and crowd the men on his right out of their places. Placed in the right column he would simply open up a gap on his left until he was marching entirely on his own several yards away from the column. Everyone was anxious to help him. Stornoway had always wanted to serve with the Seaforth Highlanders, as his father and grandfather had. Attempts were made to get him to start off facing at a different angle to the rest, but nothing worked. Eventually he was rejected on health grounds. I can see him still, taking his leave of us with tears streaming down his face. So many of us would have been very pleased to have been thrown out of the army. He, who wanted to stay so badly, was the only one we lost.

Without Private Stornoway, we who remained went on to learn the techniques of turning ninety degrees to the right and left – *Right Turn!* and *Left Turn!* – and of facing the other way – *About Turn!* We learned how to set off, and how to stop – *Quick March!* and *Squad ... Halt!* We learned how to change direction while marching – *Right Wheel!* and *Left Wheel!* – and how to march in the same place without moving – *Mark Time!*

We learned how to salute officers – *Longest way up ... Shortest way down!* – and how to acknowledge superior ranks while marching – *Eyes Right!* and *Eyes Left!*

In our final days we even learned how to undertake the Slow March for ceremonial purposes, although I doubt if we were ever very confident about the necessary movements. It was probably just as well that we were not required to take part in many formal parades.

I myself managed to learn the drill quite quickly, mostly by trying to apply my brains to the task. Everything would have been easier for me if I could have seen it written down, but that was not the method. It all had to be learned by rote, and retained in the memory. I became dimly aware that not only did the orchestral players have to be very competent, but that the conductor was not just waving his arms about. There were those NCOs whose conduct of drill made it seem difficult and hazardous, and the excellent RSM who made it all seem perfectly simple.

Weapons Training

As actual pieces of equipment began to be supplied to us, I found that the manual dexterity side of life had probably been developed by my constructional toys, and by dismantling my bicycle, and I found I was good at stripping things down and re-assembling them.

There was a good deal of excitement among the squad on the day that we were issued with our rifles for the first time. At first the rifle was drawn from the Armoury on a signature, but from then on it lived standing upright in one's locker.

The rifle had two separate purposes. It was essential for 'rifle drill', and it was used for shooting bullets. Our rifle was the standard SMLE (the Short Magazine Lee Enfield ·303), which had been around in one version or another since the first World War, and had been the main infantry weapon throughout World War Two. It fitted into our drill as if it had been there a long time. It had its own dedicated positions for 'attention', 'stand at ease', and 'stand easy'. It was brought up to rest on the shoulder for marching ('slope arms'), and brought down to the ground again when standing still ('order arms'). It could be moved smartly into a vertical position in front of the body in a form of standing salute ('present arms'), and could be extended forwards from one hip to be examined by an officer or NCO ('for inspection – port arms').

Rifle drill was learned with audibly counted pauses – as: 'one-two-three; one-two-three; one' – and was only managed in comparative silence when some degree of competence had been reached. It was very satisfying to get it right, and probably did quite a lot to instill some degree of pride in our achievements. We felt like real soldiers when we were doing rifle drill.

To this day I look at parades where soldiers are drilling using modern small arms, and think how absurd they look. I still think our arms drill looked and sounded very impressive.

The Lee Enfield rifle came equipped with a bayonet which was part of our personal issue. This was worn in a webbing scabbard on the belt. It was a pretty basic weapon consisting of a short bar of round section with a sharpened point, called colloquially a 'pig sticker.' It was united with the rifle by the command 'prepare to fix bayonets!' The rifle was then stood up on its butt between one's feet and wedged between the knees, while the top of the muzzle was steadied with one hand. The NCO would then snap out the command:

'On the command "bayonets!" the right hand will move down to grasp the head of the bayonet. It will move faster than a striking cobra.'

'On the command "fix!" the hand will pull the bayonet from its sheath and fly to the muzzle of the rifle, where it will ram the bayonet securely into position. These movements will take place too fast for the eye to follow.'

The first command would then be given, to be followed by a display of frenzied and most unmilitary fumbling, accompanied by the command: 'Don't look down!' On the second command being given there was a loud rattling sound from the company, followed by bayonets dropping to the ground all over the place, and bruised and nipped knuckles and fingers on the part of the men. It remained one of the hardest things to get right.

The bayonet was not used merely as part of drill. It was also stuck into things, particularly straw-filled sacks hanging from wooden supports to simulate human beings. The bayonet had to be thrust violently into these sacks, accompanied by blood-curdling screams which were intended to alarm the enemy. This was surprisingly good fun, although I don't think I could imagine myself doing it to a living target.

The Lee Enfield rifle was also used for shooting bullets. This was an exciting business, as 'live rounds' (as the bullets were called) were jealously guarded and handed out only under strict security. At the end of rifle practice, we handed back the empty shell cases which we collected after we had fired the gun, and also any unused bullets. This activity was followed by a loud public declaration by each member of the squad:

'No live rounds or empty cases in my possession, Sir!'

The actual business of firing took place at the rifle range, which was some distance outside the camp on an area of sand dunes. We fired from prepared positions, towards the sea, where the sand dune with the targets lay. This area was known as 'the butts', and we took turns in being on duty there. Here we signalled with a variety of long-handled markers where the bullets had hit the target, or, more likely, the direction we estimated they had missed it in. The targets could be pulled up and down, and after a session of firing we were instructed on the telephone to pull them down. We then repaired the holes by sticking pieces of the right colour of paper over them with sticky paste. It was a peaceful business, and one of the places where there didn't seem to be much actual supervision (a rarity in our training weeks). At the firing end, we were issued with our rounds and supervised as we loaded them into the small magazines, or clips, which fitted into the rifle. Firing was done in a 'lying down on the face', or 'prone' position. The idea was to close the left eye, and look out over the open sights with the right eye. Once the target was in the right position, you took in a deep breath; exhaled half of it; and while keeping everything as steady as possible, squeezed the trigger.

'Squeeze, laddie! Squeeze! Don't pull the trigger as if you're trying to snap it off!'

Despite the fact that my spectacles tended to get in the way, I surprised myself, and everyone else by turning out to be very good at this, and several times got the best score in the platoon.

'Well, Youngson! At least there's something you can actually do, thank God!'

The worst part of rifle practice came near the end of our training, and consisted of a series of shooting exercises conducted at intervals, between which we approached nearer to the target. The game started five hundred yards from the target. At this distance the entire target seemed absolutely tiny, and the black bulls-eye in the middle was invisible to me. We ran forward to four hundred yards and fired again, still in prone position. Off once more to stop at three hundred yards and fire from a kneeling position. On to two hundred yards to fire crouching, and finally to one hundred yards. At one hundred yards, the target looked enormous, and impossible to miss, however, the rifle was to be held up to the shoulder and fired from a standing position. Five hundred yards of brisk exercise in full kit had taken its toll, and it turned out to be quite impossible to keep the rifle steady enough to get anywhere near the huge targets, which escaped almost totally unscathed by the entire platoon.

On return to our barrack room after a firing session we fell into another well-tuned army routine about the care of your weapon. I suppose it was a bit like people who ride ponies having to rub the ponies down after coming home, and before they go off for their tea.

'Your rifle is your best friend in the field. Taking care of it comes before everything else.'

The care involved amounted to 'boiling out' and 'pulling through.' A small amount of hot water was introduced down the barrel, and then a small rectangle of white flannel called a 'three by two' was folded up and inserted in the loop at the end of a long piece of thick plaited string, called (surprisingly!) a 'pull through'. The bolt of the rifle was removed. The small weight incorporated into the end of the pull through was inserted into the barrel at the breech and allowed to drop the length of the barrel to emerge at the muzzle. The slack of the pull through was wound round the right hand; the butt of the rifle was lodged on the floor in the angle of a nearby wall, while the left hand kept tight hold of the muzzle. Then with a smooth and steady pressure the right hand pulled the piece of flannel the full length of the barrel to emerge, slightly soiled, at the muzzle.

That was the theory. In practice almost everything else happened. Most of this concerned the flannel having been folded too many times and becoming stuck halfway down the barrel. This caused endless panic, and such measures as tying the pull through on to some immovable object were often resorted to. The barrel was supposed to emerge from the procedure clean and shining, and was later looked down by one's officer while the rifle was held at the correct angle for inspection. Since the bottom of the barrel was in the dark, the bolt was opened, and the right thumb was inserted into the space provided so that light was reflected from the thumbnail and revealed the condition of the barrel.

Getting the Hang of It

As the weeks passed my military skills improved, and I gradually managed to catch up the others and keep up with them in everything but turn-out. I always seemed to look scruffy, and there seemed nothing to be done about it. Gradually this fact was accepted by my superiors with increasingly less comment. They had probably had scruffy soldiers through their hands before.

Other things varied in their degree of challenge. There was a lot of hardening up, a lot of running, and PE which I wasn't good at. There were assault courses to be tackled, which engaged my fear of heights, and my even greater fear of being physically hurt. There was a wretched 'six foot wall', which had to be got over in full kit. I wasn't strong enough in the upper body division to pull myself up this monster, and always flinched from hurling myself bodily at it, which was the approved method. I'm not sure that I ever actually scaled the six foot wall, but my training continued, so it obviously can't have been vital.

There were lots of lectures and demonstrations, with which I was more at home. We learned about the history of the Seaforth Highlanders, and what its mottoes meant. We learnt how to use the Bren Gun and the Sten Gun. The first was a splendid bit of equipment which I learnt to assemble very quickly.

As with my rifle, I found I was competent in shooting with the Bren Gun, and was told at that stage that I would be assigned to it later in the Battalion. The Sten Gun was a nasty little thing which I always thought was as dangerous to the user as to the enemy. I did my required shooting with it, and was glad to see the back of it.

We learned how to use hand grenades. My only close brush with danger at Fort George involved the day we were doing hand grenade drill. I had successfully thrown my grenade. You had to hold the grenade in one hand and put the index finger of the other hand through the pin. Then with a firm movement you stretched your two arms apart to their fullest extent, keeping the hinged lever of the grenade tightly in the palm of the right hand. You then threw the grenade with an over-arm action as in bowling a cricket ball. The lad who came next after me was left-handed, and panicked at the last minute. He withdrew the pin from the grenade, and threw it away – the pin, not the grenade! He then panicked again and dropped the grenade. Our sergeant picked the thing up off the floor and chucked it over a concrete barrier, where it duly exploded, on the opposite side from me.

We had to cover a number of 'route marches'. These were undertaken in full kit, and at marching pace. There were regular stops, and I don't suppose they were intended to be brutal. Still having trouble with my army boots, I didn't like them much and suffered from grievous blisters. In the final week of our training we did the famous 'twenty mile' route march, which I think everyone in our team completed successfully.

There were many regular inspection parades. These were depressing, tiring and boring. They started early in the day with kit inspection, and then we would be out on the square in formation, and waiting simply hours to be inspected first by our own subaltern, then by the Company Commander, then by the Depot Commander and finally by some visiting big-wig.

The six weeks ended with our Passing Out Parade at the end of October, probably on the 30th. I think our platoon won the award as the best of the three, but I can't really remember.

A Potential Officer!

A few days before the passing out parade I was called to an interview with the Commanding Officer, whom I don't think I had encountered before. He informed me that it had been decided that I wouldn't be going out to Germany with the rest of my intake as my education qualifications indicated that I was a potential officer. I would remain at Fort George, and in due course I would be sent down to Wiltshire to attend a WOSB! This stood for 'War Office Selection Board'.

Within a few days of our passing out parade, my platoon together with the other two platoons of my intake left Fort George for Hamburg. I parted from them with no regret, and can remember nothing about any of them, and hardly even any names. I was relocated to a different billet in what I think was called 'holding company', and found myself in a barrack room which contained some other potential officers culled from various units which had been doing their training at Fort George.

I am uncertain how we filled in our time at this point. I think we were lumped in with some other post-basic training soldiers, and inspected and drilled, as before. I know that we were given some advanced training on a variety of weapons we hadn't seen before.

While I was engaged in this extra period of waiting, my grandfather died, on 18th November, and I was granted compassionate leave to attend the funeral. P.Y. had had a heart attack. He was seventy-five.

At some time before this, although exactly when I can't remember, I must have been issued with my No.1 Dress Outfit, or 'Highland Dress', for I was certainly wearing my kilt when I went to the funeral. The kilt and sporran caused no difficulties, and the brogues which went with it didn't have to be shone like the boots.

The funeral is memorable for the fact that after it, Granny consulted her medical son, Uncle Lex, to tell him that Granda had said some awful things to her, while waiting for the doctor to come. He had apparently told her that although he was very much afraid of dying, it would be worth it to finally get away from her, after the life she had led him over many years. Lex was able to reassure her that one should not take seriously the things people say *in extremis,* as there can be an interrupted blood supply to the brain, etc. Once Granny had been put to bed, the rest of the family joyfully agreed that Granda had been very much in his right mind!

War Office Selection Board

It must have been shortly after this that the time to attend my WOSB came round. The Selection Board was held at an army camp in Wiltshire, and the train journey to Andover seemed endless. I travelled on my own, and I recall an army lorry picking me up at the station. I was put into a smallish barrack room with only five other soldiers, all from various different regiments. Six to a room was comparative luxury, and there were no kit inspections. We were issued with a kind of bib which went over our heads and tied at the waist. We were told we must never take it off, as it had our identifying number on it, front and back. The social set up was quite sophisticated. We ate together at tables with linen and napkins, and were served by orderlies as would have happened in an officer's mess. I suppose this was all done to see if we had been well enough brought up not to let the side down later. There was still a strong element of 'class' in the army at that time. We did lots of written tests, and there were several interviews. We also were formed into teams and had to undertake initiative tests. I remember one very clearly as it cropped up on television in the intervening years. There were some long planks and some empty drums, and a narrow ravine with muddy water at the bottom. We were to get ourselves and our various objects across the ravine, leaving nothing behind. We had to take turns being the leader. At one point I found myself at the bottom of a ditch on my face in the mud, with other team members walking over my back. I remember that when I got back on dry land the Lieutenant with the clipboard came over to me, and with some distaste wiped enough mud off my number plate to be able to make a note of it. I had a sneaking suspicion at that point that I was not distinguishing myself. I also remember the final interview with the officer in charge, who I think may have been a Lieutenant-Colonel. He asked me all sorts of things, and especially why I wanted to be an officer in the first place. I remember very clearly what his last question was, because I very obviously got it wrong. He said, 'Well, now Youngson, tell me, what is the first responsibility of an officer?

I knew the answer to that one and said clearly: 'The care of his men, Sir.'

A shadow passed over his face, and he dismissed me showing no further interest. I was on my way back north the next day, still without any idea what I had said that was so unacceptable.

On my return to Fort George I was called before the CO who broke the news to me that I hadn't passed my WOSB. 'Of course you haven't failed, either,' he said, 'they've called you D.W. That stands for "Deferred: Watch", so you may get another chance.' He made it clear that this wasn't terribly likely as I had by this time used up four months of my two years service, and as I would be unlikely to finally get to Staff College until well into the New Year, the army would be unlikely to train me as an officer because they wouldn't get much out of it. 'Now if I could persuade you to sign on for an extra year, as a three year regular soldier, the situation would be completely different, and I could more or less guarantee you a commission.'

The CO was evidently disappointed that this prospect did not appeal to me, and before dismissing me, he asked if I had any idea why I had not succeeded at Andover. I gave him a brief account, and then spoke of my final interview, leading up to the critical concluding question about an officer's responsibility.

'And what did you answer', said the CO.

'I said "the care of his men, sir",' I replied.

'You young fool,' snapped the CO. 'That was the wrong answer, and of course you should have known. You were told about that question before you went down.'

'Well, sir,' I asked, 'What was the right answer?'

'His men, Sir', came the reply.

I had blown it. Good old wishy-washy Peter had to include a reference to 'care' which spoiled the entire concept. I've never forgotten it. 'His men, Sir.' Life could have been quite different. It was one of those turning points.

The British Army of the Rhine

Another training intake had started its six weeks course on 6th November, and had its passing out parade on 18th December. A couple of days later this new draft was on the move and going out to join the regiment in Germany. There was no point in keeping me back in Fort George any longer and I was added to the new batch. There were NCOs and Officers in the party. We went down to London and back up to Harwich, before embarking on our ship. She was called the Empire Wandsbeck. Originally a Dutch boat designed for ferrying around inshore coastal waters, she was flat bottomed and had a reputation for rolling fiercely even in a comparatively calm sea. We piled up the gang plank, and immediately found very cosy little cabins with bunks in which we stowed our kit bags. Not for long!

A sergeant poked his head in:

'What the hell do you think you lot are doing – you're down below!'

We were! Far down below. At each deck we tried to stop but were directed down a further ladder until we came to where we evidently belonged, right against the keel, in the depths of the boat. It was hot and poorly lit, but there were hammocks, and we were told to get some rest. We had been warned that we were facing a rough crossing to the Hook of Holland, and indeed the ship began to roll about almost at once. The motion was violent and unpredictable and almost immediately people began to be sick. It was a long and miserable night before we docked at the Hook. We disembarked in the morning and boarded a troop train at the docks. Some basic rations were provided for breakfast and we set off across Holland. The train journey was in fact shorter than the run from Inverness to London, more like the distance between London and Edinburgh. We stopped at the German border and at a station called

Osnabrück, which seemed to be a major junction. Late in the day we arrived in the city of Hamburg and disembarked from the train. The usual fleet of lorries was waiting to take us to our barracks. This was located in a little outlying town called Buxtehude, which lay only about twelve miles from the city centre to the west.

We didn't learn until much later that Buxtehude is the German place name which is a source of mirth to all Germans because its inhabitants are all mad.

The well-known saying is 'Buxtehude, wo die Hunde mit dem Schwanz bellen'; which translates as 'Buxtehude, where the dogs bark with their tails.'

Our camp had been a prestigious SS barracks during the war, and had survived in good condition. It had been renamed Spey Barracks by its Highland Brigade occupiers. The photographs I have from this time show it to be a fine collection of buildings, in a spacious setting, and set off by trees and shrubs and plenty of grass spaces. The road system which ran through it was of high quality and the roads themselves were wide. First impressions were that it would be a pleasant place to stay, and nothing the army could do managed to completely dispel that early idea. We were assigned to barrack rooms, and given something to eat before the exhaustion of the journey hit us and we had our first night in Germany.

Life in the Battalion

I was now in BAOR, in the Highland Brigade and in the 1st Battalion Seaforth Highlanders. I was there just in time for Christmas!

I was posted to A Company. There were four companies, A, B, C, and D, and Headquarters. I had done six weeks longer than the intake I came over with, and moreover was a 'deferred: watch', so they gave me a temporary stripe. I became an unpaid, temporary, lance-corporal, and joined the new intake on advanced training.

There was a great deal to adjust to. We were now in the Battalion, and no longer rookies. We were supposed to take everything in our stride. Drill and inspections were probably just as rigorous, but we were supposed to know how to cope with them now that we were real soldiers. Even I began to adjust. At long last I was able to begin to swop the awful recruit's uniform for things with a better fit. I even got boots of the right size, and they were second-hand, which meant that they had already been polished. I exchanged my useless belt brasses for shinier ones, and my original and dreadful 'hat t.o.s.' (short for Tam-o-Shanter) for a more respectable version.

Everything was a lot better in Buxtehude than it had been in Fort George. The canteen food was really quite good, and there was an excellent NAAFI where you could get first class food to supplement your diet. There was always a severe shortage of money. As I mentioned earlier, the pay during my national service was twenty-eight shillings a week. This small sum didn't go very far. However, I found a small but useful additional income from the fact that I was a non-smoker. I had never experimented with cigarettes, probably because my father and mother didn't smoke. I didn't find it attractive, and was never interested in starting. In Germany cigarettes were strictly rationed and could only be purchased with coupons which were issued free to every soldier. There were plenty of smokers who would pay a lot to increase their ration, and I sold my coupons on a regular basis for a sum which was almost as much as the army paid me.

'Grannie' Tait

As well as advantages there were some drawbacks. The camp was overseen by a notorious RSM. It was literally overseen, as his office was situated within a little building on the bridge which spanned the main entrance to the camp. RSM Tait, whose universal nickname was Grannie Tait, was a very senior Warrant Officer indeed. At the time of my service he was second in seniority only to RSM Britain of the Guards, and he was immensely jealous of his position and prestige. Everyone in the camp was afraid of him, including the officers. His duties included drilling the junior subalterns, and although he was required to address them as 'Mister', he still treated them with withering contempt. He had, I think, a sadistic streak. He would spot someone marching into camp and up the main road. If he thought that the man's comportment was lacking in military precision he would lean out of his window, and bellow out that they should come back down the road and start again. He had a huge voice, and he would deliberately wait until the miscreant was almost out of sight at the top of the hill before employing it. Many a soldier doubled down to the gate and marched up that road more than once before escaping from sight. Much later, when I was working as a clerk in the Orderly Room I had a good deal to do with Grannie Tait, as I had to take papers into his office. He had obviously looked at my record and knew all about me. One day he said to me that 'unlike some people, I was not born with a silver spoon in my mouth; I got where I am by sheer hard work.' I didn't feel that he and I ever became close! The idea that I was in the silver spoon category was a novel one to me.

I think everyone shortly after arrival had a personal interview with the Commanding Officer, Colonel Graham. He was a most cultured and kindly man, and seemed to have some awareness that I was something of a square peg in a round hole. I came away much impressed.

Routine in Germany

My daily life settled down to a pretty dull routine. There were route marches, weapon training, and classes in regimental history, and in health and hygiene. At the week-end there were church parades with services conducted by the Battalion Padre, a man called Captain Gilmour. He was a friendly individual and I got to know him quite well.

Life was punctuated by big events like the visit of the Colonel of the Regiment. This was Princess Margaret, and the biggest and longest parade I can ever remember was when she came on an inspection. This event lasted all day and started at dawn. The parade was inspected at intervals by ever higher echelons of officers, until finally the guest of honour arrived. The whole performance was completely self-defeating, because the men were at their smartest, cleanest and brightest first thing in the morning, and by the time of the major event were tired and fed up and somewhat bedraggled. On the day Her Royal Highness came it rained all day, and everyone was soaked. She walked up and down the lines with an umbrella being held over her and passed within few inches of me. I had never been anywhere near a genuine Royal before. The rain had made a mess of her make-up which was thick, deep and caked. Little runnels of water had carved their way down her face, and I can still see the small ravines they had left in the Royal complexion. Princess Margaret was the guest at a dinner in her honour in the Officers Mess that evening, from which wonderful stories emerged the next day.

My Accident

It was at the beginning of April that I had my accident. We were using a former guard post tower for training, and I was demonstrating sliding down the rope when a man above dropped his rifle on my head and I fell off.

I apparently landed more or less across the rail which was set up to guard its perimeter. There was a lot of pain. An ambulance rushed me into the British Military Hospital in Hamburg where I had emergency surgery.

I remember being very miserable. I was not yet nineteen years old and far from home. As I began to feel better, and to take more interest in things around me, I got to know some of the lads in the other beds in the ward.

One lad in particular I have never forgotten. He was a Canadian soldier with the rank of private. He had been employed as a driver, and had been driving an ambulance on an army exercise. He was flagged down by one of his own officers and told by this officer to drive him to some location. The officer became impatient with his driving and told him to drive faster. The driver objected and refused to increase his speed on grounds of safety. The officer took over the ambulance and shortly after, crashed it at great speed. The officer went through the windscreen and cut his own throat, being killed outright. Our hero was thrown out of the side of the army ambulance. However, he had been bracing himself by wedging his foot under the handbrake. In the accident he was thrown clear, but his foot remained behind in the ambulance. The loss of the foot was a disaster for him as in civilian life he had lived as a trapper in a remote outback region of Saskatchewan, and felt he was unlikely to be able to go on with his normal life. He received visits from the top brass of his Canadian unit, who brought sumptuous hampers of goodies. He couldn't manage these, and they were all shared around the ward.

He was a magician with knives, which were a part of his profession. He got hold of a dartboard from somewhere, and I was nominated to hold it in my bed on the opposite side of the ward. He had several small throwing knives with which he was expert, and he would throw these across the ward into the dart board. He did this while people were moving about on the ward and caused a lot of alarm, but he had a winning manner, and after all, he had lost a foot. He would also do a party trick where you put your hand down on a board with the fingers spread. You could put a sheet of paper on the board and draw the outline of your hand if you wished. He would then bring the point of the knife down on the board between your fingers and create a pattern of stabbing movements which would go up and down between each finger, getting faster and faster until the impacts sounded like a machine gun. The pattern left on the paper would show how accurate he had been, and I never saw him scratch anyone's finger. Very many years later an android character called Bishop in the famous film 'Alien' did the same trick, but I had seen it long, long before.

Convalescent Leave

Once I had my stitches and other bits removed, I think I began to bounce back quite quickly. I was surprised to discover that I wasn't being sent back to my unit, but instead was to go on two weeks convalescent leave to the ski resort of Bad Harzburg, in the Harz mountains. Bad Harzburg was a long way from Hamburg, about 150 miles on the train. The military passes I had been given covered transport, and my accommodation and food at a nice hotel in the little town were settled by military vouchers. I had been instructed to rest and get my strength back, but I remember nothing about the visit except that I was lonely and miserable.

This seems to have been a sad waste of an opportunity, as I am sure that I would find plenty to interest me if I were to go back to Bad Harzburg now, but I was probably in no condition to take advantage of what was on offer. I have a vague recollection of splendid mountain scenery; of watching a lot of skiing, and of going up and down in a cable car; but little else. I think now that the reason for all this special treatment was that the army authorities were well aware that my injury had been due to their neglect of safety procedures, and it would be best to treat me well, lest I contact my family at home and make a complaint.

Light Duties and the Opera

I returned to Buxtehude, expecting to resume my duties, but was told by the MO that I wasn't properly fit yet, and would have to stay on light duties. I could do suitable jobs about the place each morning, and in the afternoon a car would be allocated to me with a local German driver who would take me out for the good of my health. The car provided was a post war Volkswagen, with the familiar beetle outline, and with my driver, who I think was called Hans (which seems quite likely), we explored the countryside and parts of the city. We visited the Alster lake and its canals. It was while talking with the driver, with some difficulty, that I learned of the State Opera House or Staatsoper. He believed that the afternoon rehearsals were open to the public. I desired to go, and was taken immediately. Admission was no difficulty and I was soon seated in the auditorium watching and listening to Mozart.

I couldn't get out of the camp without being in full Highland Dress, so I must have been a striking member of the small group of people who came in to listen. Certainly it was not long before performers came to speak to me during breaks between their rehearsals. All were intent on practising their English. Soon the fact that I was a Scottish soldier who had been a keen singer before the army spread through the company. I was asked to sing, and was very willing to oblige. The world famous leading bass, Herr Gottlob Frick, came to meet me, and engage me in lively conversation. His English was excellent as he was a most sophisticated world performer. He was also a great show off, and used to enjoy getting someone to punch him in the stomach while he was singing a sustained note. I was tickled pink to receive all this attention. It didn't last very long before my privileges were withdrawn and I returned to normal duties. I think it might have gone on for a couple of weeks. It remains for me a happy experience. I had been made much of, and positive opinions had been passed on the extraordinary quality and power of my voice. It was even suggested that I might be able to embark on a musical career in Hamburg once my military service was over, and I was encouraged to write from Scotland when that day came. I have often retold the story of a conversation with Herr Frick in which he foresaw my musical future – starting with him in Hamburg. I think only the general lines of the story are truly original, and I probably polished it up a bit to make it sound better.

The retold version goes like this:

'Ah! You will come back here and study here with me for three years. Then we will send you to La Scala, Milan, and you will study there for three years. After that, to Berlin – three years: and lastly to New York – three years. And then some day ... some day ... you will be *great* singer. Like me!!'

The exact places he mentioned I am not sure of, but I remember the sense of anxiety as the length of the apprenticeship built up stage upon stage, and I have never forgotten the closing phrase: 'Like me!!'

I doubt if I was able to be in my place at these public rehearsals more than about five or six times, but on this slender platform, I later constructed highly embroidered and romantic stories of my involvement with the Hamburg State Opera. I even put it about that I had been trained to sing in Hamburg, and had been a member of the chorus. My excuse is that I was very young. I desperately wanted my voice to be taken seriously, and my colourfully made up CV was very useful in getting me a more attentive hearing than I might otherwise have had. The story followed me many years after I had begun to publicly disavow its truth, and I had the unfortunate experience of being introduced at recitals as the bass who had sung with the Hamburg State Opera. It was all most embarrassing, but truly, it was only what I deserved. Later I did actually attend some performances at the Opera on a week-end pass.

By the time I returned to full duties my temporary unpaid lance-corporal's stripe had disappeared for ever, and I was back to the basic rank of private.

Orderly Room Clerk

On my return to normal duties, in recognition of my education, and probably with the 'watch' label still hanging around, I was seconded to help in the Company Office where I messed around with papers and files and lists of equipment. I had no idea what I was doing and I doubt if I was of much value. However the Company Commander obviously thought that I had some potential in this direction, and I was seconded to go off on a three months course to Bielefeld to be trained as an army clerk. This was a wonderful skive, and I remember being very content with my lot for the first time since I started in the Seaforths. Most of the course consisted of classes in typing, which of course meant touch typing. I found it very difficult, and I don't think I displayed much talent. However, there were plenty of people on the course who were worse than me, and in due course I sat and passed my trade test as Clerk B III on 30th October 1953.

On my return to duty in Buxtehude I was posted to Headquarters Company and told to report to the Orderly Room, where I joined the team of Orderly Room clerks with whom I spent the next eight months or so. There were nine of us, and we became quite a close knit group. We ran the Battalion, or so we believed. Over us was the Battalion Adjutant, Major W.C. Cheyne, MM.

William Chandos Cheyne was a professional soldier about forty-five years of age. He was over six feet tall, very fair-haired and going bald. His surname was pronounced to rhyme with chain, and so his whole name could be thought of as 'W.C. Chain', which produced a great deal of amusement. He had served with the Seaforth Highlanders for a number of years, getting his commission around the end of the war. He had recently been with the Battalion in Malaya. It was there he was involved in the action which resulted in his award. The story was told to me by a sergeant who had served in Malaya, and had been close to the event. Major Cheyne was Orderly Officer of the Day when the Battalion was moving along a long jungle path on the business of moving camp. Even in the tropics, the Officer of the Day wore his kilt, and went about with his dress claymore slung in its scabbard from his belt. It was reported to him that Support Company were lagging behind the main body as usual. Support Company consisted of the Catering Corps, or cooks, and the Pioneer Corps, the dogsbodies who dug latrines, etc. Major Cheyne was making his way back down the path to encourage them to catch up when he heard gunfire. A party of Malaysian terrorists, or, if we prefer it, a party of Freedom Fighters, turned out to be entrenched at the top of a steep wooded slope overlooking the main trail. They had lain quiet and allowed the entire Battalion to pass through without announcing their presence, but they had now opened fire on the cooks and the others.

When the Major came to the place he found men down hurt, and others being hit. The situation looked bad and he decided there was only one thing to be done. He drew his claymore and charged up the slope at the terrorists, screaming his head off. He must have been an extraordinary sight, with his bald head shining in the sun, his kilt and his broadsword. The Malaysians took only one look at him and took to their heels into the jungle. It was a bizarre episode, and no doubt worthy of his decoration. I heard that later in the campaign he was put in charge of dealing with casualties, and was involved with the local branch of the War Graves Commission. We all thought he had seen too much tragedy, and had been badly affected by it.

Whatever the cause, the Adjutant was unpredictable, irascible and given to sudden outbursts of temper. At such times it was best to keep one's head well down. Below the Adjutant, the Orderly Room staff were technically headed by their senior NCO, a lance-corporal, whom we found unreliable. He liked to feel that he was popular with the rest of us, but wouldn't hesitate to betray us to the Adjutant if he thought it would improve his situation. We all treated him with a good deal of contempt. My seven other colleagues in the Orderly Room were mostly good-natured and pleasant. Among this company I at long last began to fit in.

Orderly Room Life

Life in the Orderly Room was quite reasonable. We still had to attend parades and drills, but Headquarters Company was slightly more relaxed. We had to do our share of guard duties as well. It was the business of being on guard that got me in trouble. Guard duty was a miserable business. You had to wear highland dress, with those wretched white gaiters which had to be buttoned with a buttonhook, with the ever present risk of tearing off buttons. You had to have your entire kit as presentable as it would have needed to be during basic training. You then spent two hours on and four hours off all through the night, trying to get some kind of sleep in the guardroom, where there were no proper bunks. You had to behave the next day as if nothing had happened, and go on with the normal routine although you were half asleep. The guard itself could be a nervous business. Some of the stations, such as the one concerned with our ammunition storehouse, were quite remote. Of course there was always the chance that the Orderly Officer would take a turn round the various posts in the middle of the night. Many of us tried to get the odd few moments of sleep while actually standing up. Some tried to make sure they stayed awake by standing with their bayonet sticking up under their chin, a dodge I never dared to try. One night I had dropped off at a remote outpost. I was fast asleep, standing up, when I became distantly aware of the RSM's face shoved close up against mine. I kept my presence of mind, and straightened up smartly.

'You were asleep, Laddie! Asleep!'

'Oh no, RSM, not at all. I was engaged in meditation.'

I got away with that one, but only just.

Confined to Barracks

On one memorable occasion I didn't get away with it. On one guard duty, I had had no proper opportunity for getting my kit organised, and I turned out in a poor state, simply hoping it would go unnoticed. The Officer of the Day was a particularly unpleasant Captain, who was known to be of the opinion that Headquarters Company were all skivers and needed to be given a serious shock. He was obviously delighted to find Private Youngson of the Orderly Room on guard in filthy kit, and put me on a charge. The next morning I was on Orders. This was the daily parade of miscreants for the Company Commander's attention. You lined up outside the Commander's office door with two men who were to constitute prisoner's escort.

The CSM was there to snap out the commands:

'Escort, accused and evidence; quick march – left wheel – mark time – halt!'

We all slithered in on the polished floor. I waited to hear my fate. There was no way my offence could be overlooked. The Company Commander looked up at me.

'I'm disappointed to see you here, Youngson,' he said, 'A man of your education. Anything to say?'

'No, Sir!'

'Seven days CB.'

Seven days Confined to Barracks was a life sentence. You had to perform all your normal duties as if nothing was out of the ordinary. However, each day had defaulters parades and drills, morning noon and night. These parades were under the scrutiny of the Regimental Police (the RPs), headed by the Provost Sergeant, and they were extremely harsh. It was only too easy to be caught out with something that wasn't up to scratch, and find yourself back on another charge. Charges brought against one while actually on Jankers, as the punishment was called, were treated severely. Seven days CB could turn into a long-term sentence. This was most likely if you were isolated, or had a hostile attitude. By this time I had learned to keep my thoughts about the army to myself, and I was surrounded by pals who would put together a good set of spotless kit for me. In the evenings and the whole of the week-end you were at the mercy of the RPs, and that was the time when you could get involved in the absurdly meaningless chores which were supposed to constitute the punishment. There was the scrubbing of wooden floors, which when completed would have to be done again because the police corporal would immediately walk over the scrubbed area with soil on his boots. I thought then and still think that the Military Police and the Regimental Police attracted the kind of soldier who enjoyed this kind of thing, and took a sadistic pleasure in enforcing his will.

It was interesting to me that you could tell the worst of them by their headgear. They all affected a cap known as a hard man hat. The cap they were issued with had a shiny peak which jutted horizontally straight out above the eyebrows. These hard men had their caps altered so that the peak ran down at a sharp angle, following the line of the nose, like a Norman soldier's helmet from the Bayeux Tapestry. Over many years I have identified similar modifications to the caps of some civilian policemen. I suppose I haven't really had sufficient opportunity to test whether this means the wearers tend to a similar sadistic outlook, but I have my suspicions.

At the end of an evening on CB you would get back to your barrack room so tired that you would drop on your bunk in full kit and fall asleep. I survived my first seven days CB and vowed I would never, ever get caught out again. I managed it, but on one occasion much later it was a very near thing.

Printing and Battalion Orders

An infantry battalion contained about six hundred men, and the administration to keep it all running smoothly was considerable. Everyone in the Orderly Room had his own particular responsibilities. Each individual in the unit was kept careful track of and there were two clerks with the title of Documents Clerk who dealt with everyone's personal moves, promotions, offences, and every recorded aspect of everyone's life. There were stores to be accounted for, and military supplies and equipment. There was a motor pool. There were weapons and ammunition. There was the Battalion Pipe Band (a vital part of any Highland Regiment!). As part of BAOR we were part of the occupying power, and we had a role in border security between East and West Germany. Border patrols and their consequent reports became a fact of life in the Orderly Room.

I became personally responsible for Battalion Orders. These typed foolscap sheets contained the day to day business of the Battalion, and were posted on company notice boards throughout the camp. Much of the material in them came down from the CO and then through the Adjutant to me. They would be typed in draft on paper, and then re-typed on stencils, familiarly called skins. These would go to a nearby room occupied by the Battalion printer, a wee Glaswegian soldier of the Highland Light Infantry (HLI) called Danny McAlinden.

Danny was under five feet tall, and a happy, cheerful colleague with a great line of patter, and a strong Glasgow accent which was often hard to understand. He was hard working and reliable, and neat, clean work flowed steadily out of his print room day after day. All this description applies solely to when he was sober, for Danny, as they used to say, 'took an awful bucket.' At the week-ends he would get a pass and go out with his mates to the local pub, the Zwei Linden (the Two Lime Trees), and get riotously drunk on local German Elbschloss (Elbe Castle Beer) – taken with spirits if he could get them, which he usually could. Unfortunately strong drink filled Danny with the overwhelming desire to take anybody on. He became fighting drunk, and when the mood was on him he was virtually unstoppable. He was what was known in Glasgow as 'a wee hard man.' On his arrival back in camp, he would need to be forcibly restrained, and it could take four or more big strong men to do it. He would be put into our detention cell, and let out in the morning, when he had sobered up. He was never charged unless he damaged someone. If he had been, he would never have been out of detention. In any case he was much too valuable to the regiment. Who else would have produced Battalion Orders? On one occasion he got it into his head while very drunk that I had done something he didn't like. He entered our billet block, shouting out my name. Big men came from all around and made a kind of human wall between Danny and me down the middle of the barrack room. Danny approached inexorably, casting them aside as if they were paper dolls. About a foot short of his target, me, he was finally felled to the ground and carted away. There was a sense of last minute reprieve which I can still recollect all these years later.

Useful at Last

I should mention that Private Youngson of the Orderly Room was not only useful as a regular source of cigarette coupons, but also as a companion on nights out to the above Zwei Linden. The value of my company was that I was at that time teetotal. I was regularly approached to go out with the lads, who would keep me supplied with soft drinks until the time came to get back to camp. I was then supposed to round them up and supervise them as they shambled up the road to the barracks. On arrival, any of them who were sufficiently sober would go through the guardroom, and those who were not would get the treatment from me. I would stand them up one by one and slap some sense into them. When they could answer to their name and rank and number I would push them individually towards the gate. They would present themselves more or less vertical and give their details, and be booked in and passed through. It was extraordinary how sober they could appear to be for the short period of time that was required. I would then go through myself. At various distances inside the camp I would find my companions lying on the grass. They then had to be piloted back to their billets. It was not an arduous job, and it got me a number of grateful friends, always useful in the army.

Shortly after I joined the Orderly Room staff I had the anniversary of my arrival in Germany. Even we National Servicemen were entitled to have a home leave after one year in an overseas posting, I applied for my two weeks leave, and got it. I was going to be home for Christmas. I travelled in my battledress and the journey took for ever. However, my Christmas leave was a great success, with an unaccustomed warmth from my father, and Christmas music to sing in the church choir. Even more important was the fact that I was able to pack a complete outfit of my own civilian clothes to take back to Germany, and from that point on I was allowed to go out of camp in civvies, which made a significant difference to the whole experience of being in the army.

The Adjutant

I seem to have emerged from my course as the best typist in the Orderly Room, so I was made responsible not only for Daily Orders, but for quite a lot of items of correspondence. The Adjutant was pernickety about such work to the point of obsession. The rule was that a complete foolscap sheet of typing could be allowed one single mistake, and that only if it had been invisibly corrected. On our heavy old Olivetti machines the only way to make a correction was to scrape the offending letter off with a razor blade and type over it. This had to be done without removing the page, as it could never be got back in exactly the right spot. The corrected area ended up looking all right, but the paper had been thinned in the process, and the Adjutant used to hold the sheets up to the light and pick out the corrections. If there was more than one to a page it would come back with the whole page slashed across with blue pencil to be typed again. It often took many attempts to produce an acceptable typescript, and I remember being reduced almost to tears of vexation by this process. My father's mantra – care and accuracy – might have been formulated specially for Major Cheyne, and he often used it almost word for word, to my chagrin.

My own relationship with Major Cheyne was a curious one, and no doubt says something about each of us. It was quite different from his relationship with anyone else in the Orderly Room. I think this was not only because he respected my education and broad general knowledge, but because he probably knew that I wasn't afraid of him. The Adjutant was accustomed to getting his way, and he would reinforce his military rank, which was considerable, by narrowing his eyes to an intense stare, and shouting at people. That evidently worked very well with many people, and certainly everyone in the Orderly Room was very frightened of him indeed. One or two lived in such dread of his anger that they became quite depressed. I suppose my early experience of a person who thought that all she had to do to exercise power was to behave like this was of my grandmother, who had exercised iron control over my grandfather and over my mother and father for many years. I could never see any reason why I should be afraid of her. She was a little old woman who couldn't do anything to me, and had no power over me at all, so I never felt alarmed. I felt equally untroubled when I met people trying to exercise that kind of dominance from the position of being a teacher at my school. I knew that Major Cheyne had no power to do anything to me at all, as long as I didn't break the army's rules, so I saw no reason to be afraid of him, and I think he must have known this, although he never indicated that he did. This is not to say that I am brave in all circumstances. When confronted with real physical danger to my person, I am terrified, and would do anything to escape without harm, but I am not lacking in what might be called moral courage.

How did the Adjutant know that I was bright? Well, I wrote and spoke excellent English, using a big vocabulary. I was more literate than he was himself, despite the fact that I suspect he went to a public school. And then there was the Battalion quiz. This was quite a modest affair, completely internal and between the five companies. A to D and Headquarters. It was held in the NAAFI. I had always vowed that I would never take part in such an activity after my famous debacle in Top of the Form, but this was the Army, and I was simply instructed to be there. I was the only private in our team of three, along with a Lieutenant and a Warrant Officer. All the questions could be consulted about, and it would be safe to say that I was almost solely responsible for our team winning as I knew the answers to most of the general knowledge questions, and was often the only person who did.

Major Cheyne, though himself almost tone deaf, was a passionate lover of classical music, and had a big collection of gramophone records. By the time I joined the Orderly Room I had already appeared in one or two Battalion concerts in which I had sung a mixture of popular and classical music, so he was aware of my talent in that area, and like many music lovers who do not themselves play or perform, he admired people who could make music. In connection with these concerts, I found I was in demand to perform, and I was keen to oblige. I sent home for quite a lot of sheet music which my mother posted out to me. The Education Corps sergeant, who taught English to those who needed to improve, played very well and there was a good upright piano in the NAAFI. I sang my way through quite a number of songs and operatic arias, and felt very confident while doing it.

None of any of this meant that the Adjutant gave me an easy time. In fact he may have been harder on me than on the others, but my visits to his office would often have unexpected outcomes. He would ask me what I thought about politics or religion, and where I thought the world was going. After a lively conversation, for I was quite unabashed about entering into these discussions, he would pull himself together and say something like 'Right then! Let's get back to business!'

It was all most odd. It also resulted in me being chosen as the person who would go in to see him to ask for some privilege or favour for someone too nervous to do it for themselves. I remember going in with a leave warrant for a man whose mother was gravely ill back in Scotland, and who was consequently entitled to compassionate leave. He signed the form, and asked why the man wasn't there in person. When I suggested that he found the Adjutant a little daunting and had asked that someone else would go in in his place, Major Cheyne was plainly amazed and a little disappointed. 'How could anyone possibly find me daunting, Youngson?'

Claymore Drill

In view of the fact that a regimental dress claymore had featured in the action in which he got his decoration, it is not perhaps surprising that he had an abiding obsession with the weapon. The claymore is a beautiful big sword with a blade almost a metre long. Properly called a basket-hilted broadsword, its popular name derived from the Gaelic 'claidheamh mor', or 'great sword'. It had been in use in Scotland since the seventeenth century. The blade was straight and two-edged and the basket hilt was fitted inside with a layer of leather. Traditionally made and signed by Andrea Ferrara, modern claymores had to continue to be manufactured to meet the need to equip newly commissioned subalterns in highland regiments. I had the opportunity to look at several brand new swords, and they still seemed to be superbly crafted. The Officer of the Day was required to wear his claymore, and the Adjutant was obsessed with the idea that the ancient drill movements developed for its ceremonial use in earlier generations should be kept up and practised. To this end he held compulsory sword drill for all the subalterns and junior officers. I think this happened about once a month, and I know it was looked forward to by the whole battalion and dreaded by the officers. If we were not occupied at the time, which was possible because the drill would take place early in the morning, we would line the parade ground to watch. The perennially tricky part of rifle drill was the fixing of bayonets. The equivalent awkward move with the claymore was the sheathing of the weapon after use. To set the long blade safely back in its scabbard, the point had to be guided into the narrow opening at the top of the sheath. This delicate manoeuvre was effected by taking hold of the tip of the sword with the thumb and forefinger of the left hand. One searched for the aperture with the next finger, and delicately slipped the tip into place for the first inch or two. Only when one was confident that the point was securely located could the sword be slammed down into the scabbard with a swift and powerful movement of the right hand, before coming back to attention. The need to glance down to one's left, to see where the tip of the sword actually was, was obviously overwhelming and it took superhuman nerve to resist, combined with a lot of private practice. The problem for the young Second Lieutenants was that it was impossible to get the necessary look down without visibly moving the head. It was a complete give-away, and the slightest movement of the head would bring the command 'Keep still!' ringing out from the Adjutant in front.

On the well remembered day which provides the reason for describing this matter, the Adjutant was irritated enough by a very poor showing to demonstrate himself how the blade should be sheathed. I was myself on the side of the square and remember every detail. He shouted out to himself 'On the command – blade – sheath!' and slammed the sword down. There was a breathless pause, during which it became obvious that although down in its proper vertical position and almost touching the ground, the claymore was still separate from its scabbard and not inside it. Major Cheyne did not move an inch, but bawled out 'Carry on, Sergeant Major!', and marched smartly off the parade ground. He passed only a few feet from where I was standing, and the blood pouring from his hand left an unbroken trail along the ground. We later pieced together what had happened. He had guided the tip of the sword not into the opening in the scabbard, but into the space between it and the top leather strap which surrounded the sheath. When he rammed the sword down, it cut through the strap and ran across the fingers of his left hand, cutting them almost to the bone. He was a long time with the Medical Officer, and the hand was bandaged for some weeks. His military bearing throughout was absolutely flawless. He was, as I have said, a quite extraordinary character.

Amendments

To correct any impression I may have given that I was somehow a favourite of the Adjutant's, I can adduce some matters which prove otherwise.

The first concerns amendments. A regular and much loathed chore in the Orderly Room concerned the army's bible which was called King's Regulations. Every regiment had its own copy or copies. I think we had two. The War Office issued a continual stream of new and changed regulations which had to be incorporated into this volume. These came out more or less weekly in the form of amendments. These had to be cut and pasted. This phrase has become familiar in computer language as something you do to move text in a computer document, but at that time, cutting and pasting meant exactly what it said. Each amendment had to be clipped out of the sheet, its location in the book identified, and then it had to be pasted over the existing print. The job was tedious, and frequently evidently pointless, like so many of the procedures the regiment had to follow. We took it in turns to do the amendments. Until the day when the Adjutant sent for me.

'I've got a nice little job for you, Youngson,' he said. 'It's your turn to do amendments. Here's the latest batch. Now mind! These are to be done in your spare time.' And I was dismissed. When I got back into the main office I opened the bulky package and found the latest batch of amendments. The Queen's accession to the throne in February 1952 had finally come to the notice of the War Office, which had decided that King's Regulations would from now on be known as Queen's Regulations. Every mention of the maleness of the monarch throughout the volume was now to be replaced with a pronoun indicating femaleness. Every 'he' became a 'she', and every 'his' a 'hers', and so on. There were hundreds and hundreds of such references and I was at it for weeks and weeks. There was no possibility of skimping on the job. It was exactly the kind of thing that our obsessive boss would love to pick on. To finger through the book, and notice a surviving 'he', would give him huge pleasure, and result in one of his famous tellings off.

The Battalion Crest

The question of Battalion Orders contained one aspect which was definitely a painful responsibility and could be thought of as countering the theory of favouritism. The Adjutant was totally committed to the idea that each day's Orders had to be produced on paper which was headed with the Battalion crest, the name of the Battalion and the current date. This could not easily be managed on the equipment available to us in 1954. However, there was in Danny McAlinden's printer's room a very ancient rotary printer which was capable of doing this job. Unfortunately Danny had no love for this machine, and no great aptitude for it either, and after numerous disasters the Adjutant had me into the office.

'You're an intelligent man, Youngson, I'm going to make you solely responsible for the daily headings on Battalion orders.'

It was a heavy punishment. The printer had a steel drum about a foot in diameter which was equipped with grooves across its surface into which pieces of typeface could be slid. It was in contact with a roller which could be inked, and individual sheets of paper could be presented to it; and after turning the handle these would hopefully emerge bearing the image of whatever you slid in. There was a complete box of letters and numbers to accompany this old war-horse, whose maker's name and date put it back to about the turn of the century. You could with care and patience have used the supply of print to set up a whole page of text and print out pages with a complete story on them, but Major Cheyne didn't want this, he merely wanted the top line to read:

'1st Battalion Seaforth Highlanders . . . . 14th May 1954'.

This in itself would not have posed too many problems, but the Battalion crest was another story altogether. Someone had manufactured the stag's head and antlers, and the motto – 'Cuidhichean righ', or 'Save the King' – out of metal. The impression of this image was raised above the slightly curved surface of a square base which had four sliding fitments, two beneath the upper and two beneath the lower edge of the piece. The insignia could be slid, or more accurately forced, along the slots on the drum where it could end up sitting snugly in the middle of the line above the date.

This description makes the whole operation sound simplicity itself but in practice the old machine was appallingly temperamental. The inking process was hit and miss, and the pressure setting between the roller and the paper was neurotic. If any of the elements in the setting was the least bit wrong the impression on the top of the paper would be blurred and unclear. At the point at which I was made responsible for the operation, the previous week or two of Orders had had the headings more or less illegible and the Adjutant was reduced to incoherent rage. I decided that the machine had to be understood from the basics, and I cleaned and dismantled it and put it back together again. Once I had it all reassembled I started to experiment with the business of producing paper copies. Danny had taught me the printer's knack of riffling stacks of paper so that individual sheets could be easily grasped. It has remained a useful skill over many years of church magazines. The machine was very sensitive to speeds and pressures and I gradually began to be able to get good clean copies. The Adjutant's problem slowly melted away, and peace descended over the business of Battalion Orders. The old machine couldn't be taken for granted, and could come up with unexpected difficulties, but basically I seemed to have got the better of it. The headings remained my sole responsibility until the Battalion left Germany. The whole episode meant that I also became a kind of assistant printer to Danny McAlinden, and spent a lot of time in the print room.

How to Work the System

Danny and I now became close friends, and there seemed no further likelihood that he would try to attack me while in his cups, which was a relief. The situation also gave me the opportunity to see another aspect of the wee man's character. One day he took me quietly aside and said:

'Hey! Pee'ur!' (Danny couldn't pronounce Peter.)

'Would ye like tae see ma cubby hole?'

I said I was interested.

'Ye're no tae clipe till onybody noo!' (Clipe is dialect for telling tales.)

I said his secret was safe with me. He went into the back corner of the stationery department, which was part of his print room empire, and moved a stack of wrapped blocks of printing paper slightly aside.

'Come in here,' he said, and I followed him into a space which turned into a tiny room between the stores and the back wall. There was an army cot with a mattress and pillow, a wee bedside table and a chair, and a light with a cable leading out to a plug in the office.

'Ah'm all right here, Eh?' he chuckled. He was! He had it made. No one in the formal barrack rooms of Headquarters Company ever mentioned where he was, and his official bed and locker were always spotless. They could afford to be, since he hardly ever slept in them. If there was word of any kind of inspection, a rare event in Headquarters Company, somebody would tip Danny off and he would be there, bright and cheerful. As I said, he had it made. No one ever found out about his room, and he quietly dismantled it when it came time for the Battalion to move on. I wouldn't bet that he didn't manage to create a new one in his next posting.

Printer's Thumb

It was this close relationship with the printer and his printing that got me into my other spot of bother with military regulations. Many months after my session on CB I was due back on guard duty. Every single time that my turn came round since the bad one, I had asked for help with my kit; I had been particularly careful about my turnout, and had had no difficulty with it. On this occasion I turned out for inspection as usual.

The Orderly Officer of the Day was an elderly Major, commanding one of the other companies. The procedure at the beginning of guard duty involved an inspection of weapons. The rifle was held forward for inspection. The bolt was opened and the soldier's thumb was inserted into the breech so that light would be reflected up the barrel and show whether or not it was clean. The major looked in a casual kind of way, then stiffened:

'What is this that I am seeing here, soldier?'

'I'm sure my rifle's clean, sir,' I said.

'It's not your rifle barrel, soldier. It's the thumb-nail. It's absolutely filthy. Sergeant Major, put this man on a charge. Dirty nails on guard duty.'

It was an extraordinary situation, which my own company sergeant-major confessed to me that he had never heard of before.

'You'll just have to accept it, lad. It's quite correct, you shouldn't have been on guard duty with dirty finger nails, and they were dirty, the Sergeant of the Watch saw them.'

I felt pretty desperate. I had survived one sentence of seven days CB.

I didn't see myself likely to survive another. By this time there were more people around who knew me as a cocky chap, who probably needed taking down a peg, and the Regimental Police and the Provost Sergeant were just the people to do it.

But now I had some friends and a bit more support. The Orderly Room held a council of war. I don't remember who came up with the solution, but it was a good one, and immediately acted upon.

'Dirty fingernails are an occupational hazard for printers, and you are acting as assistant printer to Danny. You'll have to admit the offence but maintain it was unavoidable.'

Nail scissors were found and my fingernails and both thumbnails were clipped close to the quick. Printer's ink was obtained and rubbed deeply around each nail before the surplus was washed off. At the end of the operation there was a satisfactory half moon of black ink round each nail, including the thumb. No amount of scraping with a nailbrush or a sharp point had any effect on it. I was ready for my court appearance the next morning.

The next day I was on Company Orders as before.

The Company Commander looked up.

'Very disappointed to see you here before me again, Youngson, a man of your education. The charge, Sergeant Major.'

'Dirty fingernails on guard duty, Sir!'

'Disgraceful! Anything to say, Youngson?'

'Yes, Sir.' And without any pause I went into my prepared statement.

There was a shocked silence. 'Anything to say?' was normally a purely formal question, with the answer 'No, Sir'. It was probably quite some time since anyone had had anything to say, and furthermore actually said it.

I made my statement at attention, and drew to a close.

'Let me see those hands, Youngson. Oh yes! I see. Come and have a look at this, Sergeant Major. You did everything you could to get that black ink cleaned off before going on guard?'

Answer: 'Yes, Sir!'

'Well, then, I don't think in all honesty there's much we can do about this, Sergeant Major. Admonished! Take more care in future. Next case.'

I had done it! I had beaten the army machine! 'Admonished' was only a formal slap on the wrist which meant nothing. I was not starting another week of jankers. I was jubilant, and have never forgotten the wonderful feeling of having been let off the hook. We all went off to the NAAFI for a good supper.

Posted Home

It was in the summer of 1954 that word came that the 1st Battalion of the Seaforth Highlanders was to leave Germany, and was being posted to become part of the British Garrison at the Suez Canal. Since the Suez Crisis did not take place for a further two years, and since I was not party to all our Government's military commitments, I was not sure exactly what brought about this posting which evidently came as a big surprise to our Commanding Officer. Since the emergency in Malaysia had only ended in 1952, the Seaforths had not been long in their German posting and might have expected to stay there some time longer. At any rate the Battalion was to move out of Spey Barracks by the end of June, and briefly visit Fort George en route to its new location. The amount of service required to ensure that serving personnel would accompany them was a clear three months, and I fell well short of this, being due to start terminal leave on 17th September.

Last Duties as Printer

One of my last duties with the 1st Battalion was to help to pack up the Orderly Room. We were told that there would be no need for any of the material to be unpacked until the regiment arrived in Suez, as the unit would only just barely touch the ground in the UK before moving on. The Adjutant was insistent that as I had been responsible for the printed heading of Orders, I was to take personal responsibility for packing the rotary printer. In due course wooden packing cases arrived for the various items which required such arrangements, and a suitable one was earmarked for the printer. Major Cheyne had told me to make a good job of packing the thing, and as I contemplated the problems of getting it into the case, I had a brilliant idea. All the accumulated frustration and resentment I had built up over the previous year and a half seemed to crystallise into one simple plan. I decided that I would make a really good job of packing the printer.

I armed myself with a screwdriver and some adjustable spanners. I already knew how to dismantle the thing into its main components, but after I had finished doing that I went on to find that many other bits were bolted to each other, and I carefully separated everything in the machine that could possible come apart from anything else. This was not easy, as many of them had not been separate since they left the manufacturers, but I persisted. I have no idea how many bits I managed to get it broken down into. I think the final total was at least a couple of dozen. I didn't cheat. I didn't actually break anything. Then I took all the screws, nuts and bolts I had harvested, and mixed all of them together. Lastly I wrapped each individual part of the machine in brown paper and carefully fitted them all into my packing case.

Then I nailed the lid securely down, and stencilled the label on:

'Rotary Printer for Battalion Daily Order Headings.'

The Battalion and I moved home together about the beginning of July. They stayed a couple of nights at Fort George before shipping out to the

Middle East. I said good-bye to all my Orderly Room friends, and was bidden good luck by the Commanding Officer and the Adjutant. I later heard a rumour about the rotary printer, to the effect that it had defied all efforts to rebuild it and it had finally been scrapped. I found that most satisfying.

Printer at Elgin

I was moved to a military transit camp at Elgin to put in my last two and a half months. My trade test qualification as clerk went with me, together with my involvement with printing the Daily Orders. As it happened there was a shortage in that area, and I was given the temporary post of camp printer. The accommodation was perfect. There was a big duplicator, with a desk and typewriter, all occupying one half of the camp stationery store. Within a week I had constructed a McAlinden style hidey-hole of my own, from which I emerged once a week to collect my pay. Only I went further than McAlinden, and kept all my kit with me. There was such a continual flow of men through the Elgin camp that one person more or less, here or there, was of no consequence, and as long as the printing got done no one was interested in where the printer was. The great benefit was that I didn't have to go on daily morning parade. I could take my time in the mornings and go to the mess hut for breakfast. As long as I was at work in the print room by about 9 am no one seemed to be bothered. No one ever discovered what I was up to, and I left in good order.

Discharge

I was posted back to Fort George for my last two days, where Major Martin, who was still the Depot Commander, filled up my Discharge Army Book 111. The back page has a space for military conduct and a testimonial. This is not written in Major Martin's hand, but I was able to recognise it without any difficulty. The handwriting, which I knew so well, revealed that the appropriate page had been previously filled up in Hamburg by W. C. Cheyne, the Battalion Adjutant.

His entry may be of interest, and goes as follows:

Military Conduct – Very Good.
Testimonial – A very nice man indeed. Plenty of intelligence and has a ready and pleasant wit. A very good writer who can express himself excellently on paper. Clever and musical. Untidy in his thought except on paper.
Will do very well in civilian life. Is very honest. Is careless and must learn to be neater in his work and thought.

The Adjutant saw a good deal more of what was actually there than I intended him to. I would have said that I had concealed most of who I really was while I worked for him. But I couldn't conceal my untidiness, carelessness and lack of neatness in both work and thought.

On my last day I went for my final interview with the CO and collected my paperwork, including a final travel voucher from Inverness to Aberdeen. I then went to the clothing department of the stores to select my 'demob suit'. The Army issued every departing soldier with a complete suit of civilian clothes. I have always presumed that this custom arose since the clothes they had worn before their service would no longer be in style, but there may be a more mundane reason. The issue of the suit presumably meant that you could be divested of your battledress uniform, and leave it behind. In 1954 I undoubtedly retained my battledress, as I remember travelling home in it. Perhaps it was thought I would need it for my Territorial Service. I did however forfeit and hand in my dress uniform, with its very fine regimental kilt. The title demob suit was by this time something of an anachronism, as 'demob' was short for demobilisation, and by this time we were not really mobilised. However this remained its universal title. The set of clothes consisted of a shirt and tie, jacket and trousers, with shoes and socks. It was a very plain suit, but quite respectable, and a very good fit. There were a number of colours available and I chose a dark navy blue with a light stripe. I still have a photograph of myself wearing this suit outside the house in Cranford Road in Aberdeen. I kept it for best for quite some time.

I had already checked all my own stores and equipment against the list for which I had originally signed two years previously. The question of being made to pay for missing articles of kit was an ever productive source of argument and interest, and a lively black market was operated for such items. I had managed to hang on to just about everything, including the most prized individual item – my greatcoat. All weapons had been handed in before I left Germany.

When I got back to my temporary billet after getting my paperwork and demob suit, my kit had all vanished. My bed was stripped and my locker empty. I presented myself at the stores, and reported that my kit was missing.

'No kit, no signature: you'll be paying for this for the rest of your life.'

I remember my reaction.

'Look here! You're not dealing with some raw rookie who doesn't know what's going on. You're dealing with a hard man here. I've been with the Battalion a couple of years. My kit has only just been handed in by the thief who stole it. That's probably it over there.'

I was round the counter and opening an evidently recently deposited kit bag before anyone could stop me. It was mine, with all the individual army numbers on each piece. Only the big number on the kit bag and on the greatcoat had been clumsily changed.

'You never took the trouble to check all these numbers – see, 22720464 – that's me. You'll be going on a charge for this.'

The documentation was completed without a word, and I took my leave. I had come a long way from the recruit who had climbed down from the truck onto the drill square at Fort George two years before. No one was going to mess me about.

On 17th September 1954 I was discharged from the army to begin three weeks of terminal leave before formally reporting to the Territorial Army at Woolmanhill in Aberdeen. Although I was legally liable for a further five and a half years part-time territorial service, the fact that I entered University seems to have wiped that requirement out, and I heard no more of the Army.

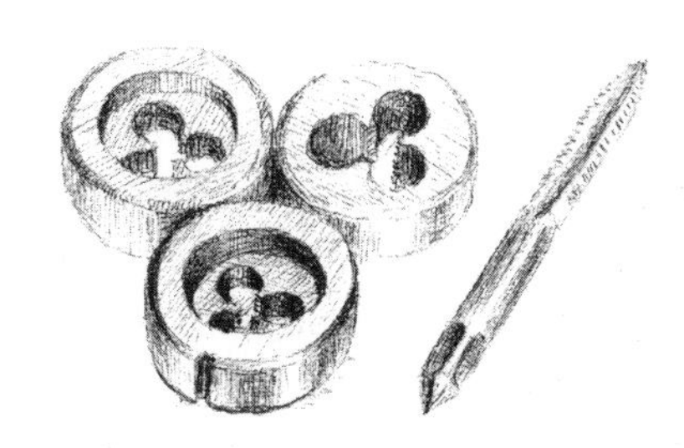

Chapter Three: Far Countries on the Road to the Ministry

I left the army on 17th September 1954, and although I was supposed to be liable for five and a half years further part-time service as a Territorial Army soldier with the Gordon Highlanders in Aberdeen, I was never required to put in another appearance – presumably because no national emergency took place to involve me.

I arrived home in Aberdeen, and went back to live with my mother and father. I think the welcome home was fairly low key. There was certainly a considerable coolness around the fact that I had been a poor correspondent during my two years away. When I left for the army in 1952 it was from my old home in Mile-End Avenue, but while I was away my mother and father had finally moved to a bungalow of their own. They allocated me a small bedroom in the new house. They seemed to take it for granted that they would support me, and certainly I had no income, nor any prospect of having one.

I presented myself at the University and was accepted to start on an Ordinary BSc based on my admission group of highers and lowers. Throughout my school days, and all through my army service, it had been made clear to me on all sides that my obvious gifts were concerned with language. I could write well, and speak freely on any subject. People often said that I had 'the gift of the gab'.

To exploit these abilities it seemed obvious that I should do Arts at University, focussing on English, and with Latin, French and History to back it up. However, I was not going to be told what to do with my life, and I had no interest in literature. I was going to be a scientist! A man of the future! I decided, against advice from all quarters, but especially from my father, that I would take the three basic science subjects: Chemistry, Natural Philosophy (i.e. Physics), and – of all things! – Mathematics. There was a fourth subject which had to be chosen from the Natural Sciences. The options were Botany, Zoology or Geology, and I plumped for Geology.

I started attending the lectures at the beginning of October. I found my old bicycle in the garage, and made a lot of use of it in those early months.

By the end of the first term it was already clear to me that I was completely out of my depth in Mathematics. Physics was difficult because of the amount of maths it required. Chemistry was more concerned with ideas which could be expressed without maths, and it seemed easier to grasp. Geology was a delight, and came easily to me.

Only in one subject was there a member of staff who was memorable. This was Prof. Reginald Jones who was in charge of the Natural Philosophy Department, and prided himself on personally conducting a first year course of one lecture a week. This took place at 9.00 am on a Monday morning, and everyone attended. Professor Jones had been a back-room boy during the second world war, and had been largely responsible, among other things, for the invention and development of 'window'. This was the creation of a multitude of fine metal foil strips which could be dropped from the bomb bays of bombers and would then show up on enemy radar, causing confusion and saving casualties. Prof. Jones was a brilliant communicator, and his lectures were usually illustrated with memorable technology – none more so than the morning we came in to find two huge glass beakers set up on the demonstration bench. One was apparently full of water, and stood in a deep tray. The other was empty. Prof. Jones came in, and drew a revolver from his belt. He fired one shot at each of the beakers. This was done in a public lecture hall with about sixty students present! The beaker with the water in it disintegrated into mush, and the water and crushed glass fell into the waiting tray. The empty beaker broke in two or three big pieces which fell to lie on the bench. The point was that the water transmitted the pressure of the bullet evenly to the glass. I can still hear the shots, and see the shape of the beaker with its contents hanging for a split second in the air before it fell. I can also see Prof. Jones bringing his revolver up to his face, after firing, pursing his lips, and giving a brief blow of air down the barrel before restoring it to his waistbelt. I can also remember the standing ovation. I can still picture the scene today, more than fifty years later, but what today's Health and Safety would make of it, I shudder to think.

Prof. Jones was a noted practical joker, and it was widely known that his senior physics year stole his treasured old Austin Eight while he was on holiday. He reported it missing on his return, but on entering the lecture hall on his first senior lecture he found it standing there, with the engine quietly ticking over. His students had dismantled the car and manhandled it into the University and up a flight of stairs, before re-assembling it and getting it running. He was thought to have appreciated the joke. Prof. Jones lived to be 86 and died in 1997.

Queen's Cross Church

Soon after I came home I returned to worship at Queen's Cross Church on Sundays, and rejoined the church choir. The church paid a small salary to the leaders of the four parts: soprano, alto, tenor and bass. Each received £25 per annum. George Duncan, the fine bass leader under whom I had sat during my last year at school, and from whom I had learnt so much, retired just after I returned, and I auditioned for the position of leading bass. I was duly appointed, and was pleased to be earning even this small amount. I was taking on something for which I wasn't really ready, as there were some difficult anthems, and a number of bass solos, but I practised hard at home, and in general I coped pretty well.

As far as any Christian belief was concerned, I think I came out of the army with very little positive feeling about religion. I probably had only one reason for going to Queen's Cross Church, and that was the music and its associated salary. I kept my opinions to myself, however, and since my parents were regular attenders, it was probably generally accepted that I was also a believer.

Although I was probably a bit too old for it, I went back to the Youth Fellowship on Sunday nights. I found there a young man called Frank Smith. He was older than I was and was in his first year of Divinity. In 1955, he was doing a student attachment to Queen's Cross. We liked each other at once, and came to know each other very well indeed.

During 1955 I got fed up with my bicycle, and my father paid for some driving lessons. I passed after only eight sessions, and was very pleased with myself.

I had quite a lively year at University, and the first year exams were a shock. I had done a lot of last minute swotting, but the results were related to whether there was an opportunity to write essays in the papers. Geology and Chemistry provided that, and I passed easily. Physics didn't and I failed. Maths was a total disaster. I had to re-sit Physics, but was told to give up all thought of doing any more Maths.

Margaret

One Sunday morning in August I was in my place in the choir, and Frank Smith was sitting beside me as student assistant, and ready to read the lesson. A young woman came into the church and sat upstairs in the corner of the gallery. Frank spotted her and whispered to me that she looked super, and that he would ask her out. The girl was called Jean Wallace, and she was a speech therapist. At the same time, I became keenly aware of the presence of a fair-haired girl in the alto part of the choir. At the end of the service I spoke to her. We seemed to get on well, and I think I offered to walk her home to the house which I discovered that she shared with Jean Wallace. The girl was called Margaret Yates. She came from Blackpool and was also a speech therapist.

Margaret and I began to spend a lot of time together, and enjoyed each other's company very much. At about the same time Frank was forming a very close relationship with Jean, so he and I had a lot to talk about. We were both invited to the girls' shared flat.

Near the end of September I made my mind up that it was Margaret with whom I wanted to spend the rest of my life, and I invited her out for an evening walk. At a certain spot on a quiet back lane, I asked her if she would marry me. Margaret accepted my proposal, and we announced our engagement to friends and family. The moment I asked her remains clear in my memory including the special blue coat Margaret was wearing, which she still had long after. I also remember that I was radiantly happy for the first time in my life! Frank and Jean also got engaged and would later marry.

Second Year Science

By now I was back at class doing second year Chemistry and Geology. The first week came as a huge shock. I discovered that second year Geology was going to be heavily concerned with a topic called crystallography. This is based on the kind of abstruse maths which I had already found impossible. At the end of an early lecture I stayed behind to ask for some advice. Would it be possible to get through the Geology course while by-passing the mathematics required for crystallography? The answer was perfectly clear, and non-committal. I knew at once that I would inevitably face failure at the end of the second year in my first choice subject. The syllabus for second year chemistry was also most alarming. It looked as if there would be hardly any opportunities for writing essays. The whole thing filled me with dread. I could plainly see that I was never going to be able to complete the degree I had chosen, and if so what was going to happen to my plans to marry Margaret?

It was a major turning point. Whether I stayed at university or not I would continue to be dependent on my father. There was no likelihood of the atmosphere at home getting any better. The future seemed altogether bleak.

I was sufficiently discouraged to discuss the whole question with my father, who for once seemed to be quite sympathetic. We had often thought of Uncle Gordon, in Hertfordshire. Gordon was married to my father's sister, my aunt Kath. He was a Welshman of Belgian descent, and an inventive genius in metallurgy, who had become very wealthy. He had interests all over the world, and since he started in a small way himself, we thought he might be sympathetic to my problem and prepared to offer some help. I wondered if he could open a door for me to work in a chemistry lab somewhere. I could enrol for a Higher National Course in Chemistry at a polytechnic, and in due course complete my degree. I would then also be earning a wage, and could become self-supporting. Uncle Gordon responded very positively, and at once. He turned out to be on the board of directors of Johnson Matthey – Gold Refiners to the Queen – with offices in Hatton Garden, and production factories in various places.

Yes! He would be prepared to get me a position in the laboratories of Johnson Matthey at Wembley. Of course I would have to start on the absolute ground floor. If I was prepared to go abroad, I could be taken on the staff as a trainee chemist. I would be given some working knowledge of the chemistry of the metal lithium, which was becoming used in the nuclear industry. I could do a series of experiments in the extraction of lithium from its main ore, petalite, which was even then being mined in Gwelo, in what was then Southern Rhodesia. Gordon had interests of his own at Gwelo. If I did well, and showed promise, I could be sent out to Africa, in a junior management role at the mine, and no doubt I would work my way up from there. Within only a few days I said goodbye to family, friends and my new fiancée, and set off for England. Suddenly the future looked more promising.

London – Another Far Country!

I stayed at first with my aunt and presented myself at the laboratories of Johnson Matthey at Wembley. I was told that I would do experiments on petalite, as requested by Mr Robiette (Uncle Gordon), to prepare me to go out to Rhodesia for the firm. I would also attend the Northern Polytechnic and study for my Higher National Chemistry. The staff were very distant to me, mainly because they were all obsessed with contract bridge, and had no interest in me once they found I didn't play.

It immediately became clear I was no chemist. I must have slept through my first year at university, and confronted by the need to conduct experiments in a laboratory I had absolutely no idea what to do. At university there had been text books with the right answers, but here there were no right answers. The principal chemist was obviously bewildered by my results. I couldn't stay on at my aunt's, so I found some digs near Enfield. The travelling was an endless succession of buses and tubes. After a month or two the manager of the plant in Rhodesia visited the UK. It was arranged that he interview his potential trainee. I made a complete mess of it by letting slip to him that had I strong feelings about the 'colour bar' and would be hoping for an opportunity to help the African workforce towards integration. I was called to the manager's office and told I would not be going to Africa, now or ever! My experiments with lithium came to an end but I went on trying to become an industrial chemist. The work I was given to do was all quite mysterious to me.

Margaret's sister and her husband lived near Wimbledon. Margaret had told them the news of her engagement. They immediately treated me as a member of their own family, for Margaret's sake, and we grew very close over the following months. I visited them regularly at the week-ends.

Margaret arranged for me to be invited to Blackpool for Christmas to meet her family. I went by train on my first visit to the north of England. Margaret's mother and father made me welcome in their house. Poppa, as the family called him, was a successful and self-made solicitor in Blackpool. He took the opportunity to inquire if my intentions were honourable, and if I thought I would be able to support his daughter in the manner to which she was accustomed. I think I was able to provide adequate answers. I also met Margaret's two brothers and their wives and children, and they also accepted me most warmly. Early in 1956 I became completely fed up with the tubes and buses to Wembley and decided to buy a motor bike. It was an Ariel 'Red Hunter' of 350 cc, and about three years old when I bought it. It turned out to be a completely reliable workhorse and gave no trouble for years and years. I could now ride it to Wembley daily and that made a big difference. To celebrate my birthday in May, I left the lab on a Friday at 5.30 pm and headed north to Aberdeen on my motor bike. The journey took me all night, and I was very tired on the Saturday morning when I turned up at my parents' house. Margaret and I had a happy week-end, and I set off south again at teatime on the Sunday. The journey south was even more tiring, although the motor bike performed faultlessly. I kept falling asleep over my work all through the Monday.

At the laboratory I continued with routine work after the New Year trying to learn about all the very rare and expensive elements that the laboratory tested and measured and purified. I didn't however, turn into a good lab technician. I found it hard to understand the value of the samples we were working with. My father's oft repeated warning – 'care and accuracy' – came back to haunt me again and again. Nothing could protect me from impending disaster. The day I washed some very expensive platinum residues down the drain marked the end of my time in the prestigious Wembley laboratory. I was finally told that I was not suitable for the work and would have to be relocated. In June 1956 I completed my first year of classes at the Holloway Road Polytechnic, and sat the exams, all of which I passed. I now had first year ARIC to add to my first year degree certificates from Aberdeen, and enrolled for the second year to start at the end of September.

Still the long-suffering management of Johnson Matthey did not dispense with my services. Instead they transferred me to their industrial department in June 1956. The works was located in a North London suburb called Brimsdown. They got the name almost right: it should have been called Brimstone, for a curious chemical smell hung about it. When I moved there I was taken on as a proper lab assistant. This meant an increase in pay, and I thought I could afford to get out of my digs. Margaret and I had decided that we would get married in September, and I knew we would need somewhere to stay.

I found a single big room in a house in Winchmore Hill, with a double bed and french windows and a small corner for cooking and washing up. The rent was four guineas per week.

Brimsdown

Back at Brimsdown, I don't think I learned much new chemistry, but I made some good friends, continued with evening classes and made no more expensive mistakes. The chemist in charge came from Aberdeen, and bore the guid Scots name of Kemp.

The plant at Brimsdown was very old and run down. This added to the dangers of working with the extremely noxious materials we handled. Here care and accuracy was part of self-preservation. Solutions of potassium cyanide were used in routine copper titrations, and had to be treated with care as they could produce HCN, or hydrocyanic acid gas, if they encountered acids. I remember one day leaving a copper estimation in the middle to have my tea break. When I returned I forgot at what step I had left the flask. I believed that I had diluted the solution until it was weak and safe, whereas it was in fact still concentrated. I dripped the cyanide salt solution into it, and bent to get a closer look at the interesting and unusual bubbles which seemed to be forming. As I did so I got the unmistakable whiff of cyanide, and ran, shouting, from the lab, across the yard and full tilt into Mr Kemp's office.

'The antidote! Where's the antidote?' I screamed.

'Laddie!', said Mr Kemp, unflustered. 'If ye made it this far, you're not needing the antidote.'

Even cyanide could be forgiving. I remember visiting the Cyanide Gnomes. These were two elderly men who inhabited a small shed where they did something mysterious in the production of cyanide. Over the years they had built up a tolerance to the stuff, and could now treat it with impunity. They would sit having their sandwiches in an atmosphere laden with dust particles rich in the poison. It posed a serious problem for the management, for any attempt to introduce a new member of staff was likely to prove fatal before the new man could develop a tolerance. I remember a colleague telling me to look carefully at the gnomes, and then tell me what was different about them. I remember the experience of meeting them had an other-worldly quality about it. There was about them an alien-ness, but I couldn't put my finger on it. I confessed later that I hadn't been able to spot the source of their strangeness.

'Next time look at their eyes', he said, and next time I did. The moment I knew where to look I wondered why I hadn't seen it before. The Cyanide Gnomes had no whites to their eyes. The entire visible eye was as black as the pupil. I learned later that cyanide in small quantities combines with albumen to form a black compound which creates the black eyes. No wonder they looked strange.

Our Wedding

Preparations for the wedding of 10th September were going on, but they didn't involve me at all. On the big day everything went as planned, but I remember very little of what happened at the church or the reception.

The telegrams were read out to the company. A lady member of Queen's Cross choir sent the memorable telegram:

'JUST MARRIED! JUST LOVELY! JUST WAIT!'

She certainly gave me my money's worth out of this economically worded telegram as I went on to quote it at weddings through forty years in the Ministry.

Margaret's mother loaned us her car for a honeymoon, and we went to Hope Cove in Devon. We had a nice room in a good hotel and everything was lovely. I have few clear memories of our honeymoon, over fifty years ago, but one single incident from Hope Cove remains clear.

The hotel lay in the village down near the shore, and the entire setting was surrounded by high cliffs with a winding, steep road down to the sea. One evening we drove up to the cliffs and found there were a lot of cars on the grass where people were sitting and looking out over the English Channel. It was a beautiful night, and it was possible to wait and see the sun go down. After a bit most of the cars moved off. We were in no hurry to go, and at last we were the only car at the top of the cliffs. Finally we decided to go back to the hotel. I started the car and engaged reverse. When I let the clutch out the wheels began to spin. The dew had come down and the grass was soaking wet. There was no grip at all. There was clearly no need to panic as we were a considerable distance away from the edge of the cliff. I decided the sensible thing would be to move gently forward and then circle round to the right, and then, keeping up our momentum we would be able to scramble up the slope to the road. I should have realised that the nearer one went to the edge the more severe the gradient became. The first part of the plan was all right, but as we tried to turn we began to skid sideways towards the cliff. The edge was much nearer now. I got the car facing away from the edge. I got the rubber mats out and tried to get them under the back wheels. I persuaded Margaret to get in the driving seat and try to gently drive forward while I put my back into pushing. Everything we tried lost us more ground. Finally we were only a few feet from the edge and there was nothing to do but admit defeat.

It would be nice to think that this experience drew us closer, but I'm afraid Margaret couldn't stand any more and began to walk down the road on her own. I was equally desperate, though trying not to show it. I left the lights on in the car and ran down the road to the village. I barged into the little pub, and tried to get the customers to listen to my story. They were too busy with their pints to pay any attention. I grew desperate and managed to drag one young man out into the street, and point upwards to the cliff edge. There was the car, apparently hanging out over the cliff with its rear lights clearly visible. He ran back into the pub and spread the word. I said I would pay to have the car pushed back from the edge, and two car loads of young men immediately set off up the road, with me in one of the cars. With that amount of muscle the job was perfectly easy, and the Austin was soon safely back on the metalled road. I happily parted with ten shilling notes all round, and the incident was over. Margaret was so relieved that her mother's car was not a write-off that I think she forgave me for my lack of common sense in getting into the situation in the first place.

At the end of our holiday we were happy to be able to deliver the Austin Cambridge safely back to my mother-in-law and take the train back to London. I went back to Brimsdown and Margaret started a new position as a Speech Therapist. Our wedding and our honeymoon were over.

Newly-Weds

We were now at Winchmore Hill and our single room in Compton Road. We didn't have a lot but we were blissfully happy. We were both keen to have a dog some day, but pets were not allowed in the room, and in any case we were both out at work all day. We decided to invest in a small tropical fish tank. We got a great deal of pleasure from our tropicals.

Then there was music. We went to a church in Enfield and there we met a fine pianist, who was the accompanist to the Enfield Grand Opera Society. Having heard me sing, she encouraged me to join. The work in progress was Verdi's early opera, *Nabucco,* which had recently been produced by the Welsh National Opera with a very good new English translation. I was quite at home with the basses. In due course there were auditions for the various leading parts and I got the role of the High Priest, Zachariah, who has four long and brilliant solos, as well as being involved throughout the opera. The other soloists were very good and I learned an enormous amount from singing in my first real opera.

Our Neighbours

Shortly after we settled in Winchmore Hill we became friendly with our next door neighbours. Two families shared the house, which was large. The husbands were Roy and Eddie and their wives Vera and Viva. All four of them were devoted to extreme left-wing politics and Roy and Eddie were members of the British Communist Party. We spent many evenings in this commune and discussion was frequently furious. Roy was a passionate disciple of Marx, Engels and Lenin, and very widely read in politics and many other fields. Running through the centre of Roy's life was his passion for classical music. He couldn't play an instrument, so he put all his enthusiasm into listening, appreciating and learning. This meant records, and hi-fidelity. How often I was called in next door to sit and listen to his latest equipment. Then there were our expeditions to 'the city' on Saturdays, to hear amplifiers and speakers and consider further purchases. The team consisted of Roy and Eddie and me together with Roy's oldest friend, Reg.

Reg was an engineering genius, who had taught and trained Roy as a machine tool-setter. He had an extraordinary talent for playing the piano by ear. He was quite untaught, but could reproduce exactly any piece of classical music. I loved it when he came to play his wonderful solo pieces on Roy's old upright piano. He was a chain smoker, and I can still see him missing a semi-quaver as he snatched the cigarette end from his lip, when it burned too close for comfort. We visited Imhof's one Saturday morning. This was a very posh establishment in town, with floor staff wearing morning coats. Reg approached a beautiful new Steinway grand, and lifted the lid. He spread his copy of his newspaper (probably the Daily Worker) on the lovely piano stool. He flipped the tails of his raincoat up and sat down. As the watchful staff member loomed up, the chords of a huge Liszt Hungarian Rhapsody crashed out. The staff froze. You could see their dilemma. He looked like a poorly dressed workman, but he played like Paderewski. Could he be an eccentric millionaire? After a short extract Reg rose to his feet, pushed in the stool and closed the lid. He turned to the attendant. 'It could do with a tune', he said, and we all strolled out.

Roy knew far more classical music than I did, although to the end of his life he could never pronounce the names of some famous composers. He always referred to Liszt as 'Litz'. It was one of his most endearing idiosyncrasies.

Not long after this Roy Hawkins began to express some concern at the amount of money we were paying out for our single furnished room. He told us that his mother was living down in Lower Edmonton, and that she had plenty of space in her house, and could certainly spare some room for us. He thought she wouldn't want as much rent, and that in general we would be better off.

Roy took us to meet his mother in Latymer Road, and we agreed to move in. She charged us £2 10/- per week which contrasted with our four guineas per week in Winchmore Hill. Our flitting to the new house was not very complicated as our possessions were few at that time and we were able to do our entire move with suitcases and boxes tied on the motor bike.

Finally the only thing we had left to move was our beloved tropical fish tank. We thought that if it didn't have much water in it Margaret could probably sit on the pillion on the bike and balance the tank on her knees, so this was the strategy we decided upon.

We bailed the water out of the tank until there was only about two inches in the bottom. The fish seemed to be all right, and we could certainly carry the tank quite easily like that. Margaret got on the pillion, and we balanced the tank on her knees, and I set off. Everything seemed to be going all right until we came to the canal which lay half way between Winchmore Hill and Edmonton. There was a little hump-backed bridge crossing the canal, and I reckoned I would need a bit of extra power to carry us over the bridge. I opened the throttle a bit and nipped over the top. Some distance down the other side of the bridge I leaned back and asked if Margaret was all right? There was no answer, so I slowed down and looked round and found she was no longer on the bike. I drove quickly back to the bridge and found her there sitting in the middle of the road. She still had the fish tank on her lap, and she was a bit tearful, but quite unhurt. When I had accelerated over the bridge she had gone slightly up in the air, and when she came down again the bike was no longer there. We remounted and reached Latymer Road safely. Margaret hadn't spilt a drop of water from the tank, and the fish went on as if nothing had happened.

The Jaguar

Travelling began to become a real problem for us as we had only the motor bike, so we decided we'd have to get a car. We finally found a second-hand Jaguar. It was a 1939, two and a half litre S.S. Jaguar. It drove beautifully and was very cheap. It had running boards, and its spare wheel was mounted partly in the left front wing. It had two huge free standing headlamps. The traditional radiator with its vertical slats was chrome, and the chrome had been laid down on brass which shone faintly through where it was worn. The wheels were held in place by big central bolts with two opposing points. You tightened or loosened the wheels with a small lead hammer with a wash-leather handle, which came in the tool-kit.

Long journeys were difficult for the Jaguar, and with families distributed between Blackpool and Aberdeen, long journeys were what we needed to be able to manage. We had several breakdowns before the final one in 1958. I see examples of my Jaguar at vintage car shows – always with emotion! You never forget your first car.

Taps and Dies

By May 1957, I was feeling that the Brimsdown job was a bit of a rut. I was also talking to Roy, and he felt that the laboratory still had too much of the 'silver spoon in the mouth' image, and that I ought to be proving that I could make my own way in the world, without family help or influence. I finished at Brimsdown and went to the local labour exchange to see if I could get work. Roy had suggested engineering. He felt if I was in something related to his own line of work he would be able to support and advise. There was a position in a factory called 'British Taps and Dies', down in Tottenham, so I said I would take it. When I presented myself at Taps and Dies, I quickly discovered that I had absolutely nothing going for me any more. I had no experience of engineering, and my previous work in chemistry was not going to be relevant. I would have to start on the ground floor. Before I started work I had no idea what a 'tap' was, apart from being something you turn on to let water into a bath, and I knew even less about what a 'die' was. I was quickly instructed. Taps and dies create screw threads inside nuts and outside bolts. I was set to work sawing off pieces from metal bars. Cutting bits off these bars was a slow, noisy and dirty job, creating dust and backache, and I did it all day, every day, for several weeks. Roy asked me how I was getting on, and was pretty horrified when I told him.

'They're just trying it on,' he said, 'They probably don't really want you there in the first place. You'd be better off with me. Just quit and come to Knight's on Monday, there's room for a feeder for my line.'

I was glad to leave Taps and Dies, and quite excited about Knight's, which lay close to Southgate, within easy reach of me and my motor bike.

Knight's of Southgate

Knight's turned out to be an engineering works centred around one very large workshop filled with machines. Knight's produced components for metal goods of many kinds, most of which were made in quite big numbers. The machines which produced these components were called Automatic Screw Machines. These were installed in lines. Six were under the control of one man, called the setter, and were operated by a lesser mortal called the bar feeder. As well as being in charge of his six BSA 48s, Roy also acted as a kind of trouble-shooter for the whole workshop as he was by far the most experienced and talented engineer in the factory.

A BSA 48 automatic screw machine stood about four feet high. It was a kind of complicated lathe, and descended from the earlier capstan lathe. It made its output by shaping the end of a rapidly spinning rod of metal, and cutting little shaped pieces off it. The rod was eight feet long, and no more than about half an inch in diameter. The rod being used lived inside a long protecting tube called the bar feed tube. This tube was swung out of line with the machine to allow the rod to be fed into it. It was then lined up with the machine, but held back a couple of feet by a catch, to let the bar feeder push the rod into the machine. He pushed the rod right on through the lathe until it was sticking out into the 'business end' area. Once the end of the rod was held by the chuck of the lathe, the protecting tube was moved forward so that it locked snugly in position against the end of the machine cover. The machine could then be switched on and the whole eight feet of the unseen bar would begin to rotate at high speed inside the bar feed tube. The cardinal sin to be avoided by the bar feeder was to leave the bar feed tube in its open position when switching on the machine. This left a two foot gap between the guard and the machine. Within the tube the steel bar was rotating at high speed, and getting shorter as each new part was chopped off. When the moment came that the rotating end of the bar escaped into the gap, the high speed of its rotation caused it to break off, and the short length of bar could go anywhere.

One bar feeder, who happened to be from the Caribbean, made this very mistake one day. He had fed his machine with a mild steel rod half an inch in diameter. When the overlooked and unnoticed moment occurred, the two foot long bar snapped off and flew like a bullet throughout the entire length of the workshop to embed itself four inches deep in a concrete wall. It passed through a crowded workshop, travelling in all about sixty-five yards and it did it without hitting anyone. In the post-mortem conducted by the manager, a long measuring tape was stretched between the machine and the embedded bar. It became clear that in its flight the steel rod had passed within a few inches of several men on the shop floor. In one case it flew between a face and a hand holding a hankie, about to blow a nose. In another place it passed over the back of a man who had bent down to pick up a fallen tool. Everyone escaped! I myself had been only a couple of feet away from the danger line, and had passed across it only a few minutes before.

The Caribbean worker got his cards on the spot: not because of his colour – there appeared to be no racial discrimination at Knight's – but because of the lethal nature of his mistake.

It would be tedious to try to describe in detail how a BSA 48 worked. Roy set up his machines for any new job as it arrived, and I fed them with the bars and checked on the quality of the parts they made. It sounds straightforward, but it was easy not to notice that the components dropping into the bucket were no longer up to standard, and if they weren't your machine had just made a pile of expensive junk. Since the whole shop floor was on a group production bonus, anyone who missed a mistake in this area caused the whole workforce to suffer through their pay-packets. A successful line of machines came from a good setter and a reliable bar feeder, and I would like to say that Roy and I made a good team, but I'm afraid that wouldn't really be true. If there was a mistake waiting to happen I would, in the fullness of time, make it, and far too often Roy had to speak up for me to Ron, the foreman, and try to cover for my error.

When everything was running smoothly, the work could be very pleasant on the shop floor at Knight's. Roy and I each used to watch the headline stories in our own particular newspaper. Roy was at that time a fully paid up member of the British Communist Party and took the Daily Worker. He would watch eagerly for any evidence of a progressive political decision coming from the Eastern block, and would be bitterly disappointed if the Kremlin came up with a political move which he felt let the side down.

'They're supposed to be Socialists!', he would exclaim. 'Have they forgotten Marx and Lenin?'

I would be happy to gloat on such days, but my turn would inevitably come to be the crestfallen one, as the British or American government would do something utterly stupid and of which I had no choice but to be ashamed. Roy would be cock-a-hoop: 'I thought you lot were supposed to be governed by Christian principles,' he would say. 'Where's the Christianity in that?'

Roy was also the shop steward at Knight's, where many of the employed were members of the AEU – the Amalgamated Engineering Union.

There was a ten-minute morning tea break at ten o'clock, and this was shifted five minutes so that it could start at five to ten. This was done by popular request to allow the workforce to listen to David Kossoff every day for his much loved five minute programme on the BBC Home Service, called 'Five to Ten'. It was extraordinary that everyone enjoyed this programme even although many of the men were not at all religious. It would have been impossible to follow it over the sound of the machines, and I still have a most vivid memory of the complete hush that fell over the workshop as Kossoff began to speak, and the sigh of satisfaction in the workshop as he would conclude with his trademark phrase: 'As we shall see – tomorrow!'

I managed to save a few samples of the many components which were churned out by our BSAs. Two of them were made for Garrard, who manufactured gramophones, and for whom we supplied the short central pillars on which the turntables rotated. I used to look at such machines in the shops and think with pride of the spindle hidden under the turntable: 'I made that!'

The day came when our line of machines started to be converted to make a nasty little brass component called a Snip-Snap. There were all kinds of problems with this job, and drills snapped off right, left and centre. To do myself some justice I should say that I think it would have been hard for anyone to keep up the pace that those machines demanded once the snip-snaps were in charge. I certainly wasn't up to it, and kept on missing breakages and losing everybody money. I started to come in for harsh criticism from Roy. My background and upbringing were investigated and my politics and religion were the obvious thing to criticise. By this time I had been thinking seriously for some time about going back to Scotland and going into the full-time Christian Ministry.

'How you ever expect to make a minister, beats me: you can't even run a line of machines!'

It became a comment which summed up much of my life in London and summed up my attitudes as well. It wasn't in fact the whole truth. I had in fact learned more or less how to run a line of machines until the snip-snaps came along, and I suppose snip-snaps can come into anyone's life, and bring ruin and disaster.

It is also interesting that Roy didn't simply give up on me. He looked for a practical solution, and found it in the works storeroom. A new storekeeper was being looked for. The manager explained to me that I was causing a good deal of disquiet on the shop floor, but that Roy and Ron both thought I might do better in the stores. I would start a trial period.

If I hadn't just spent some time on the shop floor the storeroom would have been impossible. Most things required had obscure names and titles. The shelves were stocked with things like grommets, and balata belting, and milling cutters. It was an unknown foreign language. During the first week most of the men who came for supplies came round behind the counter and showed me where they were. I picked it all up very quickly. Suddenly the critical balance had shifted and I was dealing primarily with things rather than people. It was quite like being back in the Orderly Room, only there was no Adjutant. The stores served people, but only briefly and intermittently. Long periods were spent dealing with things. I reorganised the entire place and created an orderly world where I could find everything at once. It ran, I recollect, like a well-oiled machine, and I began to come in for praise rather than blame for probably the first time for several years. This was something I really could do. I found I had a talent for organisation, and if my University career had for some reason been removed or the option shut down, I suppose I would have spent the rest of my working life in some kind of storeroom.

The end came at the beginning of August 1958, when I left Knight's of Southgate. I parted with the company with no rancour on either side, and in a friendly and happy atmosphere. Even Roy seemed to think I had made good in the stores, and although he felt that the Ministry was 'a waste of a good man' (as he put it), he wished us both very well.

The Winding Road

The most difficult topic to recall and record from the 1950s is my progress towards my working life as an Ordained Minister of the Church of Scotland. The question most often asked of any minister is: 'What made you go in for the Ministry?'.

Unfortunately for my love of a good script the true reasons don't make a particularly good story at all. They contain no hint of the blinding flash of a Damascus Road experience. Indeed, from a distance of fifty years it is hard for me to be sure what the original historical ingredients really were.

I suppose my progress towards a position of commitment to the Christian faith was a long and winding road. I doubt if my involvement with my family church of Queen's Cross as a child and a teenager had any real impact on me. I got off the church conveyer belt for a few years, but got back on in the Youth Fellowship. Fellowship members were expected to join the church, and in 1952 I went to communicants' classes, and made public profession of my faith in Queen's Cross. I was now a church member. I think I must have had my fingers crossed during the taking of any vows at that time.

I think that I did no serious thinking about God or theology during my National Service, although moral questions about one's duty to kill in following an order, or to resist such a pressure, were often discussed.

On my return to civilian life I went back to church and the choir, and was then on duty every Sunday, as the paid leading bass.

I found the minister obscure, although I remember that he would occasionally break through and for a while engage my interest. At some point in the year before I went to London he preached a series of sermons on the Seven Churches which have letters written to them in the Book of Revelation. This set of sermons had an immediate effect on me. Later in London I found myself thinking a lot about Queen's Cross in Aberdeen, and the national Church of Scotland, and then about the local congregation we were attending at Enfield.

I read the Seven Churches texts again for myself many times. One or two struck me very hard.

There was the one at Ephesus which had 'left its first love' and was asked to 'think from what a height it had fallen'. It seemed that the churches I knew had done the same.

There was the church at Sardis which was said to have 'a name that it lived; and was dead!' Queen's Cross certainly lived on its name, but seemed pretty dead to me.

Could anything be done about such churches? Certainly I wanted nothing to do with them.

Another of the seven – the church of Laodicea – was criticised for being 'neither hot nor cold; but only lukewarm'. I think I felt that if I myself decided to go into the church, I could at least undertake to be hot or cold; not even my worst enemies would ever have charged me with being lukewarm! I could resolve to try to be one thing or the other.

My minister's distant series of sermons remains a mystery to me. Why did these ideas get under my skin? Why did they take root? Why did they last so long? I have preached my own series on the Seven Churches many times down through the years. Are such things part of a plan? Part of a calling? The question goes to the heart of my doubts and of my hopes!

I am certain that I had no thought about or interest in the Ministry up until my engagement to Margaret and my move to London and Johnson Matthey. Some kind of idea of a lay Christian's responsibility for his position seems to have surfaced as I began to hear the possibility of going out to work for the company in Rhodesia.

Whatever was going on from week to week, Margaret and I settled down in Winchmore Hill during the last week of September 1956, and started attending St Paul's Enfield together on Sundays; and a little more than four months later, on 12th February 1957, I wrote a letter to the Dean of the Faculty of Divinity in the University of Aberdeen, enquiring what qualifications I would need in addition to my partial degree in order to be accepted as a candidate for the Ministry of the Church of Scotland. It seems that my thoughts about the Ministry had crystallised very quickly, and there is never any mention in later correspondence with Aberdeen that I had any doubts about wishing to proceed into the Ministry.

Something must have happened during the five months between my wedding and that first pivotal letter to Aberdeen.

One very early influence was the film of Peter Marshall's life featuring Richard Todd as *A Man called Peter*. Margaret and I went to see this during the short period between the start of our relationship and my departure for England.

The film was about the life of the Scottish preacher who went to the United States and became famous in Washington. The book of his life was written by Catharine Marshall and Margaret bought me a copy in December 1955, and sent it to me in London. It is dated 7. 12. 55, and inscribed:

> To Peter,
> With the hope that he will live up to the ideals of the 'other Peter' and also with all my love and affection,
> Margaret.

I have this copy before me as I write. It seems likely that this very early gift indicates that even at that time I was already expressing a real interest in the life of a Christian minister. It certainly suggests a perhaps unspoken admiration for Peter Marshall, and an acceptance that he was a suitable person on whom to focus my hopes. Margaret also certainly helped me to recognise how many of my decisions in work and education had been formed by a perverse decision not to accept well-meaning advice to go in for things that other people thought I would be good at. My poor relationship with my father was probably at the back of all that.

Margaret thought that it was she who raised the possibility of the

Church in an early conversation. She felt that the suggestion was not given any real welcome, but it may well have started something, as other people's suggestions always seem to have done in my life.

Fired Up for the Ministry

The minister at our new church in Enfield was not inspiring, but one Sunday a guest preacher came who set everything on fire. He was a minister of the Congregational church at nearby High Barnet. Listening to him preaching a sermon I felt for the first time that I could really begin to understand how someone could stand up in a pulpit, and by presenting a prepared talk based on a passage from the bible could get a real message across to me.

Margaret and I went a number of times to his church to listen to him, and we introduced ourselves and had more than one long talk. The question of a career in the Ministry was almost certainly raised in one of these discussions. I certainly remember coming away from services and conversations feeling inspired.

No doubt I would have tested the idea out on anyone available, as I have always done about any possible change of direction. No doubt friends at Brimsdown were asked for their opinions. I have a distinct recollection that when I finally left Johnson Matthey there was an understanding among my colleagues there that it was ultimately to become a minister in the Church of Scotland that I was headed.

What exactly it was that appealed to me at that stage I cannot say. The idea of preaching and conducting worship would have been at the top of the list. I may have contemplated christenings, weddings and funerals as a necessary service to people, at all of which I might turn out to be quite good. Turning my experiences with Youth Fellowships on their head I may have thought that I would be good with young people in general.

Opportunities to speak in public, as for example in youth groups, seemed to cause me no more stress than singing in public had done over the years. No doubt I gave no thought to aspects of the Ministry which later came to cause me my biggest problems, like pastoral visitation and congregational administration. At this time I would still be completely unaware of these.

Matters evidently came to a head in February when I wrote to Aberdeen Divinity College. The Dean replied and gave me advice about the package of qualifications I would need to put together. He told me that without a completed University Degree, Aberdeen University would not award a BD Degree on completion of divinity studies, as they termed the BD a second degree. However, the Church of Scotland Selection Board was entitled to allow a candidate to undertake the full three-year divinity course with a somewhat less rigid set of criteria. It is this course which would lead to License and Ordination to the Ministry, but without the accompanying BD degree.

It was in this letter that I first heard of 'close approximation', and it would later be this idea which would be the basis of my entry. The new Master of the College was Prof. A.M. Hunter who was in touch with George Sangster, my own minister from Queen's Cross. They advised me about the necessary packet of qualifications. I cobbled together the bits of my Science Degree with various passes from London Polytechnics, and the result satisfied the Committee on Education for the Ministry which informed me that I had been accepted as a Candidate.

Somewhere in the midst of all the above correspondence was my own personal time-bomb. This was the one which made it clear that no matter how well I did in my studies, the University would not let me sit the BD exam, and I would emerge as a Licentiate of the Church of Scotland, but with no University Degree. This would haunt me for the rest of my life.

The arrival of the committee's letter changed everything. We were now definitely going back to live in Aberdeen, where I was going to spend the next three years in full-time study to enter the Ministry of the Church of Scotland.

I could meet the committee's various requirements, but there was also an entrance exam which was a different matter. The bible exam was a simple question of getting a list of the passages from the college calendar. These turned out to be a Gospel, a Pauline letter and an Old Testament Prophet.

However there was also an examination in New Testament Greek, and this was a very different problem. I had known for some time that such an exam would be set, and had already had an offer from the Enfield minister to tutor me. He turned out to be a first rate Greek scholar and an excellent teacher. We only had three months, but I knew I would be able to study on my own right up to the time of the exam.

I remember my excitement when I discovered that it was all very easy. I quickly found I had no difficulty translating the Greek, and school experiences with French and Latin came flooding back into my mind. 'How little work I ever did at school', I thought, and how easily I could have sailed through Higher Latin if I had only been interested. My tutor set me daily vocabulary lists, and heard them at every lesson. He gave unsparingly of his time during the summer months, and I would have been in deep trouble if he hadn't been there to help me.

Prof. Hunter had spoken in one letter about 'keeping body and soul together', and now that I had been accepted for a three-year full-time course at a Scottish University I could apply for grant support for my studies. I applied to Middlesex County Council Education Committee for a Major County Award. At first I thought they would pass the buck back to Aberdeen, since I had only been living in Middlesex since 1955, and was not going to be studying there anyway. To my considerable surprise, Middlesex took its responsibilities most seriously and made what, for those days, seemed a generous Major County Award of £285, which they followed up with further awards of £223 in 1959 and £216 in 1960. If we allow an inflationary figure between the nineteen-fifties and the present day of perhaps thirty-five times, these grants were in the region of £10,000 per year. The Middlesex grant was paid in half-yearly instalments. They were paid consistently and reliably throughout my three year course and were an enormous help.

Margaret was successful in getting a speech therapy full-time appointment in Aberdeen, to start at the beginning of the school term in August. We said good-bye to friends and colleagues at work and at church, and packed our belongings, loading the motor bike on the train, and set off for Aberdeen. Our time in London was at an end.

Chapter Four: A Challenging Far Country – Divinity College

On our arrival in Aberdeen Margaret's father made a most generous offer to lend us the capital to buy a house of our own for the duration of my studies. It was understood that we would sell the house, and return the money to him, at the end of it all. The house we decided on was built by the well-known Aberdeen builder Bisset. It cost exactly £1,250. Our first house was a real bungalow with a loft. Margaret started a new appointment as a speech therapist about two months before my College term began in October.

I prepared myself to begin my Divinity studies. On arrival I found that I was to have six fellow students for my next three years. We seven were the new boys, but we were joining a small faculty in which there was a second and third year. There were seven students starting their second year and three starting their third and final year. All of the above were friendly and approachable, and I later followed their careers with interest, but from a distance.

We attended classes in Biblical Criticism and Church History, in New Testament and Old Testament Studies, and in Greek and Hebrew and Comparative Theology. We also had Practical Theology and Elocution.

My biggest surprise was to discover how few hours a week the lectures would actually occupy. They took place from nine to twelve on week-day mornings. The afternoons and week-ends were completely free. On the face of it, this was to make sure that the students had ample time for personal study. In reality it provided time for us do church visiting in our Student Attachments, and even more importantly it was to make sure that our academic staff had the free time they needed to do the research and writing of the books on which their reputations would be built.

Having just come from a life where I worked in factories during the day, and studied at night, I found all this leisure time quite a shock to my system, and it took me a long time to adjust to it.

The College

Looking back on my years at College, I am amazed when I think how deeply unsatisfactory was the standard of instruction being provided us. The majority of the nine staff members seemed to communicate rather poorly. Only three stand out in my memory as capable, gifted and effective.

Prof. James McEwen's Church History lectures were inspiring, and remain clearly in my memory. He had a huge and genuine enthusiasm for his subject, and in our second year especially, on the Reformation, he inspired a similar enthusiasm in me, as he made Luther, Calvin and his own special hero, Zwingli, come to life in his hands.

A.M. Hunter, the Master, was the author of a large number of popular books on the New Testament, and his lectures were largely paraphrases of his books. He was clear and lucid, and one could not fail to obtain considerable insight into the New Testament topics he covered. His New Testament studies were 'liberal' and he was consequently despised by the conservative evangelicals in his classes.

Neil Alexander was responsible for teaching us to understand the New Testament in 'koine Greek' (the version of Greek used in the Bible), and did a splendid job. He knew his subject inside out, and made heavy, but very fair demands on us. I learned under him to translate any New Testament passage directly from the Greek and continued to make use of this skill throughout my entire ministry. My debt to him is considerable, and he probably never knew how important his contribution was to me.

The other subjects were to a greater or lesser extent disappointing, with the most troubling area that of Practical Theology. I think we all had clear hopes for these classes, for in them we hoped to get all the information and guidance we would need about the mysteries we faced as we confronted a Ministry in the Church of Scotland. We were anxious to know how to conduct baptisms, weddings and funerals, and how to prepare sermons and hymn lists and prayers. We wanted to know the proper way to chair session meetings and the like and how to carry out a proper programme of pastoral care to a congregation. My recollection is that none of these matters was even touched upon in our Practical Theology classes. What our Professor's reasons were for not embarking on all the questions we were concerned about is something I either never found out, or perhaps cannot now remember.

I do however recall clearly one way we dealt with the problem. We tackled it by asking Professor McEwen to take time out of his beloved Church History classes to tell us, for example, what to do when confronted by the death of a child in the parish. I have spoken of this ploy before as we used it in Robert Gordon's Primary to divert Mr Cardno from Arithmetic by asking him questions about the relevant merits of Spitfires and Messerschmidts. He would always say something like: 'Now you're not going to get me off the point to speak about that'. He would turn to the problem on the blackboard, but in a few moments he would turn back to us and begin to explain about Spitfires. In the same way, Prof. McEwen would say: 'We are far too busy with Huldreich Zwingli to have time to speak about cot deaths'; and in a few moments he would be talking about his experiences in his recent pastoral charge, while we listened and hung on every word. Where would we have been without these vital digressions?

On this unsatisfactory foundation our three years of college studies struggled on. Our exams, when they came, were based on good lectures and notes on New Testament studies and Church History, and on copious background reading on everything else. The results of my exams came as a considerable surprise.

From leaving school until this point I had found everything in life was difficult. Many of the jobs I had done were completely unsuited to my talents, and things like attending night school after a day in the factory produced results which were never much more than just scraping some kind of pass. Intellectually I felt a complete failure. Suddenly I found myself in a completely different situation – one where no one seemed to be making any demands on me whatever. The subjects I was studying were obviously of the kind that I should have been devoting my time to during the previous four or five years, for here I could do everything well without apparently having to work very hard. I not only gained high marks in everything, but was awarded prizes in many subjects. In connection with the prizes being handed out, I kept a record of these, and still have a note of some of them. The cash value of each was over £100, so they not only gave me a great sense of achievement, but they made a significant contribution to our funds.

This general perception was greatly enhanced by the various class certificates which were awarded at the end of each year. I still have these documents. The 'First Class Certificates of Merit' speak of gaining 'High Distinction as a Member of the Class.' I have six of these from Church History, Biblical Criticism, Systematic Theology and Christian Dogmatics.

These documents relate to exams which were set under the University's requirements for the BD degree. I excelled in them all, and would have been awarded the BD with no difficulty. Unfortunately, as I had much earlier been told, because Aberdeen University only awarded the BD as a second degree, at the end of the three years I came away with nothing! It seemed most unfair then, and I have never had reason to change my view of the matter in the years since.

We had a life in Aberdeen which had little or nothing to do with my time in college. There was Margaret's work as a speech therapist, for example at the groundbreaking establishment called Beechwood Special School, which was a school for severely handicapped children.

In 1959 my father had disturbing news about his position with the Scottish Gas Board, his employer. They wanted him to accept promotion to a new post as Financial Director of much of Scotland. The trouble was that his office would be in Perth. He had no choice in the matter, so in October 1959 they moved to Perth. My parents lived there until they died in 1991.

In College I was always termed a mature student, in consequence of my having been out in the army and in the world of work for a few years before entering the Faculty. The normal route to a Church of Scotland parish at that time involved spending the year after you left college as an

Assistant Minister in a big town congregation. This would have meant yet another year of us relying on Margaret's salary, and was to be avoided if at all possible. Divinity students were encouraged to become involved in what were called Student Assistantships, or Attachments, during their college course. This would be usually during only one of their three years, but I was told that if I could do three of these appointments – that is, one every year – then the Church's Education Committee could exempt me from my Probationary year altogether. This was highly desirable from our point of view, and I agreed to this plan. Student assistantships also brought a small payment.

My First Two Assistantships

Once this question was sorted out I was told I would start work in my first assistantship at Mastrick at the beginning of November 1958.

Mastrick was one of the new generation of Church Extension charges established in the housing schemes beyond the ring road. The minister, a man not many years older than myself, was pretty well submerged by the work of his big new parish, and seemed to have problems keeping his head above water. He was certainly far too busy to pay much attention to me, and I was simply left to get on with it. I saw nothing of the many aspects of the Ministry which I wanted to learn about. I think my 'bishop' (as we called our supervisor) was a man of great good will, but was simply not experienced enough to know that he had responsibilities towards his assistant. My attachment largely consisted of working my way through long lists of home visits, often to the elderly. I think it was during that year that I conceived an early aversion to the pastoral routine called 'getting round'. This stayed with me to some extent throughout my Ministry. Preaching was quite a different matter and I threw myself into every opportunity. I still have half a dozen of my early attempts at preaching sermons in Mastrick, and although they now sound a bit brash and immature they still read very well, and were full of bright ideas.

I completed my first student assistantship at the end of June 1959, and was told that I would be starting my next one on 16th August in another Church Extension charge. This parish was much smaller than Mastrick, and lay to the south of the city.

My first meeting with my new bishop was unforgettable. He was a very little man, no more than five feet tall. His manse was actually in the housing scheme and adjacent to the new church. We met in his tiny office. He had an extraordinary manner. He spoke in short and abrupt sentences, as he asked me questions about myself and my interests. I found him difficult to reply to and I think I fell silent (most unusual for me!). Into the quietness he dropped a sudden question:

'Would you like to see my system?'

I said I would be most interested to learn of any system.

'Go over to the filing cabinet.'

There was a tall steel office filing cabinet in the corner of the room.

'Pull out the top drawer and look at what you see.'

I did so, and was confronted by a big and impressive looking card index system.

'Pull out the first few and have a look at them.'

The first card I drew out had the bold heading 'ADAM' on it.

'Go on! Go on!'

The second card said 'CAIN' and the third card said 'ABEL'.

I said: 'They're surely not . . . . ??'

'Yes, Yes! They're all there. All the characters in the Bible in order of appearance.'

'But how do you use these?' I asked.

'I preach on them of course. If they're mentioned in the Bible they deserve a sermon and they get one. I do them in the evening services.'

'But how long have you been following this system?'

'Since I came here!'

He had been appointed in 1950, so the system had been running for nine years at that point.

'May I ask how far you've got?' I said.

'Come this Sunday night, and you'll hear. I'm up to Job.'

'Oh, I'll look forward to that, I said.' And it was true, for Job is I think one of the most interesting men in the Old Testament.

I was in my place the next Sunday evening. I was somewhat surprised to find that the Scripture reading was from the Second Book of Samuel. When the sermon began I found the minister very hard to follow. He had a curious approach to preaching which involved him in bringing a variety of books and papers into the pulpit and reading extracts from them as illustrations. It gradually became borne in upon me that we were not going to hear about Job at all. I had misheard him in the vestry. The hero of the sermon was Joab, the commander of David's army and the man who slew Absalom as he hung by his hair from the tree. Throughout my time at the parish, my bishop remained immersed in 2nd Samuel. He dealt with Amnon, Absalom, Ahithophel, Zadok, Abiathar, and many others. Despite my very earnest efforts I was unable to extract any benefit from this work.

To return to my first interview in the office:

'Now then, regarding your work in the parish. You'll be expecting a list of visits, and I've prepared a list of people I want you to go and see. Here it is.' The list was substantial, running to several typed pages.

'Now I'm going to give you this list as well. These are the people you must on no account visit.''Goodness!' I said: 'Why is that?'

'These are the Apostles of Satan in this Parish, and I don't want you exposed to their influence.'

Shortly after this the interview was concluded and I emerged bearing my two lists.

It took very little time in the homes of the parish to establish that the names on my second list were those of people who had been office bearers in the church, but had resigned or left as a result of disagreements with the minister. There were former Session Clerks and Treasurers, elders and Sunday School superintendents. All were still living in the parish and waiting for better days. All turned out on acquaintance to be fine Christians and lovely people.

With hindsight, and now with many years of experience of people's personality problems, I realise that I should have seen from that first interview that the minister was not well, and in fact was suffering from delusions and considerable paranoia. At the time I just found him strange.

If my preaching had been well received in my first appointment, it was greeted with something near rapture in my next second. The minister's preaching at morning worship was even more obscure than in the evening, with a typical sermon leaving various newspaper and magazine sources scattered far and wide around the pulpit. The people were in fact completely starved of any kind of responsible proclamation of the gospel and were delighted to hear my efforts. The small congregation was composed of people who were determined not to be driven away from the church by the eccentricities of their present minister. 'There have to be some people still here when a new minister is appointed' was a line I heard frequently. In fact they had little hope of getting rid of him. He was known to be applying for other churches all over Scotland but the parish grapevine was well able to get information about applicants, so that prospective parishes knew full well what they would be getting and quite understandably did not proceed.

In connection with my preaching in my new assistantship, it was there that I had another unforgettable experience. It was my first sermon in the parish and I was well into my stride when a large man arose at the back of the congregation and made his way towards me down the central aisle. Although my mind froze, I continued to read on. Fortunately I had a complete typescript of my sermon. As he approached the chancel I thought for a moment that he was going to mount an attack on my person. He mounted the chancel steps and moved to the pulpit where he reached in behind me and tripped a switch. The pulpit overhead light came on, and he made his way back to his seat. He was the Church Officer, and had decided that I needed more illumination to see my notes. I didn't recover my composure, and omitted large chunks of the remainder of the sermon in order to make a quick escape. I can picture him still in his ponderous and apparently inexorable advance. He turned out to be a very nice man indeed.

There were many other strange events during my months in my second assistantship. My sympathies were strongly with the people, and I heard many bizarre stories about things the minister had said and done. He was not an easy person to be loyal to, and it was not long before he began to have his suspicions about my own loyalty, and to take me to task on a whole variety of quite absurd charges. He also made some disparaging remarks about me in public. The fact that I seemed to have joined the ranks of those under attack meant that public support for me rapidly increased.

Matters came to a head one evening in the Spring of 1960 when the bell rang, and we opened the door to find a deputation of elders from the kirk. They had decided at long last to try to mount an action against the minister under church law, and they proposed to cite his public statements about me as the prime cause of a 'fama', as such a case was called. Was I willing to be so used? I don't remember exactly how I responded, but they left seeming well satisfied. I think I decided I'd better tell someone about this development, and it was my own minister who got the crucial telephone call. Early the next morning I was called to go and see the Professor of Practical Theology, who told me that my appointment as Assistant had been terminated and I would under no circumstances set foot in the parish again. My reputation was to be protected from the damage it might acquire if I became associated with a fama against the minister who was supervising my assistantship. It was a swift and decisive move, and taken with my best interests at heart.

I never went back to my second assistantship parish, and felt that I was lucky to have escaped. I have recorded here almost nothing of the bizarre events of that year, mostly because I think they would be unlikely to be believed.

My Beloved Bishop!

The College authorities continued to act quickly in my interests and on 18th March I had a letter from the minister of John Knox Mounthooly Church. I found that it had been arranged that I go directly there to continue my series of assistantships, even though it was the middle of the year. I went off to have my initial interview with another new bishop the next day in his church office.

Alex Robertson was a remarkable man. He was short and very broad – a Friar Tuck of a man. His manner was warm and friendly and I felt instantly at ease with him. It became immediately clear that Student Assistantships of the kind I had so far experienced were to be a thing of the past. I would be at John Knox's to work and to learn, and there would be plenty of opportunity for both. I was to do a wide range of visitation; not merely to elderly and housebound individuals, but post-bereavement and hospital visits, and also visits to mainstream members and office-bearers from whom I could learn about the parish. I would attend session and board meetings when possible, and in certain circumstances I would help the minister with his heavy load of bereavement work by actually conducting funerals. I would have regular opportunities to preach and to work with the Sunday School and the Youth Fellowship.

During the following year it all came to pass and under Alex Robertson's guidance I began to learn my trade. I preached to an appreciative congregation and I heard excellent sermons by the minister. I reported on every aspect of my congregational work. I had regular staff meetings with the minister. Alex Robertson truly deserved the light-hearted title of bishop as he was completely committed to my welfare. He himself was one of the finest ministers I have encountered, and many of the disciplines he imposed on himself became targets for me to aim at in my own first parish.

A good number of the things he said to me in 1960 remain as sharp in my memory today as when he said them. The following are only a few of those I have taken with me:

'You must be responsible for your own integrity in the Ministry, Peter. If you don't do the work in a factory, you'll get your cards: if you don't do the work in the parish, no one will ever know. Only you will know.'

'Your sermons must always be typed out in full. After that you may reduce them to notes or headings which may be all you take into the pulpit, but that only happens after you have typed the text out. God will not stand behind shoddy and ill-prepared work. You must be responsible for what you have been doing week by week. No one else will be.'

'At the end of each year, between Christmas and the New Year, you must lay out all your sermons and make a table of all the texts and headings. You will be amazed at what you will find. For example, how seldom you have been in the Old Testament, and how often you have repeated yourself on your favourite hobby horses. The following year you must correct the balance.'

'Your praise lists of hymns and psalms must be responsibly constructed. Your congregation deserves no less. At the end of the year make a list of hymn and psalm numbers. Cut them out and arrange them on the table. A proper hymn list should have over 300 items in a year. You will find the favourite ones you are using over and over again. Resolve to do better.'

'During your Ministry you will find you have various people – office-bearers, elders, choir members, womans' guild presidents – who come to you and offer you their resignations. *Always accept*! The person who is holding his resignation over your head is not really on your side and you can do without him.' (I should note here that while I have always engaged in the annual ritual of assessing sermons and hymns, I have not always taken Alex's advice about resignations. What I *can* say is that when I have not taken his advice I have always lived to regret it.)

'During your Ministry you will encounter an easily recognisable hand gesture. It will happen at funerals, or sometimes after baptisms. It looks like this!' (This gesture is hard to describe, but easy to spot. The person sidles up to you, with their arm stretched downwards and the hand concealing something which is to be surreptitiously slipped into your hand.) 'You are expected to have your own hand in a position of readiness. The thing passed over turns out to be a banknote. This is your tip. You will always say the same thing to this gesture. You will say: 'I'm sorry, I do not accept gratuities. If you want to give thanks for my services you must come to worship and put it in the plate'.

'As you know, ministers are not allowed to accept payment for their services for which they are already being remunerated by their stipend. If you take money in such circumstances you will start out with the best intentions, meaning it to go into the minister's poor fund, or the building fund, or some equally deserving cause. The first note will go in your breast pocket; the next your hip pocket; the next your wallet; but they will all end up in the same place: as an addition to your income. It is a slippery slope! Set not one single foot upon it.'

This one I stuck to grimly all through my various ministries and it got me into no end of trouble. Enraged undertakers have asked me: 'Who the hell do you think you are?'

Even in my latest ministry an undertaker in the county of Angus said:

'So you're better than all your colleagues are you? They all take it quite happily.' This I'm afraid may be pretty near the truth.

Alex Robertson was also very helpful about the use of names:

'Avoid the precipitate rush to Christian names, Peter. When it seems reasonable to you, invite good friends and colleagues to make free of your Christian name. But always demand a double standard from office bearers. To a Session Clerk, or to a duty elder, you may be Peter in their house or in the manse, but on duty at the church door, in front of the members of the congregation you will always be Mr Youngson; and in a Kirk Session meeting, no matter how informal it may seem, you should always be Moderator, and you should use Mr when addressing the members of the Session.'

This was inspired advice, and stood me in good stead over many years. Although customs in the use of familiar forms of address have changed a lot since 1960, my bishop's standpoint still makes a lot of sense today.

Alex had many other rules. Some I agreed with and others I didn't, but what was impossible to ignore was the fact that he had tried to think his way through a host of practical problems and come up with some kind of prepared policy. He used to say: 'I am proud of having what I refer to as a *call*, and also of having what people often term a ministry. What is much less often heard is that a minister has to be a *tradesman* as well, and that is what I try to be!'

My First Funeral

I mentioned that Alex Robertson allowed me to do funerals for him and my first, in St Peter's Cemetery off King Street, was in the new extension, which was largely built on sand. After the coffin had been lowered into the grave I took my stance at the head of the hole. I felt the earth move as I began the famous words of committal, and as the sand fell in from under my feet I slid downwards into the hole. Mercifully in those days modern minimum depth regulations did not apply and the hole wasn't very deep. The two gravediggers climbed down and gave me a boost up out of the grave. The undertaker on duty was a very ancient individual with an aged white face. He wore a top hat with a black drape round it, and black gloves. He approached me and brushed the sand off, restoring to me my Book of Common Order.

He spoke: 'Now, young Sir,' he said, 'Shall we consider the deceased to have been committed, or would you care to have another crack at it?'

I replied that I thought we had best consider the matter finished.

'A wise decision, young Sir,' he replied, and the party moved off.

The whole event stands out very clear, even after so many years. I think the thing which drove it home was the curious use of a contemporary idiom by a man who looked as though he belonged to the 19th century. I must have seemed pretty clumsy and inept, falling into the grave at my first funeral, but no one ever held it against me.

While on the subject of funerals and John Knox Mounthooly, I must mention Alex Robertson's copy of the Book of Common Order which he loaned me for such services. He had doctored the book to make it easier to use. The pages where there were alternative words indicating whether the deceased had been a man or a women had all been slit with a razor blade to allow the insertion of small slips of paper which could be slid into one of two alternative positions. The book could thus be set up to read 'he' and 'his body' and 'our brother', or in the other position 'she' and 'her body' and 'our sister'. When doing a lot of funerals of people one didn't know well this certainly helped to avoid embarrassing mistakes. I suppose that although this treatment of the book was clever, it was not in this matter very remarkable. However, in the actual words of committal Alex had an alternative usage which was much more interesting. The passage runs like this:

'Since it hath pleased Almighty God to take unto himself the soul of our brother, here departed, we therefore commit his body to the ground, earth to earth, ashes to ashes, dust to dust, in sure and certain hope of the resurrection to eternal life.'

Alex Robertson plainly believed that this statement was tempting providence in the case of people who not only were not members of the church, but had never set foot in it, and chose to use different words for them. His version for these changed after the words – 'dust to dust' – where it ran: 'trusting in the infinite mercy and love of God.'

The book was doctored so that you could designate the deceased as a 'sure and certain hope' or, alternatively, a 'trusting in the infinite mercy.'

Alex simply used the first for people who were communicant members of his congregation, and the second for anyone who was not. 'After all,' he would say, 'I'm not in any way taking the initiative away from Almighty God, who will do as he pleases anyway.'

My year as Assistant at John Knox Mounthooly remains for me a very happy memory, and it provided the only firm foundation I had for my own first parish. We stayed in touch with Alex Robertson when he moved to his final church in Kirkintilloch, and until not long before his death.

The Round Kirk

At the start of 1960 I heard that supply preaching possibilities might develop during the summer months and I made contact with the Home Board in Edinburgh to be on the lookout for anything suitable. The Secretary replied that there was the possibility that there might be a vacancy in the Hebridean Island of Islay shortly and that he would keep me in mind. In April he told me that Bowmore was vacant, and that the Interim Moderator would be glad to have my help with the vacancy during the months of July and August. This was to turn out to be a most important development, paving the way for a lifetime of interest in Islay and its neighbouring island of Jura.

Arrangements were duly made and at the beginning of July Margaret and I set off for Tarbert, Loch Fyne, by train and coach and by ferry on Caledonian MacBrayne to the Round Kirk at Bowmore in the Isle of Islay. The parish was called Kilarrow. The congregation agreed to let us camp out in the manse. Everyone rallied round and gathered together some furniture which made it quite comfortable and we settled in quite easily. The preaching in the Round Kirk was fascinating. The building has a 'coolie hat' shaped roof which is held up by a central pillar. It was amusing to discover that the regular congregation created a kind of pillar shadow with members sitting directly behind the pillar, in a line from the pulpit, so that they could safely go to sleep behind it.

Late in 1960 I was contacted by the Home Board of the Church of Scotland. It appeared that good reports of my activities at Mounthooly were circulating, and the Home Board were considering the possibility that I might be suitable for work in a Church Extension Charge. Church Extension was the term used for modern churches erected in new housing schemes or new towns. I responded enthusiastically to say I would be interested in anything which might develop in that direction.

Lochwood – Nomination and Appointment

In November 1960 I was called to Edinburgh to have an interview with the Home Board Committee at which possible Church Extension Charges were discussed together with questions to me as to my possible fitness to occupy one. A few days later a letter from George Paterson of the Home Board arrived. It had been unanimously decided by the Home Board Committee that I would do good work in a Church Extension Charge, and that 'the Committee will nominate you for a new charge to be started in the Lochwood and Rogerfield part of Easterhouse, Glasgow.'

The letter told me: 'It is proposed to erect the halls of the new charge beginning in 1961 and to add a church later. It is quite likely that a new manse will be built on the church site. No decision has been reached on this and it is fairly certain that the initial accommodation will be a local council house.'

I wrote a letter of acceptance, and got back to my college studies and my student attachment. It was, after all, not yet Christmas 1960.

Everything worked out as planned. On 15th March I received my diploma from Christ's College. I did my 'Trials for Licence', preaching in Queen's Cross in the presence of my own minister.

In March I received a copy of a letter from the Home Board stating that having received the approval of the Presbytery of Glasgow to my nomination, the Home Mission Committee of the General Assembly would now appoint Mr Peter Youngson to the new charge to be erected at Easterhouse: Lochwood, subject to license by the Presbytery of Aberdeen. The stipend was declared at £850.

I attended the *viva voce* examination before Aberdeen Presbytery's Committee in March 1961 and passed 'Principles of Presbyterian Church Government' and 'The Westminster Confession of Faith'. On 22nd April I was licensed by Aberdeen Presbytery to 'preach the gospel and exercise my gifts as a Probationer for the Holy Ministry.'

At the end of April we took our leave of the college. I had said goodbye to John Knox Mounthooly, and we had put our house on the market. We had put a good deal of work into the bungalow, and were proud to be able to offer Margaret's father a small profit at the end of three years. Most generously, he left it in our bank account as a starting donation. At the end of 1960 we had sold the motor bike and bought a black Morris Traveller. This would be the first of several such cars.

Our three years in Aberdeen had been a very happy time. With firm plans for a future in the Ministry, Margaret and I found we enjoyed a more settled life, with lots of friends and good company. We both looked forward to Glasgow, although with a certain amount of apprehension.

By 7th May we had flitted to Glasgow, and on the 14th I was Ordained and inducted into the Church Extension Charge of Lochwood. The representatives of Glasgow Presbytery were all unknown to me, and their presence was somewhat daunting, although the laying on of hands was as meaningful then for me as it again became when I myself took part in it in later years. The sermon was preached by a young newly-appointed minister, on the basis that the most recently ordained member preaches the next sermon. He knew nothing of the candidate, not even my name. But he chose as his text:

'Thou art Peter, and on this rock will I build my church!'

It was a strange way for my first parish appointment to be launched.

Chapter Five: The Far Country of Easterhouse

The two titles Easterhouse and Lochwood were almost interchangeable for us, but strictly speaking Lochwood was the name given to Unit Six of the huge sprawling system of housing scheme units called Easterhouse.

Life in Easterhouse was immediately more complicated than anything we had previously experienced. First there was the business of living in a Glasgow Corporation Council flat on the top floor of a three-storeyed council block. There was the matter of beginning work with the newly formed congregation of Lochwood, at worship and in all the other tasks of a minister.

The temporary manse was perfectly suited to my new situation, as people seemed to see me as very much identified with them in my domestic setting. Indeed many people in trouble presented themselves there who would probably have been deterred by a traditional manse. Our house was on the main bus route from the centre of Glasgow, and the bus stop just outside was at the terminus. At the other end of its run was an equally huge housing scheme called Castlemilk. Passengers would board the bus in the city centre in a state of intoxication, and on being put off at the end of the run, would ask the conductor where they were. It was not unusual for them to find that they had arrived in the unknown land of Easterhouse, when they had been planning to go the other way.

You could hear loud complaints floating up from the street:

'Easterhouse! Where in God's name's Easterhouse?'

Worship in Lochwood

Worship was already being held in the school hall of Bishoploch Primary School just across the road. I conducted services from a table on the hall stage, while the people sat on rows of stackable chairs with a central aisle. There was a big and very enthusiastic group of worshippers, who had been eagerly awaiting the appointment of a new minister.

A notable feature of worship in Lochwood was the enormous number of requests for infant baptism. This was a Glasgow parish, and the Roman Catholic halves of mixed marriages were anxious for early baptisms. With so much pressure for Christenings, I absolutely insisted on keeping them to the first Sunday of every month. If I had not made that a rule I would have had infant baptism at every service. I had decided that I would follow Alex Robertson's practice at Mounthooly of taking the babies into his own arms, and I did this, and would frequently hold them longer than was expected. This went down very well with the congregation, and I got the reputation of being good with babies. Indeed, the fact that crying babies often stopping crying when I took them in my arms was frequently commented on. I always explained this by saying that the mothers and baby-carriers were nervous, and this communicated itself to the babies, whereas I was at home in the church and they could sense my relaxation. I privately also noted that many of the young people held the babies in an artificially horizontal posture which they didn't like, while I always supported their backs and held them more upright which they enjoyed.

With the monthly routine of baptisms it was not often that there was only a single baby, and frequently there was a group of some size. In 1962, one such service produced twenty infants in one service. This attracted some attention at the time and I still have a press cutting and photograph of the families gathered outside the school. The group contained three sets of twins and one set of triplets. The parents of the triplets were both very short in stature, and with three of the mother's sisters holding the babies there was no one in the family party over five feet tall. The father had become quite famous locally, as triplets were not common at the time, and he had been receiving complimentary baby food and other articles promoted by various firms. It was our practice at this time to have a small plate on a table at the door of the hall. This held a retiring collection which went to a minister's benevolent fund. I used this for hand-outs of coal or food where there was a need. As the baptismal party was leaving the hall the father of the triplets spotted the plate. He made his way directly to it and tipped the contents into his jacket pocket. 'Thanks very much,' he said as he left. You couldn't fool him. He knew that any loose change around was earmarked for him.

The Sunday School

Easterhouse had an enormous number of children, and consequently its churches all had big Sunday Schools. At one stage the Sunday School of Lochwood Church was over 1,000 strong. It met in Bishoploch Primary School, where the children attended during the week, and this gave rise to some curious situations. It was often found most simple to have the children sit in their own classrooms on Sunday, and even sometimes at their own desks. On one famous occasion a young and inexperienced Sunday School teacher was tormented too far by a child who challenged her authority, and when asked to be at peace, went on to say:

'Why should I, Miss? You canna dae anything. You canna belt me like my teacher does.'

'Can I noe?' said the hard-pressed lassie, and getting the teacher's leather strap out of her desk, applied it to the child.

We found out that this had happened when the aggrieved parent presented herself at the manse, demanding to know what I was going to do about it: 'My Willie got the belt at his Sunday School.'

The huge Sunday School meant big numbers of children present during the first part of the morning service, and the urgent necessity to keep up a high standard of what in the church are entitled 'children's addresses'. Good stories, then as now, were hard to find and many a Sunday I'd have paid good money for a fresh one.

In those first few years one of the most memorable of our annual events came from the fact that the enormous Sunday School continued the universal Glasgow tradition of Sunday School trips, or outings, at the end of the summer term. In our case these involved a great convoy of double-decker buses wending their way through Lanarkshire to favourite locations such as Strathaven or Stonehouse. On the first of these I remember being ill-advised enough to let the juggernaut set off ahead of me, which faced me with the need to overtake an endless line of buses on narrow country roads, with torn off pieces of toilet paper floating down upon us from the upstairs windows. A wonderful time was had by all, and many photographs still survive of the children's races on these outings.

The Christian Year

The Church of Scotland tradition in which I grew up was typical of its time, and paid very little attention to any of the Christian Festivals, but I always thought that Christmas and Easter were both important. At Christmas 1961 we were worshipping in the school, but I got permission to have a service at 11.30 pm on the night of Christmas Eve, and another on Christmas Day. The new choir sang carols, and I encouraged everyone to wish each other a Happy Christmas once I had finished the sermon, just after midnight. This service was immediately popular, and in later years the Watchnight Service was packed.

Christmas was also celebrated in school, and since I was now chaplain at Bishoploch primary I had services to take there, and was present at endless class nativity plays. The last Sunday before Christmas involved the enormous Sunday School, and was supposed to be a *tour de force* by the minister. I certainly used to pull out all the stops. There were also Christmas parties for each department of the Sunday School. These required a vast amount of preparation, and I was always involved up to the hilt, usually in helping to organise games. The format was completely traditional with a break in the middle of the games for sausage rolls, jelly and ice-cream. The whole event ended with the children being sat down; the lights dimmed; Jingle Bells being sung; and Santa making his entrance with a sack of toys which would be distributed to the children. It was also predictable that some child would be left off the list, and depart tearfully without a present.

I tried to make Easter special as well, with Palm Sunday for children, and a service on Good Friday. I even tried small evening services on each night of Holy Week. Some folk did attend these, probably out of loyalty to the young minister!

Music had been important to me since childhood, and Christmas and Easter became the foundation of a tradition of music and drama in my ministry. I began to prepare the choir and others to exploit their possibilities.

Palm Sunday presented special challenges, as I focused strongly on children, and I managed various processional events, with singing and waving branches. Where do you find hundreds of palm branches in a Glasgow Housing Scheme? Ingenuity was often taxed to the limit, and rhododendron bushes were raided from far afield.

One year I decided to approach a farmer for permission to borrow a very young lamb to take into the church as a symbol of Spring. The lamb was willingly given, and I hid it under my voluminous preaching gown throughout the early part of the service, to reveal it to the children at the appropriate moment. The lamb was a huge success, and the service was long spoken of. What was not widely known was that during the afternoon and evening of the Sunday, I became conscious of a large number of unwelcome guests, crawling and jumping on and inside my clothes. The lamb had been heavily infested with fleas, which were delighted with their new host, and I had to strip down in the bath to be finally rid of them.

One year, once we were in our new church, I thought that we might be able to go one better than the Easter lamb, and I had the idea of having a live donkey in the church on Palm Sunday. A farm just a short distance from Lochwood had several donkeys, and its farmer, one Mr Fyfe, was an approachable though somewhat rugged man, who had come down to Lanarkshire many years earlier from Aberdeenshire and still had a broad Aberdeen accent.

He listened carefully to my proposal, and agreed at once not only to lend the donkey, but to bring it to the church in a trailer and supervise leading it round the church. He had one practical point to raise, however, and I remember his words as if they were said yesterday.

'Aye, Meenister. Ye can hae the beast, a' richt! But fit if it dungs?'

I agreed that that would be a consideration, but that we would just have to have a bucket of sawdust handy and hope for the best.

The visit was a great success, and the donkey was perfectly behaved throughout the procession. The children were robed as disciples and crowd members. The donkey did not dung. I repeated the event several times during my ministry – in Glenrothes and in Kirriemuir – and there were never any accidents. The Easter lamb may have been memorable, but the donkey was never forgotten, and I have been reminded of it many times over the years. One year I was approached at a General Assembly in the 1980s by a young minister, who had been in Lochwood Church as a Sunday School child, and was still excited by the memory of the donkey.

I mentioned Christmas carols. In our second Christmas in Bishoploch School, it became borne in upon me that since the enormous population of Easterhouse was not crowding into our services, it was up to us to take our services out into the streets. I suggested that we should go out as a congregation and sing carols in Dalilea Drive and Lochdochart Road. This was treated with some scepticism, but I was very determined, and I was personally equipped with an enormous singing voice which could probably make an impact even from a street pavement. We set off one evening before Christmas. I still treasure photographs of this strange event. Two leading elders are there handing out carol sheets. There is a Glasgow policeman in attendance. There are about twenty adults, with church members well represented, and, this being Easterhouse, there are over a hundred children. One photo shows me standing at the front conducting and singing lustily outside a Lochwood block of houses. The actual reception we were given was quite friendly and polite. People leaned out of upstairs windows, and some joined in the singing. This venture created a certain amount of anxiety in the Kirk Session, and I don't think it was repeated, probably on the grounds of being responsible for the children.

The New Buildings

Most Church Extension congregations start without churches and halls of their own, and we relied on a school. But new buildings were planned for us and things quickly started moving. The ground for the church was on an exposed hilltop. The site was superb. We were to have a set of halls first, to be followed by a church. The question of a manse was left open.

The chosen architect was delightful and keen to involve me in the plans. He told me that according to his contract with the Home Board of the Church of Scotland, he wasn't supposed to have any direct contact with me. He said he thought this was crazy, and insisted that we two would have to have a close relationship.

He asked me for any thoughts about the church and I told him of the time we had spent in Bowmore in Islay, where I conducted worship in the famous Round Kirk. Mr Ramsay was immediately enthusiastic.

'I've always wanted to build a circular building,' he said. 'Wouldn't it be wonderful if my first one was a church?'

By the time I left his office, the architect was on fire with his new idea, and after only a week or so I was back seeing some of the ideas set down on paper. I can still remember the excitement with which I looked at his first drawings of the future church. The walls curved round in an opening spiral. The outer wall rose steadily round the circle, gaining about six or seven feet. This created a pie-crust slice of vertical window where the higher roof edge met the lower one. The chancel would cut off a part of the circle, and would be backed by a huge wooden screen pinned on the wall. There would be a very long communion table, and an enormous free-standing cross. The font was to be a mighty boulder. The pulpit was a striking white structure, and there was a place for an organ.

The architect had said that a modern roof would not need a central pillar like Bowmore. The roof was an umbrella, only without the long handle. The ribs were huge laminated timber beams. A central post projected some distance down into the open space. This was called the dumb-bell. The ribs of the umbrella were metal tie rods running through the beams, with bolts to be tightened up on the outside, and connecting into a round metal ring at the bottom of the dumb-bell.

In June 1962 it was decided that the future manse would be built on the same parcel of ground as was going to contain the halls and the church. I had had my way! The principle of having a modern church and halls with this minister living in his own house on the same site as his church buildings had been accepted.

The first turf was cut and the work on the church hall was begun in October 1962, less than eighteen months after my own Ordination. It was an exciting time for the congregation as the walls began to rise.

Life in Easterhouse

Life in Lochwood was a busy time for Margaret and me. She had been determined not simply to fit into the expected role of minister's wife. Both of us felt that 'two for the price of one' was not how we saw the Ministry. Margaret had no difficulty finding speech therapy posts in Lanarkshire, and was soon doing four days a week in schools in places as far away as Hamilton and Wishaw. This involved her in a lot of travelling, and she had the car more often than I did. Fortunately Lochwood was a very compact housing scheme, and I was able to do afternoon visiting on foot. I had the use of the car to go to visit all my hospitals, and my knowledge of the layout of Glasgow is still based on the location of each of them.

In church Margaret was a constant and supportive presence in worship every Sunday, and went back to singing in the church choir, as she had when we first met. She took the lead in setting up a Woman's Guild, and was its first president.

The Royal Visit

In the early months of 1963 I learned that it had been decided by the powers that be that because of the high profile of Easterhouse as a vast Glasgow Housing Scheme, with significant social problems, Lochwood would be put on the agenda of the Lord High Commissioner to the General Assembly. An official visit would be made to the half-completed church building at Lochend Road. I would be the on-site host for this visit, as the parish minister, and Margaret would share with me in this. I would be supported by the Purse Bearer, and by officials from the Presbytery and the National Home Board. The only slight complication foreseen was that the Lord High Commissioner for 1963's General Assembly was the Duke of Gloucester. Although never very committed to the monarchy, I wished them no ill, and even found it possible to include 'The Queen and members of the Royal Family' in my intercessary prayers from time to time. I made inquiries and learned that the Duke of Gloucester was the late King George the Sixth's younger brother, and the Queen's uncle. Born in 1900, he was sixty-three at the time of this visit.

He was married to Alice Montagu-Scott, the Duchess. She was reputed to be warm, friendly and charming, while he was known to be extremely vague. It was established that when the Royal Party arrived on the church building site, Margaret would be responsible for conversing with the Duchess, and I would get to cope with the Duke. This is indeed how matters turned out.

The superb scarlet royal helicopter landed in the playing field behind the Secondary School. The Royals disembarked and met the Glasgow Corporation and the Church Establishment party and embarked in a fleet of cars which took them seventy-five yards to the foot of what would become our manse drive, and the main access to the church site. The Duke and Duchess emerged from their car and I welcomed them both, and presented Margaret. From then on Margaret was part of a relaxed and happy group in which Alice was the central figure, and I was left on my own to accompany The Duke. I couldn't get a single word out of him, and got more and more desperate. No one responded to my signals which clearly indicated that I would appreciate a bit of support.

Finally, looking round at the great crowd of kids who were crowding round the site, he looked up and said:

'Um! Many children!!'

Feeling pretty desperate, I jumped in:

'Yes, Sir, lots of children, but not here to see you of course. They've come to see the helicopter.'

I thought I'd probably gone over the top, and wondered if they still put people who were impertinent to Royalty in the Tower. There was a long pause, and then a slow guffaw as his Royal Highness finally got the point, and expressed amusement. Even in my unenviable position, I found myself really quite sorry for the man, who looked about eighty-five, but was not yet even at the age of retirement.

The helicopter took off in due course, and our moment in the unusual limelight was over.

The Church Roof

In October 1963 the new halls were dedicated and we moved out of Bishoploch School for good. The foundation stone for the new church was laid in the same month, and the round building began to rise and take shape.

There were some memorable moments. The works foreman had a Glasgow accent which made him hard for me to understand, and about this time I had a conversation with him about the provision of the various lintels for windows and doors which would shortly be required.

'Oh!', said he, 'We'll be casting them in City.'

'Ah!', said I. 'Up in Glasgow, then, and bringing them out here later?'

'No! Here! We'll be casting them in city! Here on the site!'

The penny finally dropped. They would be casting the lintels 'in situ'; or in Glaswegian, 'in sittie'.

Another exciting time was the construction of the church roof. The laminated beams for this structure each weighed three and a half tons. The central dumb-bell was balanced on top of a mighty tree trunk in the centre of the church. This timber was from a huge larch tree, and was sawn with four square faces. The post was stayed in place with ropes like the mast of a sailing ship. The dumb-bell looked precarious as the crane slowly dropped the first of the radial beams into position to span from the top of the wall to the top of the dumb-bell. The key man in this operation was the spiderman, a wee Glaswegian, who was lowered on to the top of the dumb-bell to wait for the arrival of the first beam. He was set down on this little circular platform on his knees and had no room to stand up at first. He shouted down to the watching crowd:

'Is the Minister down there?' he asked. He was told that I was present.

'Hey, Minister!' he cried. 'You can tell your congregation that the first man to kneel inside their church was a Catholic.' (He pronounced it 'Kafflik'.) He got a big roar of laughter from everyone present.

The beams went in one after the other. No two were the same length because of the spiral structure of the wall and the increase in height. It took twelve to complete the roof and I am pleased to have a photo which shows one of them, I think the fourth, being set in place. It took very little time to set all the beams in place and insert all the metal tie bars. The nuts went on to the threaded ends of the rods and a huge spanner was used to tighten them up. A good deal of time and effort went into getting the nuts really tight. Once this job was complete the great larch post had to be taken away. This was achieved by the foreman with a sledgehammer. Everyone's eyes were fixed on the circle of beams overhead as the beam fell. There was a lot of creaking and cracking as everything took up the strain of over thirty tons of timber. No actual settlement was apparent. The centre post was set up again, and when fitted against the dumb-bell it was clear that it would have fitted back underneath the centre with only about an inch taken off it. The roof was voted a complete success by all concerned, and our architect expressed enormous satisfaction at the completion of this critical phase of the building.

The Dedication

Soon a date was able to be set for the dedication and opening of the building. I had long cherished the idea of inviting George Macleod to come and dedicate the new church. Not only was he the leader of the Iona Community, but he had been Moderator of the General Assembly some years previously in 1957. We had had some vigorous discussions, and some fairly profound disagreements, during my college trip to Iona in 1958. I had not been prepared to become a full member of the Community, but had been immensely impressed by George Macleod.

I knew that a building in the round, standing on a hill in the midst of a new Glasgow housing scheme, would appeal to him. He could also be expected to respond to the imagery of the huge communion table and the free-standing cross, not to mention the font, carved out of the living stone. I wrote a suitable letter, asking him if he would be prepared to undertake this engagement, and received a reply in the affirmative.

George Macleod was at Lochwood Church for the Dedication Service, which was conducted by the Moderator of Glasgow Presbytery. His sermon was powerful, and everyone present felt it was a memorable occasion.

Perhaps even more memorable was the sit-down meal for the dignitaries after the congregational social. George Macleod was in sparkling form. It was asking him to say grace before we ate that started him off. Here is Macleod speaking as I recall him:

'It was in 1650 when Cromwell was in Scotland dealing with Montrose that he was billeted in Glasgow. He went to worship at the Cathedral on the Sunday, where the Minister, Melville, was an enthusiastic Royalist. Melville went through agonies trying to decide whether he should be true to his opinions in his sermon, and finally decided that he could do no other, and preached a Royalist sermon. At the end Cromwell's aide said to him:

"Shall I pistol-whip the fellow now, sir, or wait till later?"

"Nay, sir," replied Cromwell, "Ask him to come and dine at our lodgings; I have a sweeter punishment in store for Master Melville."

Melville was amazed at the invitation, but had no choice but to attend. He was shown into the dining room where Oliver Cromwell was, and on his arrival Cromwell welcomed him and said grace – for an hour and a half!'

George Macleod's second story was on a familiar topic but in an unfamiliar setting.

'During my year as Moderator I was involved in a wedding at St Giles, which you could only call a society wedding. Both the young couple were titled, and as I stood up to put their vows to them, it suddenly occurred to me that it was only as "The Marquis of such-and-such", and as "The Duchess of so-and-so", that I knew them at all, and that I hadn't the faintest idea what their Christian names were. The important part of the service was almost upon me, so I said to the young man:

"By what name do you wish to be married?" He looked a little startled, but replied clearly: "Charles, Sir."

I then said the same to the young lady, who replied: "Catherine, Sir."

I proceeded with the question, "Do you Charles, take Catherine. . . ." and so on.

I thought the whole crisis had actually passed off rather well. Later, at the reception, I was approached by the elderly Bishop of Durham, who was a relative, and who wanted to congratulate me on the service.

"My dear fellow," he said, "What a fine service! I was particularly impressed by the rubric you made use of in asking the couple to declare their own names. I've never seen that before, but I plan to include it myself in future."

I felt I had made a significant contribution to inter-church affairs.'

George Macleod told several more good stories at what was a very happy meal.

The Open Door

One of my lifelong obsessions has been about church buildings being open. Certainly I remember hating finding churches locked up even when I was cycling about the countryside in my childhood.

I raised the matter of the Open Door with my Kirk Session.

'You must be mad to even think of it, Moderator. This is a Glasgow Housing Scheme. This is Easterhouse. The church wouldn't last a week. Think of the damage! Think of the cost!'

The elders seemed unanimous. I could see them insisting on locking a building I thought of as my church. I tried to explain my position. I spoke about the desperate need to recover the idea of 'sanctuary' in our day, and especially in a place like Easterhouse. I explained that it wasn't our church, it was everybody's church. I spoke of my confidence and hope that everyone in the community would be on our side if we opened it, and would be against us if we locked it up. I explained that I believed that news of any damage to our new building would bring a wave of sympathy and support from the community and could do us nothing but good. This was the kind of argument the Kirk Session liked, and the motion was finally made in those terms, and passed unanimously.

After the dedication in October the open door policy was begun. Lochwood Church stood open during the hours of daylight in the middle of Glasgow's turbulent Easterhouse Scheme from October 1964 until I left in October 1969. During those five years there was not a single example of damage to, or theft from, the church. I would have to admit that folk didn't beat a pathway to the door, but individual accounts from people met in trouble, sickness or bereavement often indicated that they had at some point 'just gone in for a minute', and felt all the better for it, so I suppose it was all worth while.

Funerals

I considered myself fortunate to start my ministry in a young community where death was a comparatively uncommon event. In Lochwood death, when it did occur, tended to be untimely. Children would be knocked down on the road. Others would succumb to meningitis or, at that time the great killer, leukaemia. Some teenager would not survive a beating or kicking in a gang fight. There were industrial accidents to men at work, and deaths on the road. There was an occasional suicide. Most of these involved what might be called 'circumstances of unusual distress,' and in dealing with most of them I felt myself pretty far out of my depth.

My very first funeral was an infant cot death. I had only been a few days in my parish when word was brought to me that a baby had died in a house literally just across the road from our manse. I put on my new dog collar and went to call. I still remember the scene that met my eyes. There was a youngish woman sitting by the fire with her head sunk on her hands. In the corner was a cot with the baby's body still in it. The room was threadbare and dirty, and there was no light on. The helpful neighbour who had shown me in, spoke:

'Yes, Minister, it's just like I always say, it's just a wee flower given to us to bloom for a moment and then withered away.'

Nothing had prepared me to respond to this, but I remember an anger rising up within me as I said to her, loudly and very coldly:

'Madam! My God doesn't kill babies!'

I don't suppose it was a well thought out answer, and it certainly sounds rather crude now, but it engaged the mother's interest and she looked up, and I sat down and we began to talk about what had happened. Later I conducted the funeral, which was a sad event.

Healing

One resident who was unwell I have never forgotten. She was called Marie and she lived with her husband and two children near the manse. I received a message that she was ill and at home and would like a visit from the minister, so I lost no time in making a house call. Marie was in bed and her husband, who was at home, showed me in to see her. She was in her late thirties, and looked pale and drawn. She told me that she had been diagnosed with abdominal cancer some time ago and had spent a considerable time having treatment in hospital. She had now been sent home. The medical authorities were saying that there was nothing more they could do for her, and that she was incurable. I expressed my sorrow, which was genuine, and I asked her if, since she had called for me, she would like me to say a prayer. She said she would, and I did. When I had said 'Amen', I rose to go.

'Is that all, Mr Youngson?' she said.

'Well, what more do you want?' I replied.

'I want you to make me better' was her reply.

'I'm afraid I don't do that,' I said.

'Well in that case you're going to have to be like a GP and get me a specialist.'

It became clear that Marie had heard about Christian healing somehow, and that it was 'healing, with laying on of hands', that she was looking for. I explained that I would have to find out about it, and promised to be back as soon as I had some news.

A minister friend said: 'The man you really want to find is Cameron Peddie. He is the founder of Christian Healing in Scotland nowadays. I think he's still alive, but whether he's still active and whether he would help, you would have to find out.'

I looked up Cameron Peddie. He was retired from his parish and living on the south side of Glasgow. I was soon speaking to him on the phone.

He sounded a bit distant and somewhat frail, but he was interested and positive. Yes, he would be prepared to come and see my lady.

I arranged to collect him as he had no car. He was ready and waiting for me. He looked to be about eighty years old (he was actually seventy-seven at the time). He was extremely thin, and his face was deeply lined and pale with a kind of papery appearance. He had almost nothing to say, and we sat in silence for the journey out to Easterhouse, which probably took about half an hour. He leaned on my arm to the top of the stairs, and we were admitted by Marie's husband, and conducted into her bedroom.

I introduced Mr Peddie, who greeted Marie, and said:

'It is my custom to begin with a prayer.'

His prayer was old fashioned and formal, and quite long. When he had finished he got up and went to stand beside the bed. I myself stood near the window, about four feet away. I suppose I was one corner of a triangle with Mr Peddie and Marie's head at the other corners.

'There is nothing to be alarmed about,' he said. 'You don't have to take off your watch, or any jewellery. You may experience heat, or perhaps cold. It will seem like a wind blowing over you.'

I was already very anxious, and nothing had happened to make me feel any better. From my point of view everything was against him: his frailty; his prayer; and the comment about the watch, and the hot and cold winds, which seemed to me to be pure mumbo-jumbo.

Mr Peddie stood up by the bed and stretched his hands out over Marie's chest and abdomen. I was watching intently and saw that he was not in fact touching her body, but that his hands were poised in the air about an inch or so above it.

As Cameron Peddie stood there, I experienced the most extraordinary sensation. I could only describe it later by saying that 'power was flowing through me'. It was like being connected to some kind of electrical current. I felt as if my hair was standing on end. My hands were tingling and there was a faint roaring in my ears. I gazed at Mr Peddie, and was conscious that he no longer appeared to be frail, but strong and confident. His back, which had been much bowed, was straight and his shoulders were back. He no longer gave any impression of great age.

After a few minutes – perhaps as long as four or five – he removed his hands from their location over Marie's body, and pronounced a brief benediction. His voice was strong and vibrant. He moved back away from the bed and turned to face me and Marie's husband who had been standing by the door.

'Thank you,' said Marie's husband, 'Now if you and Mr Youngson come through the house, I'll get you both a cup of tea.'

'You will come and sit with us, Sir,' said Cameron Peddie. 'Your wife will bring us the tea.'

There seemed to be no discussion about it, and we three went into the sitting room and sat chatting together. After only about five minutes Marie came into the room with a tray, and served us with a cup of tea. She was wearing a dressing gown and slippers, but she seemed to be moving freely, and she came and sat and talked with us.

'You understand that we have not finished here,' said Cameron Peddie. 'There is much still to do. We will come back and see you again next week.'

Shortly after that we left and I took Mr Peddie home. He had returned to his former fragile aspect by the time we were back in the car, and he climbed his own stairs with some difficulty. He was plainly very tired. We confirmed an appointment for the following week and I went home.

I called on Marie the next day, and found her up and about, though she said that she got quickly tired and needed a lot of short rests. It was the first time she had been able to manage to do anything for many months, and she was immensely pleased and radiantly happy.

We repeated the happening the following week, when everything went very much as before, although Marie was up when we arrived. I experienced exactly the same set of sensations as I had the previous week. We left in due course but this time there was more to talk about in the car.

'We are not quite finished with Marie,' said Mr Peddie, 'but I will not be coming back. The journey is too difficult for me. In any case I am no longer needed.'

'What do you mean, "no longer needed"?' I stammered. 'Who is going to go on with the case?'

'Oh, you'll be all right', he said. 'Just do exactly what you've seen me doing. You have the same talent. The gift has come upon you. If you need to know a wee bit more about it all, I'll give you a copy of my little book "The Forgotten Talent".'

'But how will I know what to do and when to stop?' I asked.

'Don't worry,' he said: 'You'll know.'

I went back to Marie's house three more times, at weekly intervals. I did the same thing I had seen Cameron Peddie do, although I used my own prayer, with modern words I was comfortable with. The sensations which accompanied the 'laying on of hands', as I have become used to calling it, were much stronger when I was doing it myself, and I felt as though a strong hot wind was blowing over and through my hands and in and out of the body beneath them. In anticipation of going on with all this myself, I had been prey to all kinds of doubts. Had I really seen what I saw and felt what I felt? Was I about to make a complete fool of myself? Would someone jump out of a cupboard and shout: 'Candid Camera!'? However, once I was there in the house, and actually doing what I had been told to, everything felt absolutely right, and I didn't feel silly or embarrassed. In fact, I found afterwards that I hadn't been thinking about myself at all. This is an unusual experience for me!

By the time I stopped going to see Marie, her life was more or less back to normal. She had been to the hospital for a check up, and had been told that they had no explanation why she was apparently so much better as her cancer appeared to be still present. In fact she remained quite well through the rest of my time in Easterhouse, and I have no reason to think that she didn't live a normal life span, or for that matter may not be living yet.

My encounter with Cameron Peddie was a turning point in my life. Before that I had been a rational Christian. I believed in the gospel because it was sensible and seemed like a good idea. No one in college had ever asked me if I actually believed in Jesus or in God, and I'm not sure what I would have said if asked. I knew that I had had no mystical experiences in my life. The nearest I had was a variety of strong feelings, usually associated with preaching sermons, during which activity I often had a powerful idea that I was 'where I was supposed to be' and 'doing what I was supposed to be doing.' The feelings associated with Cameron Peddie's visits, and my own subsequent practice of laying on of hands, were the first time I had experienced anything which suggested the 'gifts of the spirit' that St Paul was so concerned with might actually be a reality. I had plainly received a gift of healing. I knew that I had received it rather than earned it or learned it, because I had caught it, like a kind of infection, from being close to Mr Peddie. I certainly felt a bit isolated with it, and kept pretty quiet about what was happening to me, but I didn't feel any lack of confidence, and was sure that I would put the gift into practice if it became clear to me that I ought to do so.

From that time on various individual people more or less self-selected themselves for laying on of hands. It was not that they knew that this was something they could ask for, but in meeting them at home or in hospital, I would make some leading remark about a service that was available, and while some ignored the hint, others simply jumped at it. Cameron Peddie had said that it would become clear what I was supposed to do. It appeared to be true, and with that I had to be content. The activity of Christian Healing went on to become a continuing thread through my life and ministry, and in due course came to involve Margaret as much as me.

Margaret at the door of our home in Lower Edmonton. She works as a speech therapist: I am at the factory.

In London we shared our life with our tropical fish and our S.S.Jaguar, which often didn't run. It is seen here approaching the point at which it had to be scrapped.

While I was at College in Aberdeen we lived in a bungalow bought with money my father-in-law lent us. Margaret loved it and its fine garden.

We were able to have the first of several black cocker spaniels. Both photographs show us here with Jet, of whom we were very fond.

Plate 6

Lochwood: the view down Lochend Road from the site of the new church.

The bus terminus and our Morris Traveller. Our manse was in the top right flat.

Carol singing in Rachan Street, with the minister leading in the front right corner.

Lochwood Parish church was modelled on the Round Kirk of Bowmore. Here the mighty roof beams are being dropped into place. The spiderman is in the centre.

The finished suite of buildings has its various church halls in the foreground with the circular worship building standing beyond them.

Plate 8

The superb chancel of Lochwood Church. Set against the great wooden screen are *(left to right)*: the organ – the font – the cross – the table – the plaque – the pulpit.

The Duke of Gloucester was Lord High Commissioner to the General Assembly in 1963. He and the Duchess visited Lochwood to see the church, which was being built in this housing scheme. Here he is with the minister. Margaret is with the Duchess.

For Goodness' Sake – Say Something!

My First General Assembly was in 1966, and I had to attend the supplementary meeting called the Commission of Assembly in October. It was at this meeting that there was a big report on behalf of the Home Mission Committee. There was a new plan for the Kirk to use a five-strong group of laymen to solve the church extension crisis. The plan was to ask for an extra £1,500,000 for Church Extension over the next five years, and speaker after speaker came to the lectern to urge that more time should be given to consider this plan. In other words there were many ministers who did not want it to pass. I was amazed by the general lack of enthusiasm for something which I considered to be absolutely vital. Things were evidently going very badly indeed.

A note was passed to me by a steward. It had been scribbled by the Secretary. It said: 'For goodness' sake stand up and say something! We're being slaughtered!' I rose at once, and was immediately spotted by the eminent Moderator, Dr Leonard Small of St Cuthbert's. I whispered my name and parish, and he introduced me.

'Peter Youngson, the minister of Lochwood, in Easterhouse, has the floor.'

I had no speech prepared, but I hardly needed one. I had been in Lochwood for five hard years, and there was plenty to say. A pretty full report appeared next day in the Daily Express, and I quote from it here:

'I live and work in Easterhouse. It is violent, tense and difficult to survive in. One focus of sanity and hope in it is the existence of our brand new church building. In schemes like this, only the churches provide a focus for Christian life, Christian action and the possibility of future development of the community for the future. When I look round the faces of the fathers and brethren here I recognise few faces of men working in the new housing schemes. Perhaps this is why the matter isn't seen as a crisis. What conceivable danger is there in a scheme to raise urgently needed cash for the Kirk's church extension work? These places are jungles. Are you going to leave the men who have committed themselves to work there without any focal point, without any possibility of inspiring hope for the existence of future congregations? There are many in these housing schemes who are afraid that they are not going to get new buildings in the next few years. How long will you withhold their churches from them? I appeal to you not to hesitate about this action, but to allow the courageous undertaking of this work to go on.'

Although it doesn't appear in the press cutting, I certainly also said that being in Easterhouse was like 'fighting wild beasts in Ephesus.' (St Paul!!) I think I also said that we were at the sharp cutting edge, trying to proclaim the gospel in difficult areas and the church was going to withhold the very basic tools we needed – our halls and our churches. It must have gone down well, for I got a standing ovation from the General Assembly, and walked back to my seat through applauding Commissioners. The vote went in favour of the scheme. Leonard Small, who had added his own complimentary remarks from the chair, never forgot me, and always crossed over to speak to me in later years, often recalling my maiden speech.

Tom Allan

I had only been in Lochwood a few weeks when the phone rang one morning.

'Is that Peter Youngson?' a voice said.

I answered that it was indeed he.

'You'll be feeling a bit strange! Everything a bit new?'

The voice was rich with a strong gravelly, Glasgow accent.

'Yes, I am,' I replied, 'Who is this, please?'

'This is Tom Allan, St George's Tron. I just thought I'd give you a wee ring to say that some of us meet in the vestry here on a Friday morning for a bit of bible study and fellowship, and you'd be very welcome to come along.'

I had heard all about Tom Allan, the founder and instigator of the well known Tell Scotland movement, and a supporter and colleague of Billy Graham in his Crusades in Scotland. I also knew him to belong to the wing of the church that I call Conservative Evangelical. You could call it less politely fundamentalist. I felt I had to come clean with him.

'That's very kind of you, Mr Allan, but I think I should warn you that where the Scriptures are concerned I'm something of what you might call a liberal!'

‘Och! Come along anyway. We can always find room for a liberal!’

The invitation was hard to resist. He was, after all the only representative of the kirk in Glasgow who had shown the least interest in my arrival. I went to the meeting as invited, and remained as a loyal and enthusiastic member for several years.

The group of ministers I joined in the Tron was a curious one, but they all made room for me, and the issue of the bible and its authority seldom arose, and never came between us. Tom had a genius for bible study, and I learned an enormous amount from him. He held rallies in the Tron as part of the Tell Scotland Movement, and I tried to support him by attending them. It would have been at my first rally that I was seated on the chancel and singing in the bass section of the church choir. The singing I remember was full-throated and the Tron was packed.

Tom did a kind of warm-up session with the people present, and he was absolutely brilliant at it. He was as at home and relaxed with his material as Dave Allen would be later on TV. He welcomed various groups who he knew had travelled to the rally in coaches, then he asked if there was anyone present for the first time.

‘If you’ve not been here before, could you stand up!’ he announced.

As one of the newcomers I stood up in my place in the choir directly below him. After picking out several people around the church, he looked down at me. He knew me well by this time, but you wouldn’t have thought so.

‘Hello! What’s your name?’ he said.

‘It’s Peter, Mr Allan’, I replied.

‘Pee’ur!’ (He couldn’t pronounce the ‘t’.) ‘That’s a grand Christian name.

Where do you come from, Pee’ur?’

‘Aberdeen, Mr Allan.’

There was a ripple of amusement.

‘Aberdeen? Do you know they were playing today, Pee’ur?’

‘Yes, Mr Allan.’

‘Do you know who they were playing?’

‘No, Mr Allan.’

‘They were playing Rangers.’ There was a strong murmur of delighted appreciation all round the building. I sat down in my seat. Tom Allan turned towards his next subject on the opposite side of the kirk, but at the last split-second he turned back to me:

'They lost!' he said.

The congregation broke into a huge roar of applause. Within a very few minutes Tom Allan was preaching the Gospel, and going for the hearts and souls of everyone in the congregation, including mine. He had been softening up his audience, and he did it with consummate artistry. Tom remained a close friend and a great support to me until he died in 1965. I still miss him.

The Clinical Theology Association

In the 1960s I heard about an organisation based in England and called the Clinical Theology Association. CTA was about to hold a series of seminars in Glasgow, aimed at offering experience and skills in dealing with the various forms of personality stress to be met with in pastoral work. These seminars were particularly aimed at the clergy. I signed up, and set off to my first meeting. It was there that I encountered Frank Lake. He was a doctor and a psychiatrist who lived and worked in Nottingham, where there was a Counselling Centre. The seminars were Christ-centred, and the theories behind them, developed by Dr Lake, were represented as being in agreement with the Christian gospel. He taught that there was a healthy normal cycle of spiritual and psychiatric life, and various deviations from it were manifest in people to various degrees as conditions to which labels could be given. There was the depressive position; the hysteric position; the schizoid position. There were the problems of paranoia and of phobic anxiety. After every class I attended in those early seminars I came away convinced that my personality had been accurately described, and my condition diagnosed. To some extent this was an accurate enough perception, as we do all in fact have elements of depression and of withdrawal, and of fear that people are against us, which in most of us are kept in some kind of balance.

Frank Lake was himself a quite amazing person. He had enormous gifts of clear explanation, and he backed them up with a huge amount of practical experience, which meant that his lectures were punctuated by vivid case histories – anonymous to us, but obviously intimately known to him. I could not know then how vital to my own survival Frank Lake and CTA would later become.

Roman Catholic Encounters

The presence of Roman Catholics in my parish was at first a mystery to me. I learned that the proportion of Roman Catholics in Lochwood was about 40% Roman Catholics to 60% Protestants. I didn't really know anything at all about Roman Catholics when I arrived.

My very first experience came with the Brownies. There was a Brownie branch in Lochwood when we arrived, and they had arranged a small display especially for the new minister. This was held on the evening of their regular meeting, and was in Bishoploch School Hall. I ought not to have been surprised that the Brownies had gained an early foothold in Lochwood. It would not have surprised me later if Neil Armstrong had found some Brownies already established on the moon, when he made his giant leap for mankind. Margaret and I were enjoying the display when there was an accident. The game in progress was some form of leap-frog and a little girl fell and as she hit the floor there was a clearly audible click. On examination it became clear that she had broken her arm in the fall. Her parents were absent, and no one knew where they were. I was anxious to help, and since I lived immediately opposite the school it was decided that I would bring my black Morris Traveller to the school door. The child would be wrapped in a blanket from the school medical room, and I would take her up to Glasgow to the casualty department of the Royal Infirmary. Attempts would be made meanwhile to discover the whereabouts of her parents and bring them up to date. Her arm was put in a makeshift sling, and she was propped up in the back of the car. She seemed to be all right, so I set off. I was driving along the main Edinburgh road at about fifty miles an hour when the police car overtook me and flagged me down. A big burly policeman got out and approached.

'Where are you off to in such a hurry?' he said.

Then he saw who I was: 'Oh hello Father, is there some kind of trouble?'

I said: 'I'm sorry officer, I know I was exceeding the speed limit, but the little girl in the back has a broken arm and I'm taking her to casualty.'

'Say no more, Father,' said the officer: 'Just follow us.'

And off we went. I think we probably touched about seventy going in Alexandra Parade. I know it was all I could do to keep up. We arrived in the forecourt of the hospital, and the two big policemen were all over me. One held the door open, the other took the child. Together we arrived at the reception desk, and I told the story and handed over a slip of paper with the child's name. The girl on the desk knew about the accident already; a phone call had come in and had said that the parents had been contacted and were on their way there. My police friends and I left the patient in good hands, and made our way back to the car.

The conversation was warm and friendly. We obviously all of us felt that we had done a good job.

'Have you been out in Easterhouse long, Father?' said one of the policemen.

'Are you enjoying it, Father?' said the other.

As I got ready to take my leave, the moment of decision arrived. I could not leave without telling them who I really was, even if it meant a speeding ticket.

'Look officers: you've been very helpful, but you've got one thing wrong. I'm not a Roman Catholic Priest, I'm a Church of Scotland Minister.'

There was a pause, after which the one policemen turned to the other:

'Sure, Paddy,' he said, 'We've been helping the wrong side!'

There was much laughter, and they sent me on my way rejoicing.

In the dark on the road they would only have had a glimpse of the dog collar, but I learned later that they would probably have sorted things out in the hospital had it not been that I was wearing the wrong uniform. The suit that I had bought in Aberdeen for my new position in Lochwood had been black, as I thought proper. I discovered that only Roman Catholic Priests wore black in Glasgow at that time. The proper attire for ministers was charcoal grey. In due course I bought another suit – this time of the correct shade.

Most of my lessons about Catholics came in Lochwood, but some had to wait till later. Father McMeel in Glenrothes became another close friend and used to come to the manse for a coffee. One of his visits must have been during the season of Lent.

On his arrival this day there was evidently something a little bit unusual about his appearance, and it confronted me with the familiar problem of whether you tell a friend that his trouser flies are open. This, I may say, was not his problem. His problem was a dirty mark on the middle of his forehead. His housekeeper had let him out without washing his face after making up the fire. I suggested that he might like to use the toilet, thinking he would catch sight of himself in the mirror. He did, but he returned with the smudge on his face still there, so I decided I'd better tell him. It was only then that he gently told me about Ash Wednesday. When Palm Sunday is over, some of the palm leaves are burnt in a wee container, and then crushed to ashes and the ashes are put away for the next year. The ashes are smeared on one's forehead on Ash Wednesday, as a sign of repentance for the beginning of Lent. Why did I think it was called Ash Wednesday? I had had no idea. Aberdonian Presbyterians had no knowledge of such things.

The Parish Priest of Lochwood in my first years in Glasgow was a giant of a man called Father Docherty. He had a strong Irish accent, and he was very traditional, as his members often told me. He was not much interested in attending to the needs of the youngsters who were running wild in the scheme every night.

'Do they come to mass, Mr Youngson? Do they attend confession? No! Let them start coming to mass and confession and I'll see what can be done about them.'

His members knew that this attitude was at odds with my own attempts to do something for the gang boys, and would continually apologise to me about it.

'Don't be too hard on him, Mr Youngson, he's one of the old school!'

Father Docherty's successor was Father Donnelly. He was more my own age and a very small and dapper individual. We got on very well. It was during his period of office that St Clare's was built beside Drumlanrig Avenue. The building was completed in August 1966, and Father Donnelly invited Margaret and me to attend. The service was to take place on a Sunday morning, and if I was to be there it would mean that I would miss conducting my own service in our own church. I decided to consult the Kirk Session. My Session Clerk expressed the views of the whole body:

'You're an ordained minister of the Church of Scotland, Moderator! There no chance whatever of you turning! You'd better go!' The matter was decided and we both went. The sermon was preached by the Bishop of Motherwell, Bishop Thomson, and it was a splendid exposition of the Good Samaritan which would have done credit to any Presbyterian preacher.

There was one strange experience which came in the immediate aftermath of the opening of St Clare's. We were by that time already living in the new manse. It was on the Monday morning, when I was working in my small study by the front door that the bell rang. I opened the door and for a moment thought there was no one there until I glanced down. A very short man was standing there wearing a cloth cap.

''Scuse me!' he said, 'Are you the minister?'

'Yes', I replied.

'Are you the minister who went to the Kafflik Church yesterday?'

'That's right,' I said.

'Well I know you're a busy man, and I'm not going to take up much of your time; but it's a disgrace!', he said: and he hit me.

He hit me right in the solar plexus. I doubled over and smashed my face into the top of his head, and immediately passed out.

When I came to he had left. As he said, he hadn't wanted to take up much time. I had slid down the door post, but in due course I got up and went inside. My spectacles frame was snapped, but I was otherwise unhurt. I suppose it wasn't a high price to pay for Christian Unity, but I have never been hit that hard before or since.

Presumably my visitor was an Orangeman – a member of the Orange Order, fierce and traditional opponents of the Roman Catholic faith. There seemed to be none of them attending Lochwood Church; at least, I never found anyone who would admit to being a member. However they made their presence felt from time to time.

Shortly after the new Catholic church opened in 1966, I had a telephone call from a representative of the Orange Order who said that since I was the minister of a new Church of Scotland in Easterhouse, he would like to bring a couple of members along with him, and discuss the possibility of having a church parade to my church. I said that I would welcome him and we set a time on a morning a few days later. It occurred to me that my kirk had been open since 1964, and this was their first contact. I prepared for the event by telephoning the Presbytery Clerk, who by this time was a friend, and potentially a mighty ally in any situation. I described the phone call, and he listened.

'They're not interested in attending your church,' he said, 'but only in embarrassing the Roman Catholic one. They will be planning to march past it with the band playing. Say they'll be welcome, but don't let them set the timing.'

The three men who came to see me were quite polite and made few demands.

There was a spokesman:

'Would it be all right to have our banners in the church?'

'Quite all right,' I said.

'Could a member read a lesson?'

'Absolutely,' I said.

I asked them about their route.

'We would be marching through the Housing Scheme to arrive at your church in time for worship, and then we'd be leaving by a coach which would be waiting.'

'That would surely mean you arriving here a bit tired', I said, 'It would be much better if you were fresh when you arrived. I would prefer you to come by bus, and do your marching afterwards.'

The spokesman and his companions all swore at me politely, and left.

Social Issues

I had had my first real encounters with people who were living under pretty poor circumstances in my assistantships. There were problems with debt, a lot of domestic violence, and there was too much alcohol being drunk. Lochwood demonstrated all of these problems in a more severe form.

Debt was everywhere, and many people were facing a future in which they would never be out of it. There were many other forms of irresponsibility in the community. We felt a great deal of concern about the way many families treated their small children. This could manifest itself in the fact that very small toddlers could be seen sitting in the middle of busy roads, and that accidents involving them always brought an angry crowd of women screaming at the driver of some bus or van.

I was called to an incident in Lochdochart Road. I found a crowd of angry women surrounding a stationary van.

I approached the van driver, who was afraid to get down from his cab until I offered him protection. The little boy who had been injured was lying on the pavement, unconscious, and the people around him were waiting for an ambulance which had already been summoned.

'He hit me,' said the driver. 'I didn't hit him. He was moving like a bullet. Look, here's the dent where his head hit the van.'

The dent in question was several feet back from the front of the van. The child had in fact run into the side of the van. I pointed this out to the women in the street, and a kind of grudging calm ensued. No one ever seemed to consider that perhaps they were themselves partly responsible for accidents by allowing the children to be on the street in the first place.

'Ye canna' watch them a' the time' was a commonly heard statement.

I was called out one night to a house in Lochdochart Road. A neighbour knew the parents of three very small children to be out, and the children to be alone in the house. She could hear children crying, and it was getting late. I arrived into a small group of folk on the street.

'All very well,' I said, 'but what do you want me to do?'

'We'll give you a boost up, and you can go in the verandah window. It'll no' be locked. The front door's bolted.'

I objected that shinning up drainpipes wasn't what I had been engaged for, and pointed to a young man in the crowd.

'You're in a far better state for going up to the verandah than I am,' I said, 'You can do it.'

'No' me!' came the reply: 'No' wi' my record.'

After considerable negotiation it was finally decided that the person to climb up to the verandah would be me! The willing crowd pushed me up almost the whole way. Inside the house I found a terrible situation, with three small children tied into a cot with electric cable. The parents turned out to have had a win at the bingo, and had gone off drinking. They were currently in custody. The children were taken into care.

At the end of 1961 a woman turned up at the manse in distress. Her son had killed her boy friend. His father had left and the new man had moved in, and he didn't treat the boy very well. It was a Saturday and the lad came in from somewhere: he was about fourteen at the time, and found the man sitting with his back to him, watching the television in what the boy considered to be his father's chair. He went into the kitchen and found the tool box. He came back and hit the man on the head with a hammer. He was taken into custody, and the woman was at my manse seeking asylum, having found it impossible to get rid of the press. In due course reporters turned up at the manse and demanded to interview the woman. When told that that would not be possible they became abusive and threatening. It was an early example of a relationship which was later to deteriorate even further, especially with the Daily Express.

Up until Lochwood, my experience of drunks was mostly limited to the army. In Easterhouse I was to become only too used to dealing with them.

'Hey, Minister! There's a drunk man on the bonnet of your car!'

The cry floated up from the pavement beside the bus stop. I had left the Morris Traveller outside the manse. I often used to think regarding this situation that the Priest and the Levite in the story of the Good Samaritan would not have had the opportunity to go by on the other side, if the man who had been beaten up was lying over the bonnet of their car. I went down to the car and found that the man lying insensible on the bonnet was our local coalman, who had been put off a bus at the terminus. I knew him and I knew where he stayed. I manhandled him more or less erect, and with the help of a passer-by I got him into the car. When I got to his house he was still unconscious, but quite responsive to being wheeled out of the car and over to the close entrance. That was as far as he was going. I knew that he lived in the top flat. I managed to get him into a fireman's lift, and made my way up the first flight to the landing. He was a big man, and I needed a long rest before tackling the second stairs. By the second landing I could go no further, but I sat down on the steps and hitched myself backward, one step at a time, pulling him up behind me.

I knocked on the door. It was answered, but not by the wife of the coalman. I had come up the wrong stair. He lived in the next one. I left him where he was and went next door. His wife knew me.

'Oh hello, Mr Youngson, what are you doing here?'

I told her I'd brought her husband home and that he was drunk again.

'Oh dear,' she said: 'Where is he then, Mr Youngson?'

I explained that he was at the top of the stair in the next close and that she'd have to deal with the problem from this point on. She looked a bit surprised, but I still left. I felt I had done enough.

A similar incident started like the coalman's but had a different outcome. This time I found the drunk man near my own front close, as I was walking back to the house. I got him into the car front seat, and set off to take him home. I realised as I was going up Lochend Road that although I thought I recognised him, I hadn't the faintest idea where he lived. I stopped the car near the Secondary School and spoke loudly to him without eliciting any response. I tried shaking him hard, but it seemed that nothing could rouse him. With all my ideas having been unproductive I decided I'd better see if he had any means of identification on him. I reached across his body and pulled open his jacket, reaching into his inside breast pocket for his wallet. He came stone cold sober and laid me out. I don't know exactly what he hit me with, but when I recovered consciousness he was long gone. I had a splitting headache and a bleeding nose, but I had found the way to sober up a drunk man. It was a method I didn't try again.

Fatalities in a Crash

By 1967 we were living in the new manse and we were woken by a very loud noise at about three o'clock in the middle of Saturday night. I scrambled into my clothes and ran out. There was a wrecked car wrapped round a big overhead lamp standard on Lochend Road just past the church. I was the first to approach the wreck, and found it was full of people. There was the driver and the front seat passenger, and there were three adults in the back seat. The wreck stank of petrol, and the people inside stank of drink. The driver and the front seat passenger were evidently dead. As a couple of neighbouring residents approached I got one of the back doors open and pulled a woman out of the back seat on to the pavement. She was also dead. I went back for the woman sitting in the middle of the seat, and as I pulled her out, she made a faint moaning sound. As I sat on the pavement with her in my arms, she died. The third woman in the back seat seemed also to be alive, but was dead by the time she was brought out. I found myself there on the pavement in the middle of the night with five dead people.

All of them had evidently been drunk. They had been coming back from Coatbridge, and hit Lochend Road travelling very fast. At the top of the hill the driver was not ready for the right hand bend and carried straight on into the lamp standard. The police arrived, followed by ambulances, and the authorised people began to establish who these folk were by looking at the papers they had on them. They were able to come up with firm identities for them all. They had been nearly home, and all lived in Easterhouse, although not in Lochwood. I gave a statement to the police, which also confirmed for them that I was the local minister. They asked if I would be prepared to go round the various addresses with them, and break the news to the families of what had happened. I went back to the manse and put on my dark suit and dog collar and we set off round the various houses. The job lasted the rest of the night, and I got back to the manse at about half past nine with only a short time to get my thoughts in order for morning worship, for which I was fortunately well prepared. I think at the end of the day there were nine children who had lost a parent, including three who were orphaned.

I conducted the morning service, and as I came out to the front door of the church, I was approached by two men, one with a camera.

'We're from the Express, Mr Youngson. You've been at the homes of the victims of the accident. Will you tell us how you found the relatives and survivors to be. We're particularly interested in how the children took the news.'

I said that I had nothing to say to the Press.

'That's not good enough, Minister. You are a man of the cloth. You have a public duty to speak to us. This matter is in the public interest.'

At this point several of my kirk elders, who knew what had been happening and could see that I was distressed, moved quickly forward and threw the two men down the front steps of the church.

The photographer picked up his camera and the reporter his notebook.

'You haven't heard the last of this, you know: you'll go on our blacklist!'

I may not have achieved much in my time in Easterhouse, but one thing I am proud of was that I made it onto the blacklist of the Scottish Daily Express. That's at least something.

More Music

I have already made it clear that music was an important part of my life from childhood, and everywhere I had been since. It was no different in Glasgow, and once settled there I decided to do something about the fact that I had had no formal musical training. I auditioned for the Royal Scottish Academy and was admitted. I studied in 1963 with Miss Lillian Liddell. It was she who memorably told me: 'You seem to think that "p" in the music means powerful'.

After I completed my year in 1964, I got a good report and was asked to sing solos in Academy concerts.

Mr Hyde, my old music teacher at Gordon's College, was by now head of Music at George Watson's in Edinburgh, and got in touch with me again as an adult. In 1967 I sang the solos in Brahms' *Requiem* for him and in October 1969 I gave a musical evening at his Music Society entitled *The Role of the Bass.* I presented the Operatic Bass as Mephistopheles, or the Devil, as the High Priest and as the Clown. I spoke about these themes and illustrated them with operatic arias.

In 1965, in June, I was invited to sing the part of Noah in Benjamin Britten's work *Noye's Fludde* at a performance in Govan Old Parish Church. All the other parts were sung by children, and Benjamin Britten had insisted in his stage directions that the children should be encouraged to believe in Noye, so that he should not appear in their presence without being in costume and make-up. This made for an extraordinary experience. I had a wonderful time, and thoroughly enjoyed myself.

Amahl and the Night Visitors was a Christmas opera which was seen on television in the early sixties. Using some of my contacts from the Academy, I produced it in Lochwood in 1965. A local mezzo-soprano and boys with treble voices were memorable.

At Easter, 1968, we produced a huge Passion Play in the round kirk. This was a dramatised version of the last two plays in Dorothy L. Sayers' great radio series, *The Man Born to be King*. We produced the Crucifixion on Good Friday, and the Resurrection on Easter Day. The cast was quite outstanding. The platoon of Roman soldiers came from the Youth Fellowship as did many of the crowd. Members of the congregation had the key roles. The production was a unforgettable event for all those who took part and for many of the congregation. For myself it presented the practical difficulties of representing an actual crucifixion where the dialogue meant three men being on crosses for almost half an hour.

Our Family

The most important thing to happen in our lives during our years in Lochwood was the arrival of our two children, Lyn and Donald. Lyn was born on 27th February 1965. She was christened Caroline Ann, but was always called Lyn, and uses the name still. At that time the new manse was not yet open, and we had the interesting experience of bumping a pram up and down three flights of stairs. We also had close neighbours who doted on the baby, and an unlimited supply of carers and baby-sitters.

Donald was born on 7th May 1968. I had always resented having only the single Christian name of Peter, and was determined that our son would have two. He was christened Donald Mark, although I think he only heard the two names when he was in trouble. We left Lochwood when he was only eighteen months old, and he has no memory of it. Lyn attended a playgroup in our new church hall for some time before we left.

In 1963 our black cocker spaniel Jet was three years old, and we decided it was time she had some puppies. We found a fine golden dog with an excellent pedigree. The happy event took place and Jet had six puppies, three black and three gold. We had no trouble finding homes for them, but we made it public that the purchase price would go to the Church Building Fund, and this was in due course credited with £60, which showed in the accounts as Jet's Puppies. The puppies were absolutely gorgeous and we still have three good photos which show them lying in the sun.

Holidays from Easterhouse

We had become very fond of Islay during our stay in Bowmore in 1960, and it seemed an ideal place to escape to after a year of work in Easterhouse. We bought a tiny caravan and got permission to leave it in an area of sand dunes at Sanaigmhor, on the north coast. There we spent many wonderful holidays, going for a full month each summer. There were rock pools to visit and wonderful flowers on the machair. The island was full of wild birds to study, and since I had qualified as a sub-aqua diver at Ibrox, I went on many exciting dives. The entire scope of natural history study fulfilled my earliest dreams of actually getting to know and recognise birds and flowers and shells. These holidays bred in us a love of the Inner Hebrides which would go on to have far-reaching consequences in our later life.

The Drummy Gang

I became aware almost as soon as I arrived in Lochwood that there was something different about the children I saw on the streets of the parish. They moved about in small groups of various ages. I very early saw slogans painted on walls and closes. The local gang seemed to be called The Drummy; and Drummy Ya Bas was the common message daubed up everywhere, with variations like Young Drummy and Tiny Drummy. Had I only known it, I was following in the footsteps of my hero Cameron Peddie, who had made his own discoveries about Glasgow gangs in the Gorbals in the 1950s. I quickly learned that the local gang in my parish was called The Drummy, after Drumlanrig Avenue, and that it had territorial problems with The Pak, from the nearby part of Easterhouse, and further afield The Bar-L which came from Barlanark. There was also a Toi, with an Easterhouse location, and another notable Easterhouse group called The Rebels.

Once the local team's reputation spread in towards the city, there were the notorious Calton Tongs to be reckoned with. These lads thought nothing of coming out to Easterhouse to show the local boys that they couldn't have it all their own way. The gang was well organised along age group lines. The oldest members were simply The Drummy, and membership there would go right up to very late teens. The gang leaders came from this age group and I got to know them well. They could be basically peaceful and slow to anger, holding their position by having good planning and control, like John, or by their capacity to go berserk and be unstoppable in a fight, like Billy. The Young Drummy had members who were as young as ten or eleven. The Young Young Drummy were about nine or ten, and the Tiny Drummy were as young as you could be and still be able to run and keep up. There were promotion procedures with flying-up rites of passage. One such which I had described to me, for a Young Drummy member seeking to become a Drummy, was the breaking of a landing window – a 'stairheed windae' – on the top floor, from the inside. The challenge in this was that once the candidate had been sent off up the stairs to do the deed, his companions followed a little way behind and knocked loudly on all the doors on each landing so that his escape would have to be managed through angry residents who had been called out to stop it.

The fights, which mostly took place at the week-end, took the form of running street encounters where a number of one gang, either in its own territory or the neighbouring one, would come upon a smaller number of the other and give hot pursuit. The weapons at my time tended to be primitive. The commonest was a length of the chestnut pale fencing that the corporation used to designate the front garden areas of the housing. This was useful because it could be found ready to hand and you didn't have to be tooled up in advance, and so could deal with enquiries from, for example, the police. There were belts and bicycle chains in use, and occasionally broken bottles, but in the early 1960s in Lochwood there did not seem to be very many blades of any kind on the streets, although the senior members would certainly carry them. Guns had not yet been thought of, and were not encountered. The normal development of the fight was that the pursuing group would rush through a close to discover that the boys they were following had run into reinforcements of their own gang, and that they, the pursuers, were now outnumbered. After a number of blows had been struck in face to face conflict, they would now be the ones who took to their heels.

I reckoned that not very much harm was done by these fights. The most dangerous scenario seemed to be when a single lad was cornered by a sufficient number to cause him considerable harm. He might then be desperate enough to produce a real weapon in defence, and lash out with it, inflicting a serious wound. This was when knives and Stanley blades put in an appearance. The other way serious injuries were inflicted was when someone was unlucky enough to be knocked to the ground. This was a signal for others to gather round and kick his prostrate body. Dreadful wounds could be caused in this way, especially to the head, and I think most of the number of gang boys who died on the streets of Lochwood during my years there died in this way. The number of casualties that I myself buried during the years from 1961 to 1969 was probably eight.

It was interesting to me that the gang was not organised along lines of religious affiliation, although the children of Protestant and Catholic families were educated in separate schools at both primary and secondary level. The point was often made to me that the gang would have been weakened by such divisions when it needed to be strong to protect its territorial base. It was all about territory. I consequently had as much to do with young Catholic boys and girls as with Protestants, and they were as often in my halls attending Beat Dances as my own kids. For this their parents were hugely grateful and they gave me great credit for everything I was trying to do.

In connection with territorial allegiance, it often occurred to me that most of the tenants in Lochwood considered it to be a terrible place and couldn't wait to get out of it and move somewhere better. The gang boys considered it to be the greatest place in the world. It was theirs! It was the best! It was worth fighting for, and if it ever came to it, it was worth dying for! I often felt that no one ever gave them credit for these feelings.

Beat Dances

From October 1963, when our new halls opened, I began to try to get into some kind of relationship with the members of the Drummy gang, although I found them suspicious of me, and inclined to treat me as a comic figure. 'There is nothing to do in Easterhouse' was their constant complaint, and in terms of amenities for them that was literally true. I decided that we should try to do something about this and discussed with the Session and Board the proposition that we should run events for young people in the church hall on Saturday nights. These would have live Pop Groups playing, which would be funded by admission charges. They would be called Beat Dances and be held once a month. They would be organised and patrolled by me, with Alec Mason, our church officer, on the door, assisted by as many burly church elders as could be persuaded to support him.

These dances were immediately successful. There was no difficulty in getting groups to come out to Easterhouse to play these gigs, and I used to remember a lot of the names. The only one which has survived in my mind to the present is The Dream Police, who were very popular. The hall was cleared to a single row of stacking chairs round the perimeter. The band were on the stage. The police were completely in favour, as they could more or less have a night off knowing that the trouble was off the streets. They could put in an appearance as the young people emerged at the end of the event and see them safely home. The church members were pretty hostile. The Sunday School staff would come in the next morning and find evidence of sick in the toilets, and even sometimes of blood. They complained that our halls were being abused by young people who were merely taking advantage of the church and would themselves never set foot in it.

We did our best to keep these problems to a minimum. Alcohol was not allowed on the premises and we searched our customers as they came in. Bottles however still managed to get through, and would turn up later smashed in the toilet pans which themselves would be broken by the impact. A young lad in the gang was an apprentice plumber, and he said that if we could get a job lot of toilet pans, he would replace any that got broken. We found a load of toilets at a cut-price store at Bridgeton and came home with a dozen or so, which we stored under the stage. This worked very well, and we even made a small profit.

On the other hand these Beat Dances could also be very scary. One of the things their success depended on was getting good intelligence well in advance about any gang members who had unfinished personal business which they might be inclined to sort out in the hall. I used to go out on the streets and try to find out the latest feuds and vendettas and then approach the two participants and tell them they were banned from the dance. They mostly accepted these rulings.

Once the dance was in full swing I used to sit up on the stage alongside the band. This gave me control of two vital switches. One of these cut the power to the loudspeaker system so that the deafening sound of the music was stopped and the other brought up the main hall lights so that you could see what was happening. During one dance in particular I saw an area of confusion in the middle of the dancers and knew that there was trouble. I hit my switches and dived off the stage into the crowd, arriving at the face-off I had seen before any of my helpers could get there from the door. I came between a boy I didn't recognise and the fellow he was bent on attacking. The aggressor was drunk, of course, and brandishing a knife. It was an open switchblade.

Unwisely I said: 'If you want to get at him, you'll have to go through me first!'

'F---ing right!' he said, and lunged forward. All my army training in unarmed combat deserted me instantly and I thrust forward a weak right hand. The knife slashed across the back of it, opening a deep long cut. Everything happened at once. Two big men grabbed him. Screaming girls climbed on chairs and the stage. The fire doors were thrown open and numbers of young folk spilled out into the open air, and amidst it all I sank to the floor in a faint. I was taken up to casualty where a few clips were put into my hand. My intelligence had been good, but I had not been able to cope with collusion from within the hall which had resulted in an accomplice opening the fire doors and allowing my assailant in. I preferred no charges as a result of this incident – which had, after all, only resulted in a flesh wound, and this lack of police action no doubt did me a lot of good in the teenage community. A couple of nights later I was walking home along Lochdochart Road, when two big lads whom I didn't know fell silently into step on either side of me. My hair stood on end, especially when my greetings to them were met with silence.

One spoke:

'See the Dance, Saturday?'

'Yes.' I replied.

'See him that cut ye?'

'Yes.'

'Don't you worry, we fixed him!'

I stopped in my tracks and stopped them as well and asked them what they meant. For a terrible moment I thought they'd killed him. However, he had only been worked over. I found out where he stayed and went to see him. He didn't remember the incident, having been out of his skull on cheap VP wine, which was the preferred drink at the time. However, he fully accepted that he had been responsible, and he was full of remorse.

'I should never have done it, Father. You can't go hitting priests and ministers. If you're going to hit priests and ministers there's no knowing where it'll stop.'

This dance probably took place about the spring of 1966, which seems to have been the height of the Beat Dances. In September of that year I was contacted by Dennis Duncan, the then editor of the British Weekly. There was to be a new television series on STV called 'This is the Day', and he asked me if I would be prepared to be interviewed on it. I have an account in front of me that Dennis later published in his column in the British Weekly of 15th September, and I quote from it, as it is probably quite accurate:

'Peter Youngson was very critical of the church in his outspoken comments. Indeed his congregation might feel he was unfair in his strictures. So may the authorities in Boys' Brigade and other similar circles. Mr Youngson wrote these off as entirely irrelevant and therefore quite useless: typical of church organisations. They demanded conformity – in other words wearing a uniform – quite unattractive to the teenage gangster type of which he has not a little experience.

Mr Youngson's complaint was also very much centred on the unwillingness of the church to accept the street corner teenager. Parents objected to their children mixing with them. Office-bearers feared for the premises if they turned up in bigger numbers.

If anything can be done to fulfil the kind of ministry Peter Youngson has in mind, the church ought to do it. It suggests the need for premises and people to help, quite distinct from the normal Christian activity we know. But Mr Youngson's intuition is sound. This is how Christ would have been found – not inside the church preaching about the problem, but outside dealing with it, in love.'

I think Mr Duncan accurately catches my mood, and expresses much of my true feelings as I struggled to come to terms with my problems not long after my thirty-second birthday. I am sure that I did not come across as attractive when I spoke on this issue to my members and my elders. On the other hand I was deeply involved in a rounded parish ministry, and just as many people were unaware of the existence of gang warfare near their homes, they would have been equally unaware of my involvement with the young people concerned.

More Gang Trouble

I think it was about this same time that I found myself being involved more directly in the gang's activities. Some of the girls who attended the Beat Dances came to feel that they could trust me with their confidences. Although there were several girls who craved the excitement of the gang fights and would be there on the sidelines whenever they happened, there were more who were afraid of them, and even more who were apprehensive that the lads they were seeing might get hurt. Some of these took to coming to look for me as the week-end approached, to tell me there was a fight planned, and where and when it would be. I found the possession of this information very nerve-wracking, as it was evidently given me to enable me to do something. On these occasions I got into my bullet-proof outfit. (I didn't really have one of those, but I always thought my dog collar was almost as good.) I headed off to the prearranged area, and if I managed to get there before the boys had set off to invade the other territory, I was sometimes successful in getting them talking with me instead. If I could get them on to one of their major topics – that of complaining that no one paid them any attention, and that there was nothing for them to do – they sometimes simply dispersed without heading off to the fight. It may be that they also felt that I would be in possession of evidence of their intent, and might inform on them later if anything serious happened. I found these encounters deeply terrifying, and they caused me a great deal of anxiety. I discovered that I was liable to feel very cold at such times, and might be overtaken by violent shivering which would rob me of my only weapon, which was my hopefully witty conversation. I took to wearing several extra thick sweaters before going out on such missions, and that helped.

Some time later, probably in the spring of 1969, I was urgently called to what was supposed to be going to be a major confrontation on the edge of the parish. I took my car, and after parking it began to make my way towards where there was a gathering of boys.

Four big lads that I didn't know moved towards me and crowded me against a wooden fence.

'Are you that minister we keep hearing about?'

'Well we're the Calton Tongs, and you'll not interfere with this fight! You'll stand here.'

There was a knife in his hand and I didn't manage to talk my way out of that one, although I did persuade them that they had nothing to fear from letting me go, and I went straight home. The incident went very deep. I began to think that I might very well get myself killed if I persisted in acting like this. I think, looking back on it that that night with the Calton Tongs was a major contributory factor to my later nervous breakdown.

Saturation Policing

It was in the winter of 1966 that there were increasing complaints from all quarters that the violence on the streets of Easterhouse was getting completely out of hand, and that confidence in the police was being seriously undermined. Indeed it was true that the policy of housing a small number of uniformed officers in tenements within the scheme had clearly not paid off. They lived in some fear, being so well known, and were always anxious that their wives and children might be victimised. It was decided that a new initiative was required, and the Chief Inspector of the Northern Division was given responsibility for this, and the resources to apply it.

Suddenly a very large number of policemen made their appearance on the streets of the parish. These men were in uniform, and were largely on overtime. I had got used to recognising 'hard men' during my military service. These were hard men. Such men were not to be trifled with, and enjoyed being harsh. They were present in large numbers and were backed up by several elderly vans. These were big, shapeless things, painted a neutral gray. They were known as Q vans, and the men on the patrols were called The Untouchables. The van would stop at a pavement.

The back doors would open. Some policemen would jump out, pounce on a small group of teenagers walking along the pavement, hustle them into the van and drive off. They would be disgorged at Millerston Police Station, often the worse for wear, having offered resistance when arrested, and having been restrained – with the use of minimal force. They were then charged and released to make their own way home. It was boasted that by this method the saturation police were able to make 600 arrests within their first month.

Extraordinary things happened in these first weeks. The regular beat men had at least known the local lads, and a certain amount of cheerful Glasgow banter was accepted. The new overtime men didn't know anybody, and they believed that every man's hand was against them. One evening two of them were watching four lads walking on the other side of Dalilea Drive.

'What are you doing, boys?' the policemen asked.

'Walking', came the reply.

'You're walking too slow!' the police said.

'If we walk any faster we'll get where we're going too soon' was the reply.

That was impertinence and they were picked up.

One Friday evening I was visiting in a ground floor flat overlooking the street and saw some lads being forced into a Q van. The man of the house said:

'Mr Youngson, it's Friday night! I think I saw a B.B. Uniform.'

I ran out of the house and started the car, taking the householder with me, as his son was in the Boys' Brigade. As we drove through nearby Garthamlock with the van up ahead of us, he shouted. 'Stop, Mr Youngson! That's a bugle!'

I stopped, and he ran out, coming back to the car with a bugle and a B.B. hat. They had been thrown out of the van. As the van went along, more objects of Boys Brigade uniform and more instruments turned up by the side of the road and we collected as many as we could. At the Police Station I went in.

'Good evening Sergeant,' I said, 'We'll have the boys out now who've just been brought in.'

'No one here, Sir', he said.

I walked quickly past him and into the squadroom. There were sounds of distress and activity coming from the locker room and toilets. The sergeant came past me and said:

'All right, bring them out!'

Four dishevelled but lively youngsters emerged. There was damage to their jackets where Boys' Brigade badges had been ripped off. They had been on their way home from band practice, when they were lifted. It had been an error of judgement on the part of the police, and they were all set free with no charge.

In the vast majority of these arrests a minor charge was dug up out of ancient legislation and forced into use. This was loitering. Most of the boys picked up by the van were simply loitering. When their parents complained that they were respectable, as many were, and had never been in trouble before, they were told:

'That's all right, dear. Loitering doesn't go on your record.'

This cut no ice with the parents.

'Our son doesn't have a record', they would say. 'There's no record for this offence not to be recorded on.' It sounds funny, but it was very far from that.

Get a Good Lawyer

Suddenly my vestry hour was inundated with angry parents who wanted something done about the intensive policing. At that time there was a very famous criminal lawyer in Glasgow called Joseph Beltrami. He was well known for defending notable villains and frequently getting them off. I contacted his office and got an appointment to go and see him. He received me most warmly and listened with growing interest to what I had to say. He immediately volunteered to come out to Lochwood and set up a surgery in my church hall where he would give free interviews to anyone who felt aggrieved by what had been happening. On the afternoon in question the church hall was packed with people wishing to bring him their complaints. At the end of it all, he told me that he had decided to settle on a group of ten 'test cases', which would comprise complaints against the police, such as wrongful arrest, harassment, and injuries sustained while in custody.

When completed, this dossier was sent to Glasgow's Chief Constable. A few days later, the Untouchables disappeared. The Q vans vanished. The Chief Inspector was shipped to a posting somewhere in outer Siberia, and a Unit Beat Policing System was set up in Easterhouse, under the direct hands-on control of two volunteer sergeants of great experience. One, I remember, was called Sgt. Hamilton. There were new patrol cars and experienced local staff. There was to be a strange new being called a collator. They would all operate out of a newly erected small police office on Westerhouse Road.

Things got back to normal immediately and started to improve. The Unit Beat system seemed to have a real effect on crime in the scheme. Information flowed in to the collator about those individuals who were most responsible for housebreaking and other property offences, and the incidence of these crimes went down. The new system probably had no great impact on the sub-culture of the local gangs, which went on much as usual, but then this was by no means a phenomenon found only in Easterhouse. A gang structure was established here, as it had been for generations throughout Glasgow.

Another episode concerning the gang boys comes from about the same time, probably soon after the end of the Untouchables. I was doing some visiting in Dinduff Street, and was walking from one close to another when I heard the unmistakable sound of a police whistle. It came from the wood just beyond the houses. I scrambled down the bank and hurried through the trees in the direction of the sound. There I found a young policeman with his back to a tree, and surrounded by about twenty youths. His hat was lying on the ground and his truncheon was in his hand. He was very much at bay, and it was evidently only a matter of time before the boys got organised enough to attack him, in which situation he wouldn't have stood a chance. I walked into the midst of the crowd, many of which I knew by sight.

'Well, now lads!' I said, 'What are you up to here?'

'He was chasing us, Mr Youngson, but he got a bit of a surprise.'

I knew the spokesman and I addressed him:

'Now, we none of us want any trouble, and this can only end in trouble. If we go on like this it'll end with a lot of people being banned out of the dances in the hall. Now we'll all go back up to the scheme together. The constable and I will lead the way, and we'll have a favourite song. We've sung it before. We'll have: 'Follow, follow; we will follow Jesus.' I know you'll all be singing your own version of the words, but I don't mind that.' (I was referring to 'Rangers'.)

I spoke quietly to the young officer. 'If you put your truncheon away, and come with me, we'll be all right. You wouldn't want to carry out any reprisals on any of these lads? There's been no real harm done, has there?'

He agreed that nothing further would happen.

'You hear that, Lads! The Officer here says that he'll let the whole matter drop. Off we go then.'

And I started off up through the trees singing at the top of my voice, and keeping the policeman close by my side. Back up on Auchingill Road, I and the lads made our way towards Drumlanrig Avenue, and the constable went in the opposite direction. The incident was over and no one was any the worse.

It would have been during the following week that I had been doing my hospital visits, and was driving home when I was stopped by a police car, whose occupants told me, very politely, that I had been driving at 45 mph, and that I would be charged with exceeding the speed limit in a 30 mph area. They didn't make the mistake of calling me Father, and they were quite apologetic when they found that I was a minister, but they felt they had gone too far not to proceed to book me.

This incident annoyed me considerably as I had a clean licence at the time; indeed I had never in my life been in any kind of conflict with the police, and I was jealous of my public reputation for being a law-abiding citizen. It must have been on the Saturday evening following this that the door bell rang, and on going to answer it I found a police sergeant and a constable standing outside. I invited them in and they sat down. Margaret offered them tea, which they were happy to take. We had a long discussion about Easterhouse – the church; the gangs; probably even the state of the nation – but they never mentioned any reason for their having come to call. Finally they stood up to go.

The sergeant spoke. 'I believe I am right in thinking that you came to the assistance of one of our officers about a week ago here in Easterhouse. He had got himself into a spot of bother.'

I agreed that it was so.

'I understand that things might have gone badly with him if you hadn't intervened. You may find it helpful to have possession of this.' He handed me a folded slip of paper.

'It's the formal note of the occasion on which you were exceeding the speed limit on the Edinburgh Road last week. You'll be hearing no more about it. We like to think we can remember who our friends are.'

So saying they left. It was a happy and memorable visit.

'24 Hours' in Easterhouse

Frankie Vaughan's involvement with Easterhouse seems to be the only episode which is remembered widely through the country in connection with the violence in Glasgow's housing schemes and the 1960s. What is not so clearly remembered is Lochwood's earlier connection with the BBC's attempt to investigate the problem.

It was in June 1968 that a member of the Probation Service came to see me, to tell me of a plan that the BBC had to investigate the pattern of gang violence in Easterhouse. Ivor Dunkerton was to make a programme for the 24 Hours team and felt it would be useful to have someone on the spot who was able to persuade some members of the local gang to speak to his interviewer Philip Tibenham. The interviews took place, but a report that they had been conducted was leaked to the press and gave rise to banner headlines.

As a consequence of this an investigation was conducted into the making of the programme by the BBC's Controller, Scotland, Mr Alasdair Milne, who sent me a copy of his report. This report was written before the programme was actually broadcast the following Friday. In connection with my own role this report states that I personally invited several young people of my acquaintance to meet the producer with a view to being interviewed on film. I wrote to Mr Milne immediately to say that this did not quite agree with what had actually happened.

My own response to the probation officer was to say that if a boy or boys from the Drummy gang could be persuaded to be interviewed I would be prepared to host the interviews in the open air on my church grounds just outside the manse, and that to see fair play I would be prepared to be present. I said that I certainly could not undertake to produce gang members to order, and would not be willing to attempt to do so. However I said that I was prepared to put the word about through boys I knew well, and wait to see if anyone turned up. I think I put the matter to one of the leaders of the Drummy.

I think I made this approach on a Thursday, and on the same day the crew filmed a wedding which I conducted in Lochwood church. On the following day some boys turned up at the arranged time, having been told about it, and the interviews with the boys took place. I was present as I had agreed to be. I recognised all the boys as being lads who attended the Beat Dances in the church. Philip Tibenham asked them questions about the kind of fights that took place between the gangs and the kind of armaments commonly carried and used. As far as I can recall both the questions and answers were quite low key and the conversation on both sides was pretty sensible.

It appears that someone on the ground then contacted the local SNP councillor, to complain that they did not approve of what the BBC had been doing, and he brought the matter to a meeting in the City Chambers. He appears to have declared that what the BBC was up to was not fair. The Lord Provost said at the meeting that he was aware the programme was going to take place. The Chief Constable said he had been asked if he would provide police backing, but had refused.

The news coverage the next day said that the BBC had asked the boys concerned to bring weapons to the interviews, and had then staged fights, and paid out money to the participants. Mr Milne writes in his report that the 24 Hours team did not stage gang fights or 'incidents' or pay money over to young people interviewed, although a small payment would later be made in the usual way to any people whose filmed interviews were actually used in the programme. He stated that no one asked the boys to bring weapons to the interviews, and that one boy who did turn up with what he termed 'a rudimentary weapon' was sent away immediately. He also records my presence at the interviews, and states, quite correctly, that in my opinion the 24 Hours team acted with complete propriety.

The Express reporter made a number of claims in his article the following day. These claims were typical of the sensationalist coverage of the Express, and were quite unsubstantiated. He claimed to have spoken to one of the youths who was interviewed, an 18 year old apprentice furrier, and to two other boys. He represented them as telling him that they had been more or less picked up by Ivor Dunkerton at the corner of Dalilea Drive and Canonbie Street, and that he had asked them to bring weapons to the interviews.

He reported the boy as having said to him:

'We were told by the BBC man that we wouldn't get money. I gathered we would probably get paid if the interview was used, but I'm not quite sure. We were asked all about the gangs and weapons. I think we told them what they wanted to hear, and we exaggerated a bit here and there. We go to Mr Youngson's club. He tries to help everybody by getting us something to do, a place to go other than the pub. There's nothing else in Easterhouse. That's why we get in trouble.'

It seemed likely to me at the time that the reporter did actually manage to speak to one of the boys, and I imagine I know which one. I am sure that he never met anyone who said Mr Dunkerton had had an interview with them on the street corner, or that the nonsense about bringing weapons was true.

To do him justice, when the reporter spoke to me on the telephone, I told him these things, and he reported some of my answers fairly, although they didn't support the boys' story. He says:

'Said Mr Youngson: "I invited some of the boys from the club to appear on the programme. I wanted them to tell something of life in Easterhouse. There was a reasonable discussion; and I can tell you there was no person there with any weapon. I am sure they were not asked to bring weapons, and I am surprised to hear them say the BBC producer spoke to them on the street and asked them to appear. I do not believe this."'

The reporter tried to extract a comment from Margaret, who said: 'I am not prepared to discuss this. I am not entirely sympathetic to the Press.' They found a small photograph to print of her over the single word –' REFUSAL!'

The 24 Hours programme was duly broadcast but aroused no great interest, and the fuss about the way it was made simply fizzled out.

Frankie Vaughan

It was in the middle of July, about a month after the 24 Hours programme, that there was another quite serious gang fight in Easterhouse, although this one did not centre on Lochwood. One of the boys received a fatal wound and two others were put into hospital. The national press the next day carried reports of 'More Easterhouse Violence.'

The singer and variety artist Frankie Vaughan had become well known in recent years for the interest he had been showing in the problems young people were facing in society, and had evidently taken a number of initiatives in London and in the Midlands in starting to get some facilities for disadvantaged youngsters. His own background had been tough, and he had had a difficult struggle to get status and acceptance for himself. His approach seemed to be that, trading on his own background, he could claim a natural kinship with violent and disaffected youngsters. It seemed that when he promised to support them, in several projects, they had come half way to meet him, and progress had been made.

Presumably it was with this current interest of his in mind that the BBC sought him out for an interview on the subject of the violence in Glasgow, and in Easterhouse in particular, since it had just resulted in this fatal stabbing. The interview was broadcast on the Home Service after the six o'clock news that night, and I listened intently. Frankie Vaughan was quite clear about it. He said that the young people had no sense of status, they had no club premises or other facilities, and they felt that every man's hand was against them.

'What is needed is for someone to take them seriously, point out where this behaviour is going to get them, and broker some kind of deal with them where in return for better behaviour they would get some kind of respect, and some kind of place where they can meet without danger of being hassled or moved on. It would take someone with a bit of authority to manage it. I would help if I was asked to!'

I was really fired up by the programme and I set to work to find out where Frankie Vaughan was, and how I could get there. The programme went out on the Thursday. By Friday I had got the name of the club in

Manchester where he was performing till the end of the week, and had discovered that there was a good chance that I could get a stand-by flight from Prestwick to Manchester Ringway Airport the following afternoon. I drove to the airport on the Friday, and everything went well. I arrived at Manchester late in the afternoon, and a taxi took me to Frankie's Variety Club, where I presented myself at the stage door. I sent a note in to the artist saying who I was and asking him to see me. He had me brought to his dressing room and we had our first meeting. I told him all about my involvement with the Drummy Gang – about our Beat Dances, and the 24 Hours programme, and I challenged him with what he had said on the radio.

'You promised you would respond if you were asked,' I said. 'Well, I'm asking now! Come to Easterhouse. You can stay in my manse. Come and see if you can do anything to help!'

Frankie Vaughan was as good as his word, and immediately agreed to come up to Glasgow. His run at the club would finish on the Saturday night, but on the Sunday I would see him at Lochwood manse, and he would be prepared to stay until something was achieved. On the Saturday I got a flight home, and on the Sunday Frankie Vaughan arrived at Lochend Road, just as he had promised.

Frankie had a warm and pleasant personality, and an easy way. He was friendly towards Margaret and delightful with Lyn, then three years old and Donald, then two months. Nothing Frankie did was done without publicity and we soon discovered that his arrival was known to the press. I went to the Drummy leadership to explain what was happening and a large group of the senior members came to the church hall to meet Frankie Vaughan, with myself present as proprietor of the premises and host to the meeting. Television cameras were present, although we didn't allow them inside. I have a copy of one of the films which were later put together about this episode, and it shows me coming out of the hall immediately behind Frankie Vaughan, and surrounded by Drummy boys. The atmosphere looks hopeful. Frankie is emerging to address the large crowd of onlookers gathered at Liff Place and Lochend Road. He then headed off with an entourage of supporters and staff, and I lost contact with his movements from then on.

A consensus of a kind can be pieced together from the various newspaper accounts of what happened next. A meeting was organised by the Drummy leaders with the leaders of the Rebels, the Pak and the Toi. The papers named the four concerned in the talks as Shuggie of the Drummy, George of the Rebels, Gerry of the Pak, and Denn of the Toi. This meeting appears to have taken place in the cellar of a pub in Provanmill. Hugh Murphy, who had been a leader of the Drummy, was in the Young Offenders' Institute at Barlinnie for a stabbing assault, and Frankie got permission from the Governor to have an interview with him which resulted in a letter from Hugh urging the members to support Frankie.

Things moved rapidly and amidst a good deal of confusion. It emerged that Frankie had offered to broker an amnesty during which weapons could be surrendered without penalty, and that if this was successful he would throw his weight behind a move to get premises started which would give the gangs somewhere to meet.

There followed a handover of weapons on waste ground near St Benedict's School, witnessed by about 200 folk, with cameras and television crews, including a team from the National Broadcasting Corporation of Canada. A clip of this event is in my TV collection, and shows crowbars and butcher's cleavers being thrown into large waste bins. The weapons surrender caused deep divisions among the public, the press and civic figures. The Lord Provost of Glasgow, John Johnson, felt it had been a worthwhile exercise. Sir James Robertson, the Chief Constable, said: 'It was a success; we got possession of a lot of weapons we would not otherwise have got.'

Hugh Brown, the MP from Provan, said he was impressed by Mr Vaughan. Hugh Brown had taken the trouble to go to the weapons handover, and appears in a press photo I have of the event. In his comments, it is he who is on record as saying:

'Mr Vaughan has come along at the right time, perhaps because of the '24 Hours' programme on gang violence, with the right approach and the correct solution.'

I later got to know Mr Brown very well, and he remains in my memory and my affection as the most honourable and honest politician with whom I have had dealings. Baillie Frank McElhone was also in favour of some initiative. However Baillie James Anderson, the Convener of

Glasgow's Police Committee, described Frankie Vaughan's plan as Pie in the Sky! He said: 'It is a giant publicity stunt by the gangs, and Mr Vaughan has been taken in. I do not trust them one little inch. I am sure of one thing; the police cannot do any deal with them.' Frankie Vaughan resisted Mr Anderson's comments and said publicly that he had been wrong about the amnesty.

Matters moved very quickly after that. Frankie Vaughan stayed in Lochwood Manse for about five days and nights while he held all kinds of meetings with all kinds of people and then returned to his professional work.

It becomes harder and harder to build reasonable bridges between memory and contemporary reports. I have a paper column of the time written by one Colin Smith, which mentions me and my opinions. He says of an interview I gave him:

'The Rev. Peter Youngson, a Church of Scotland minister, has a 3 inch purple scar on his right hand where he was stabbed trying to stop a fight during a church hall dance. He is a boyish thirty-four. It took him seven years of hanging about on street corners to get to know the Easterhouse gangs. In the early hours today the minister was at the Cresta Club in Birmingham, where he had been talking to Frankie Vaughan about the situation since the amnesty.

He said: "Look, I don't mind admitting I had reservations about Mr Vaughan. This amnesty was farcical. No members of the Drummy gang handed in weapons, and those that were handed in were mainly kitchen junk. Not only that but some boys who went to him saying they were leaders of the Drummy were nowhere near the leadership. These boys' first rule is never on any account to tell the truth. But having met Frankie, I am absolutely convinced of his sincerity. He asked me what he should do, and I told him the only way was to speak to all of them individually, and not to representatives. He has agreed to this."'

This newspaper account is a fine example of the worst that can happen in journalistic reporting. There is no doubt that an actual interview between myself and Mr. Smith did take place, and that it lies behind his report. Some of what I said to him does actually appear in print, but the article contains many extraordinary inaccuracies, and is barely recognisable as a record of what I said.

It was certainly very soon after this that legal minds put together what would need to happen to come up with Frankie's side of the bargain, and an organisation called The Easterhouse Project came into existence through the formation of a group of Trustees. I myself was one of these Trustees, and attended many meetings in the early months to sketch out how the Project could be expected to take shape. I shared my place on this working committee with some very interesting people. There was a core of political personalities like Hugh Brown and Winnie Ewing who were MPs and Frank McElhone, the Councillor. The Lord Provost and the Chief Constable were also involved. One of the Roman Catholic priests was appointed. Frankie Vaughan had promised that he and his friends from the world of show business would get the funding for the Project up and running by giving a variety show in Glasgow, and donating the proceeds to the Project. He involved Jimmy Tarbuck, Jimmy Logan, and Bert Lynch in this venture and I met them all a number of times.

When the event took place, members of the various gangs took part, and some of the girls sold programmes. Further meetings with young people on the ground resulted in developments which never hit the press in the way that the amnesty had, but which were in fact far more important and far-reaching. The key to this period was the concept of a truce. This was to be an end to inter-gang warfare while Frankie's project was coming to fruition. Frankie's promise was it would all move very fast, and the truce was the condition for that progress. The truce would be 'for the future of the Project', but the real truce was really 'for Frankie'.

A number of discussions took place about the nature of the truce, but the heart of the matter was that you would be safe from attack in a hostile territory. Previously, if you ran out of money, and didn't have the bus fare to reach home, and the conductor put you off in someone else's patch, it could be virtually a death sentence. This would change under the terms of the truce. It was decided that a notable member of the Drummy would be chosen to test it out. The boy chosen was a small boy with a big reputation, and a number of assaults to his credit. He would walk across the boundary near Glengyre, and through the Pak part of Easterhouse, returning to Drummy Land up Lochdochart Road.

'You'll have to follow me in the car, Mr Youngson,' he said, 'or I'll never come out alive.'

'That would not be in the spirit of the truce, son,' I replied, 'But what I will do is this. I will drop you off at the start, and come to the other end of the route and pick you up.' This was agreed on and I put him out at Easterhouse Road. I watched him set off, a lonely figure, walking down the middle of the street. I could see small groups of boys standing silently on the pavement. The test run had been well publicised. I made my way round to Lochdochart Road, and in due course our hero came in sight. He was still in the middle of the road, had his hands in his pockets, and was trying to look jaunty. When he reached the car he got in. He was sweating profusely. He spoke:

'F---ing Hell! Mr Youngson. This beats fighting any day!!'

The Project goes Downhill

During the remaining months of 1968 and throughout 1969, I and the Easterhouse Project had an increasingly shaky relationship. Frankie committed himself to appointing the manager of the Project, and his assistant. The army became involved in the erection of a concrete building. Most of this was in the teeth of my own advice. I had wanted the Project to result in a series of small regional, or district, huts which could be cheaply erected, and which would give a place where each of the local gangs could meet without fear of being harassed by the police. These would also be locations where you would know that someone from the territory could be contacted. Everyone agreed that my assessment was sound, and it was coming from the only one of the trustees to have lived for a number of years in the community. However my plan foundered on one immovable rock. This was the Project's public image. You couldn't point to a group of small huts and say 'There is the Frankie Vaughan Easterhouse Project.' It was decided that there would have to be a single building, and it was erected on Westerhouse Road, smack on the boundary between the Drummy and the Pak. The completed building could hardly be opened without bloodshed as each of the territorial gangs tried to claim it as their own. On the question of the single building, and on the question of his chosen appointment of an unsuitable leader, Frankie Vaughan and I fell out. He considered me to have become disloyal to him personally by publicly disagreeing with his judgement. I believe that most of the trustees believed Frankie to be sincere and well-meaning. I felt he had a tendency to naivety which left him open to being conned by any smooth operator who came along. The consequences of him getting his way on the two issues where I opposed him was disastrous for the future of the deal. The building was controversial, and the manager of his choosing was a poor choice, and so nervous of trouble that he would keep the new building closed on any pretext. The young folk who had trusted Frankie in the early weeks of his initiative became disillusioned and the truce was soon dead. I know that in the following years, after I had left Lochwood, the Easterhouse Project came under much better management and did in fact do a lot of good work, and I am still happy that Frankie Vaughan's project did not ultimately come to nothing. I never bore him any ill will, and shortly before his death we planned a meeting which would undoubtedly have represented a reconciliation, if indeed he still remembered our disagreement so many years ago.

Unfortunately he didn't manage to make the meeting and I had to abandon my plan to see him. Later, and sadly for me, he died.

We Leave Lochwood

Looking back at 1968 and 1969 from thirty-seven years later it is very hard to remember the details of the process by which my life fell apart during that time. By Christmas 1968 all was far from well with me. I was suffering from attacks of diverticulitis, and I was also finding it hard to stay in touch with my responsibilities and relationships. During the early months of 1969 I was evidently able to continue to just about cope with all the various aspects of my complicated life. I never missed conducting worship on a Sunday, and I responded to most of the demands of a busy housing scheme parish.

I now know that I was moving towards an 'anxiety state' and suffering from what would now be called 'ministerial stress.' If I had to pick out the main things that contributed to the problem, I suppose I would have to mention the growing sense of tension and fear as I tried to stay in touch with the increasingly unstable situation within the teenage gang community. There was also some strain as I watched the Easterhouse Project going in what I felt was the wrong direction. My isolation from Frankie Vaughan and other committee members was very painful. I think I was conscious of tension within my Kirk Session and congregation, and the responsibilities of being a family man with a wife and two small children in the middle of that turbulent parish certainly didn't help. I was moving more and more inside myself, and trying to find some magic solution which would make everything work out all right. I can't begin to imagine what it must have been like for Margaret to be getting on with life while trying to stay in touch with me.

In the months following the summer of 1969, I was like the carthorse, Boxer, from Orwell's *Animal Farm*. If only I could work harder, and get more achieved, everything would be all right. As late as October, I was still putting a huge amount of effort into producing my big programme of operatic talks and arias which I took to Edinburgh on the 25th. Only one week later I had left Lochwood for good. By September 1969 I had made up my mind that I couldn't go on in Lochwood. I knew that I simply wasn't coping at all. My GP was well aware that I was in a bad way, and tried to persuade me to apply for sick leave. However, I had heard something of the confusion into which churches were thrown when the minister was sick, and I stubbornly wanted to protect my beloved Lochwood from such a fate.

Against all advice, I had a meeting with the Secretary of the Maintenance of the Ministry Committee in Edinburgh, and told him I was going to demit from Lochwood. He strongly disapproved, but was, I suppose faced with more or less a *fait accompli*. He looked around his church world, and came up with a vacancy in the little island of Coll in the Inner Hebrides. I could go there in the meantime. There was hardly any population. There would be no real demands on me, and I could take my time and make a full recovery.

I demitted my Charge at Lochwood on the 31st October 1969. The chapter was closed.

Chapter Six: The Farthest Country of All – Breakdown!

We went to the island of Coll as arranged, but I was too unwell to stay and Margaret found herself suddenly in charge of the entire situation. She drove us all back to Glasgow where she found a hotel where we stayed for a few days.

The Edinburgh Secretary was inclined to wash his hands of us, but Glasgow's Presbytery Clerk, Andrew Herron, responded immediately. He grasped the situation and he said he would take care of everything. He was as good as his word. With the Edinburgh committee he took the position that whether I was legally and technically still the responsibility of the church or not was neither here nor there. As he said, quoting *Romeo and Juliet*: 'He took his hurt under our arm'. He pointed out that whatever had happened during the last months, I had been the minister of Lochwood for eight and a half years, and it was as a result of that experience that I was now in the midst of having a breakdown. The committee capitulated and put into action procedures which restored my status as a minister of the kirk. I was granted sick leave, and a monthly salary continued to be paid. Andrew Herron found an empty manse in Pollokshields, and we quickly moved in. The manse was furnished, up to a point, and we were soon very comfortable. With Andrew Herron's help, Margaret had single-handedly saved the day, and bought us invaluable breathing space in which she, and our families and well-wishers, hoped that I would be able to make a recovery.

With the responsibility of Lochwood no longer on my shoulders, I began to find the daily routine slowly becoming possible, although I remember being in great distress at this period. In the New Year we made contact with Frank Lake in Nottingham, whom we had already informed of developments. It was agreed that I would go there with Margaret, and receive deep analysis and therapy aimed at getting to the bottom of the problems with my personality which had resulted in my being unable to cope.

Margaret and I settled in at the clinic in Nottingham, which Frank Lake had called Lingdale, and our few days there were a major turning point in my life. There was a group of people living in at the centre. Some were members of a help and support group who had been working with Frank. Some were patients who had been before and some, like ourselves, were there for the first time. It became clear that Frank Lake was engaged in conducting deep psychoanalysis of a kind that he called Primal Therapy, which involved clients attempting to revisit episodes from the earliest period of their childhood. Primal Therapy has been well documented, particularly in Janov's books, so I won't go into it here. Dr Lake was following a practice pioneered in Holland and using the drug lysergic acid diethylamide (better known as the hallucinogen LSD) to assist clients in making their journey.

Frank Lake thought I would be a suitable person to benefit from this treatment. The LSD was taken in the presence of a support group. In my case the treatment revealed to me a world of early experience of which I had no memory. After my first session with Frank Lake I could identify many aspects of my adult life with painful early experiences, and it seemed to make sense to interpret my later problems in terms of these first sad and difficult days. I could see the possible source of many of my defensive patterns: my tendency to give up when seriously challenged, my fear of pain and painful encounters, and my need to shout very loud to keep people at a safe distance. I came to see myself as someone who, while I needed to take responsibility for my actions and behaviour in adult life, could also see where their roots lay in my early days. I was immensely hopeful that this new awareness would put into my grasp the tools I might go on to use to make positive changes to my adult behaviour.

It became my turn to attend to the other members of the group as they had their own treatment. I found this very demanding, but it formed relationships which developed more quickly and went deeper than most others I had experienced. After this intense experience was over, Margaret and I kept in touch with other members of this group for a long time. Almost forty years later we are still very closely in touch with one lady from those days. We returned from Lingdale with much to think about, and I spent a great deal of time transcribing the taped records of my long sessions with Frank Lake, and trying to extract as much benefit from them as I could.

Lyn, our little girl, was five at the end of February 1970 and was able to start to attend the primary school at Pollokshields. In those troubled days my old friend Roy Hawkins found his way to Scotland to be of support and encouragement.

During April and May of 1970 I began to feel a real benefit from the sessions with Dr Lake, which seemed to have unlocked many previously closed doors, and offered the hope of acquiring the equipment to live a more constructive life. The combination of aggression and defensiveness which had been my technique for coping with stress, and which had ultimately let me down completely, could now be seen to be unnecessary. It looked as though it might be possible to move forward into a new kind of openness and confidence. I could look forward to a more adaptable personality with which I might be able to get on better with my life, and even with my ministry.

I wrote to the Secretary of the Maintenance of the Ministry Committee in June:

'I am happy to inform you that I now consider myself completely recovered from my breakdown of last year, and feel that I should start to look for another church. I have been given a clean bill of health both by my GP and by Dr Lake. I would be very grateful if you could inform me of any vacancies for which you think I might be suitable.'

After some time, I heard that a church in Glenrothes was vacant. This was a famous Church Extension Charge, now at full status, about which I knew a good deal from my Lochwood days. At our annual Church Extension Conferences, David Levison, its minister, and I had often got into debates about the different problems of housing schemes and new towns. We were even seen as the spokesmen for the two camps. It was astonishing to think that his church in the new town of Glenrothes might be available to the former minister of Lochwood. I sent off an application right away. I hadn't planned to go back into Church Extension, and yet might that not be exactly what Lochwood had best prepared me for?

I was given a date to preach. The interview with the Vacancy Committee went well and I was made sole nominee. The date for the induction was set for 31st October.

Chapter Seven: Someone Else's Country – Glenrothes

On Wednesday, 31st October 1970 at 6.45 pm I was inducted to the Charge of St Columba's, Glenrothes. Andrew Herron sent a wonderful letter. Horace Walker of the Home Board was there and spoke, as did George Sangster, my own minister. Andrew Flockhart came. He had become a youth worker in the Church of Scotland, but had taken the part of one of the two thieves in our crucifixion play in Lochwood. He was able to say to the folk of St Columba's:

'I hope you enjoy Peter Youngson as your new minister. He crucified me!'

St Columba's Church was more or less in the exact centre of the town. The parish consisted of three residential areas: South Parks, Rimbleton and Warout.

On our arrival in Glenrothes, Lyn went to school at South Parks Primary and Donald started at a nursery in Pitteuchar. Margaret got a new appointment as a speech therapist, but from 1970 onwards she worked only part time.

My ministry settled into the usual pattern of a Church of Scotland parish. A great deal of activity centred on the church buildings in worship and in organisational life and activity. The main hospital and the nearest crematorium were both in Kirkcaldy. There were no cemeteries in Glenrothes, and burials mostly took place at nearby Leslie. There were three primary schools with associated chaplaincies for the parish minister, and a chaplaincy appointment at Glenrothes High School, which also lay in the parish. The overwhelming majority of the people on the congregational roll of St Columba's lived in the parish. Domestic visits were very simple.

The first meeting with my new Kirk Session turned out to be a daunting experience. There were more than fifty elders present. The composition of the group by occupation was surprising. The Session contained thirteen teachers and two doctors. There was an architect and two accountants. There were many administrators, managers and supervisors. Tradesmen were thin on the ground. I remember a railway guard, a plumber and a factory worker. All this was the more strange to me when it became clear to me that the population of the parish was solidly working class. It became clear that since the first minister was committed to the Iona Community 'house church movement', he had felt he could only make elders of people who were prepared to lead such groups. It was in this first meeting that I first came face to face with the presence of my predecessor, David Levison. I could hardly miss him, since many of the elders in the meeting used his name when addressing me. This was a strange phenomenon which continued throughout my entire five years, and was even manifest in meetings of the entire congregation. It made me feel oddly invisible.

The Church Buildings

St Columba's church was impressive. Its structure was based on a square, rather than a circle, but the design was actually more radical than Lochwood's, and altogether bolder in terms of the use which could be made of it. The chancel was central, and leading worship from anywhere on it you were in the middle of the congregation. Indeed, if you chose to use the communion table for anything, including the sacrament, you had people on all sides. The pulpit was the only fixture, and was set so far back that it often felt like a retreat from the people. Behind the pulpit the raised chancel floor ran back to the rear wall, forming a long rectangle with a low ceiling, laid with rows of chairs, and used for small services. The back wall was covered by the famous fresco by Alberto Morocco which portrayed elements of the passion. I was attracted to the church from the first moment I set eyes on it. I felt it had all kinds of possibilities for innovative worship. The church occupied one corner of a square site, with the church halls and offices on two more and the manse on the fourth side with a small garden in the middle.

Once more we were in a Church Extension Charge which had its manse incorporated into the suite of church buildings. This was an arrangement for which I had argued strongly in many ministers' conferences. Glenrothes changed my mind. Our little garden had a door out to the car park, and so was a continuous passage for all kinds of people. The family rooms were very closely overlooked, and there was very little privacy. The pressure was so intense that Margaret and I took to having Monday as a day off, and would set off very early and stay away all day exploring the fascinating Kingdom of Fife. By the time we left Glenrothes we knew every small road in the county.

Margaret went on with her speech therapy, working in the many primary and secondary schools of the new town. Much of her previous work had involved her in a lot of travelling. She much enjoyed the compactness of Glenrothes, and was soon a valued visitor in its schools.

Baptisms

There was still a continual stream of baptisms, and I still was very firm about gathering them all into one Sunday. It was in Glenrothes that I first I heard a christening story which would have suited Lochwood perfectly.

The minister, apparently as unfamiliar with the west coast as I had been, takes the baby from the father and says:

'Can you tell me the baby's name?' The father replies: 'Spindona'.

'Spindona', says the minister, 'My, that's a very unusual name; I don't think I've ever heard that one before. Does the child have another Christian name?'

The father says: 'Yes! It's Spindona Jaykit.'

'My goodness, Spindona Jaykit, that's even more unusual,' says the minister; 'However, anything you say,' and he makes a move towards the water.

'No, no, no,' says the mother, 'You've not got it at all, he means her name's *pinned on her jacket*.'

The christening then goes on uneventfully.

My most unusual baptism in Glenrothes was I suppose no less strange than that. I was in the middle of my sermon on a Sunday morning, sometime about May 1973, and I think I had got to about my second point when the main church door opened, and a group of people entered and advanced down the aisle. There were five or six adults and several small children. They were led by a rather swarthy looking middle-aged man, who came to the front of the chancel and spoke:

'We've got a new baby, and we've come to get him christened. Will you do it?'

I had left the pulpit as they advanced and was more or less at the chancel steps as he spoke. The baby was indeed present and very tiny. Several elders had got up and one or two clustered round the group. Someone murmured in my ear:

'They're from the tinker's camp site on the edge of town'.

'Well! Will you do it,' said the leader again.

'Of course I'll do it,' I replied.

The Session Clerk said: 'You'll be needing some water then', and he went off to the vestry with the bowl from the font.

While he was away I said some of the words of institution for the sacrament – said them by heart, for I had no Order Book with me. The parents were both present and when Bob came back with the bowl, I asked them if they believed in God as their Father, in Jesus Christ as their Saviour and in the Holy Spirit, and they said they did.

I took the baby, as was my custom. I think the name was straightforward; something like James. I baptised the child, and the congregation sang 'The Lord bless thee and keep thee.'

The leader produced a birth certificate and asked me to sign it, which I did, and he then swept his party together and turned to leave. As he did so he left money on the communion table. I think it turned out to be five pounds. The church door closed behind them. I didn't return to my sermon, but we sang the last hymn and had the benediction and we all went home.

Later I went to visit their camp, and was made very welcome. A few days later they had moved on and I never heard of them again. I came in for no criticism for the way I had dealt with this case.

Evening Worship

I approached my evening services by using bible passages and constructing meditations or studies on them, and this seemed acceptable to the smallish group who regularly attended. I used to have only a couple of items of praise and a service which lasted no more than about thirty-five minutes. I very much enjoyed these services held behind the chancel, in front of Alberto Morocco's striking mural, where the scenes of Christ's passion created a powerful atmosphere. One thing that happened there is worthy of mention.

We had in the congregation at that time a very aged retired minister who came from Lewis and had had a number of parishes in the northern and western isles. He had had a ministry in the wilds of Canada, and had strange stories about possession and exorcism. He and his wife lived in the high flats, just across the road, and he came regularly to the evening service. One night he approached me after the service was over and said he wanted to speak to me.

I said that I would be most willing to hear what he had to say.

'I wonder,' he said, 'if you know what it is I come for when I attend this service?'

I waited for him to go on.

'Do you think it is to listen to your very fine sermons?'

I shook my head.

'Is it because I value your inspiring prayers?'

I remained silent.

'Perhaps you think it is because I wish to listen to your splendid singing of the evening hymns?'

I essayed a quiet negative, and waited some more.

'No! It is for none of these things that I come. I will tell you what I come here for. I come for your blessing. Your Benediction! And you are sending me away without it.'

He then went on to explain that I had been using the informal wording in my blessing which said 'us' instead of 'you'. As in: 'The peace of the Lord Jesus Christ be with us all. '

He said that I was an Ordained minister of the Church of Scotland, and it belonged to my office to be entitled to pronounce the benediction.

The form I had used was not a benediction. It was merely a prayer. I must give up the practice and never again fail to give a proper blessing at the end of the service.

I was profoundly shocked. I took what he had said completely on board, and I never forgot it, and have followed his instruction throughout all the intervening years until the present.

Watchnight Services

Over the years I felt that my attempts to make the message of Christmas more real and relevant had become a major problem. I held a Watchnight service every Christmas Eve, and tried hard to present a really challenging sermon on that occasion. The presentation got increasingly difficult as the prevailing social atmosphere brought all kinds of undesirable people and behaviour to the service. One year we had young people setting fire to hymn books in a back pew during worship, while on another we had a young man with a guitar standing up during the service and announcing:

'This is f---ing awful! I'm going off to see what the Priest has to say.'

In 1974 it seemed to me that I had to take some kind of stand, and some of the modern Christmas music must have been at the forefront of my mind, especially the carol by Ian Fraser whose chorus line ran 'In a Shakedown in a Garage lay the Saviour of the World.'

I created the shakedown in the garage in the entrance vestibule of the church. In this small area between the outside and inside doors I created rough wooden walls, hung with netting and coats. Mary was a figure with a shop mannequin's head and dark wig, lying under a rug on a palliasse on the ground. Beside her the infant lay in a wicker basket. Joseph was a stuffed figure sitting on a hall chair with his back to the entrance. The whole effect was so realistic that you might have expected the baby to cry, or Joseph to pick it up. When you were going in to the church for the watchnight service you had no choice but to pass close to this scene. It caused enormous offence! I attracted fierce criticism on all sides for making the Christmas scene cheap and tawdry – which was exactly what I wanted to do. Looking back on the incident I think it did point out to me just how phoney and sentimental many people's views of some aspects of their faith really was, but the wedge it drove between myself and some of the congregation was probably quite deep.

Holy Week

As Easter approached, I longed to be able to follow up the event with the live donkey in Lochwood, and after a year or two I was able to arrange it. The donkey behaved well, and there was no bad publicity from this Palm Sunday. My stock stood high over that one. I had held Holy Week services every year in Lochwood, and I continued at St Columba's. These reached a climax on Good Friday, when I usually presented the events of the crucifixion in place of a traditional sermon.

For the Thursday of Holy Week I developed a script which followed the events of the Last Supper. Ladies set the communion table with a cloth and with bread and wine and baskets of fruit. When everyone was seated I wrapped a towel round myself and took a basin of water round the people so that they could dip their hands. I was followed by an elder with a towel. I made the point that although we no longer washed our feet before meals, we all washed our hands. It was extraordinary to me to discover how completely natural it was for members to dip their hands in the basin and to dry their hands on the towels. Each individual member seemed to have their own personal way of doing this. The activity produced strong and positive emotions in those present. We had breaking of bread and drinking of wine and we passed fruit around, with quiet conversation. Afterwards we stood up and sang a hymn and then I led the way out to the manse garden where we took our leave of each other. We followed in fact all the actions the gospel records from the Thursday night. This service became important for the people who took part, but it didn't spread to the wider congregation, and never numbered more than about twenty-five members.

By Easter 1974 I felt that we were probably ready to tackle the Easter play, *The Man Born to be King*, which had been so dramatic in Glasgow. We modified the chancel to take fixings for the crosses. We had a superb cast once again, with local members and a professional actor as Jesus. I myself was the centurion and producer and director, and once more a keen Youth Fellowship provided the roman soldier detachment which carried out all the dangerous manoeuvres connected with the crucifixions. The play was just as dynamic in its new setting, and I'm sure it had the same impact on those who took part and on those who saw it as it had in Easterhouse.

Music at St Columba's

The opportunity to use my position as a parish minister in Lochwood to create musical events had been important to me, and I could see all kinds of similar possibilities in Glenrothes. I started a series of evenings called Music at St Columba's shortly after my induction.

There were all kinds of events. There was an opera by Telemann called *Pimpinone.* I produced *Amahl and the Night Visitors* again, in a new setting. In 1974 I gave my lecture recital on *The Role of the Bass* again, which was popular, but the most notable event in Music at St Columba's happened in October 1972 when we had a concert given by The King's Singers. These were by far our most famous visitors. They all came to the manse for a buffet supper after the performance. They were memorably quite charming, and all fell in love with Sheba, our Great Dane.

Holidays from Glenrothes

After Easter 1971, we gave some thought to having a summer holiday. We remembered happy visits to Islay during the 1960s, which had been founded on our visit to The Round Church in 1960. I asked the Edinburgh committee if there was a similar vacancy I might be able to fill in the summer of 1971. We were told that the neighbouring island parish of Jura was vacant and no doubt the Interim Moderator would be delighted with any offer. It turned out to be so, and we contracted for four Sundays in July and August. To keep the cost down we offered to camp in the vacant manse. We booked the car ferry to Islay and set off. By this time our family included Simba, our Siamese cat, and we discovered that he could only cope with a car journey by singing all the way at the top of his voice. Sheba the Great Dane was no trouble, but on the large side. Lyn, our daughter, established that she was car sick on long journeys. The Jura folk furnished the empty manse and we moved in.

Sunday worship was a joy, and the congregation was swollen with its usual summer visitors. Everyone was most appreciative of my preaching and of my useful singing voice. I felt very much at home, and even made a few house calls to the sick and housebound. We found Jura to be a magical island for a holiday, with superb beaches at Corran and wonderful rock pools everywhere. The manse lay only a few hundred yards from the beach and the children were in seventh heaven. During our month on Jura we were able to arrange for future holidays and spent a summer month in a cottage there each of the next three years. These holidays established Jura as the perfect place to visit and explore.

It was in May 1974 that Margaret's father died. Her mother had died some nine years before. We used Margaret's inheritance to buy Corran House, on Jura, and spent a lot of time in it during the next few years.

Friends in Glenrothes

We made many new friendships in Glenrothes both in and outside the congregation and some have lasted to this day.

One of my elders was a charge hand at the famous Frances Colliery near Kirkcaldy. In conversation he asked me if I had ever been down a mine. When I said that I hadn't he followed up by asking if I wanted to.

There was an obvious challenge implicit in these questions, and although I was a bit scared I told him that I couldn't wait, and presented myself at the main gate by appointment on a Saturday, when the mine was partly closed. I was given a helmet and shown into the cage, as the lift was called. It dropped like a stone, and I left my stomach above ground to be collected later. Once at the bottom of the shaft we took our places on crude benches on tiny metal trolleys on rails and began to roll along the line towards the coal face. My host kept up a continual flow of interesting commentary throughout this entire journey, so that my interest was in conflict with my nervousness. Everything seemed very wet, and I was told that the Frances pit was one of the group of coal mines where the coal-bearing seams ran out under the Firth of Forth, so that the sea was directly overhead. We walked the last few hundred yards to the pit face, where a cheerful group of men were engaged in actually getting coal out. The conditions seemed very bad to me, with very little head room, and the actual coal seam rising upwards at a very steep angle. As we stood and chatted and I asked questions, a lump of coal about the size of a small cabbage detached itself from the coal face some feet above us and bounced down, landing on the thumb of one of the men as he stood with his hand on the handle of his pickaxe.

He dropped the axe, and jumped up and down, wringing his stinging hand:

'Oh, deary, deary, deary me!' he exclaimed.

'For God's sake, men', I called, 'Don't do yourself any injury on my account. I was in the army you know. I've heard it all before.'

There was widespread laughter and much handshaking, before we set off back to the trolley. The men had been warned that a clergyman of the Church of Scotland was coming on a visit, and that no strong language would be tolerated. It remains one of my most precious memories.

Funerals

My parish of St Columba's was similar to Lochwood in containing a very large proportion of young families and a comparatively small number of elderly folk. This resulted in a quite limited number of funerals, and indeed a week or two could go by without any.

One funeral I had to conduct will remain with me for ever. The elderly gentleman who had died had a name I will never forget, although for the purposes of this account I will call him Mr Lyle. I had known the family through visiting, as he had been in poor health, and in due course he died. There was a funeral service in the house and a burial to take place at Leslie cemetery. I knew the undertaker quite well. He was in charge of the Co-op funeral establishment at Buckhaven. It was a bitter winter morning when we arrived at the cemetery. The coffin was duly lowered into the waiting hole and I took my usual place at the head and opened my service book for the words of committal. Mr Lyle's son, Jim was standing beside me, and as I began to speak he went:

'Pssst! – Pssst! – Mr Youngson!'

The sound he used to attract my attention was drawn from the school classroom, and he was also speaking out of the side of his mouth, as children did then.

I adopted the same technique as I replied: 'What?'

'Mr Youngson! That's never my Dad!'

'What!!'

'My Dad was over six foot. That coffin's no more than about five foot six.

Besides, I've been trying to read the name on the brass plate, and I think it says "Barbara somebody"!'

At this moment I realised that we were not facing a minor technical hitch here, but a major problem. As I paused, uncertain what to do next, the undertaker bustled over:

'Is there a problem, Mr Youngson?' he enquired.

'Well, yes, I think so,' I replied. 'The deceased we have here does not appear to be the late Jim Lyle: it appears to be much shorter, of a different sex, and apparently called Barbara.'

'Oh my God!' the undertaker exclaimed. 'I had the twa of them in the parlour and I've brought the wrong yin!'

I made a short announcement to the mourners and we stood back while the undertaker and the local gravediggers climbed down into the grave and handed up the cords with which, with some difficulty, the coffin was extracted from the hole and put back into the hearse which then set off for distant Buckhaven.

The mourners occupied the next half hour in the freezing cold by trying to construct a scenario to be told to Grannie Lyle, who had not come to the cemetery. (It was the custom in those days for the elderly widow not to be present.) Various suggestions were made such as the hole wasn't ready; the hearse broke down; and all were dismissed on the grounds that they would cause great distress.

Finally a small boy approached me.

'I've got it,' he said: 'We'll tell Grannie Lyle that everything went off fine at the cemetery, but when we were on the road home a lorry shed its load of bricks on the road and we were held up behind it for half an hour.'

As far as I can remember that was the story that was settled on, and I think accepted and believed by the elderly widow until her death some time later.

We were very lucky to get away with it. Had Jim's son not noticed something was wrong, and had we gone on to complete the committal of the coffin we had put in the grave, the family of the late Barbara would not have been able to get the six foot coffin into their five foot six hole and the entire matter would have come to light. We would then have had to get an exhumation order from the Sheriff and start all over again, and no concocted story would have got us out of that.

I shall never forget the surprise I felt when at such an inappropriate moment the young man beside me said: 'Pssst!'

Weddings – The Missing Bridegroom

Lochwood may have been the parish of the mass christening, but St Columba's, Glenrothes was equally the parish of the mass marriage. My busiest Saturday contained six weddings, with two in the morning and four in the afternoon. The only benefit that came from having so many matrimonial events on the same day was that I had a good excuse for being unable to attend more than one of their several receptions!

Two weddings from my Glenrothes years remain memorable, the first being as close as I ever came to not being able to complete the ceremony.

The bridegroom on this occasion was a serving soldier, who I think was at the time stationed abroad. I always recommended the bridegroom and the best man to be at the church about twenty minutes before the appointed time, and I was always there to meet them. There were last minute things to be arranged. The Schedule of Marriage had to be given to me, as had the fees for the organist and church officer and the use of the church. There was also the matter of the ring (or rings) to be settled. On this occasion the best man was in good time. He was also in uniform, and he assured me that the bridegroom would soon be with us, but that he would be making his own way to the church. By five minutes to the hour, which I think was probably two o'clock, the church was full of family and friends, the organist was playing and the bridesmaids were on the premises. There was no sign of the bridegroom.

A little earlier the best man had set off by car to try to collect him, and just before the set time he arrived back to say that he couldn't find him. At that point the bride and her father drew up in the car, and after photos were taken they came into the church (radiantly, of course!). She had to be told that her future husband had not yet arrived. On hearing the news she burst into tears and was taken into the vestry to be comforted. The story emerged from the best man. The bridegroom had been put up for the night by some friends up in Newcastle, one of the town's newest areas. The friends had been contacted at work and had said that they had woken him up and checked that he was all right, and then set off for work. The house where he spent the night had now been visited, and there was no sign of anyone. He had vanished off the face of the earth. Where could he be?

The time was about a quarter past two, and I and some other folk were standing at the front door of the church when we saw him. He was sitting in the front seat of a milk float which was coming slowly down the hill towards us. Its batteries were evidently very nearly flat, and it was only going at a slow walking pace. As it neared the church the milkman, whom I knew, waved cheerfully, and shouted: 'Here's the missing soldier!' – and in due course, after a tearful reunion, the wedding started. After it was all over the story came out. Our bold bridegroom had got up in good order and had his breakfast, and in due course a shower. He got dressed, and realised that he was far too early, it being only about half-past nine in the morning. The arrangement had been that his best man would pick him up good and early at about half-past eleven. By half past ten he was fed up of waiting, and getting nervous. With so much time in hand he thought he'd be as well to make his own way into town and just turn up at the church. He left the house and walked to the nearest bus stop. He waited about three-quarters of an hour for a bus until a passer-by asked him what he was doing.

'Waiting for a bus', our stalwart said.

'You'll wait a while, Son. Its a new service and it isn't starting until March.'

He still had lots of time, so he asked the way to the town and set off walking. He saw no sign of churches, and his chosen route took him nowhere near St Columba's. He asked someone where the church was, and was asked which church he meant. He didn't know the name of the church he was going to be married in, so was directed to St Margaret's, which did actually have a wedding on that Saturday. It was the wrong wedding! He visited the Episcopal Church in the town centre, before chancing upon the milkman, who knew St Columba's and knew me and thought it would be the right church. So, ultimately, all was well. It was the wedding that nearly didn't happen. Not because the bride didn't turn up, but because the bridegroom got lost.

Trouble with the Ring

In my second wedding reminiscence all the arrangements had worked out all right, and we were well into the actual service. I had put the vows to the young couple, and the promises had been successfully negotiated. It was time for the ring. I moved sideways to stand in front of the best man and said the next words in the service:

'Will you please put the ring on the book?'

The young man answered: 'No!'

I said: 'Just put the ring on the book.'

He said again: 'No.'

I said: 'Don't mess me about, son, put the ring on the book. I know you have it; I checked before we came in.'

He answered: 'Ah canna! It's stuck!'

I looked down at where his clasped hands were engaged in a fierce private wrestling match with each other. The boy had put the wedding ring on his finger to keep it safe, and, since it was rather small for him, he couldn't get it off again. The finger in question was swollen and raw and bleeding.

'What's the matter?' asked the bride and groom in unison.

'Its the best man,' I said, 'He's got your wedding ring stuck on his finger'.

'That's your stupid brother!' exclaimed the bride, 'I told you we should never have had him as best man.'

I explained that it wasn't a problem, I had my own ring available. I showed it on my hand, and said that the ceremony could go ahead with the loan of my ring.

'That's my wedding ring', said the bride, 'I chose it and we paid for it, and if I can't get married in my own wedding ring I'm not getting married at all.'

I made a short public announcement to the congregation, explaining that there would be a brief intermission while the wedding party would leave to deal with a problem concerning the wedding ring. Meanwhile if they remained in their seats the organist would play for their entertainment.

We all adjourned, and the unfortunate brother was marched into the minister's toilet, from which yells of pain shortly emanated. It was all in vain – the ring would not budge. Suggestions were bandied around, and someone proposed that an axe be fetched and the offending finger chopped off.

As the impasse continued, the church officer approached.

'I've got a possible solution, Mr Youngson,' he said, 'but I'm not sure if you're going to like it. There's a wee boy here who says he's a Boy Scout and that he can get it off.'

He was right! I didn't like it, but any port in a storm. The lad was ushered into the vestry. He was small and neat and bright. He was in full uniform: shorts, shirt, neckerchief complete with woggle. He also sounded a bit Glasgow. He spoke:

'Is it a question of a stuck ring, Sir?' he asked. 'Don't you worry, Sir, I'm a Boy Scout. We're prepared for this. I'll get it off.'

He disappeared into the toilet, and no more than a couple of minutes later he emerged with the ring on his outspread palm.

'There you are, Sir', he said, and saluted smartly and rejoined the company.

The wedding continued with no further hitch. At the reception I sought out the best man and asked him what had happened when the boy scout came to see him.

'Oh, Minister', he said: 'He was magic. He had a bit of string in his pocket and he wound the string round my finger. Very close it was, and very tight, like whipping a bit of string on to a knife handle. Then he started to unwind it slowly and the ring slipped into the groove the string had cut in my finger, and then, a turn at a time, it came over the knuckle and off. Imagine some scoutmaster teaching all those kids how to do that?'

Yes indeed! Imagine!

Before I leave the topic of weddings I should say that it was in Glenrothes that I had to develop some kind of criteria for what to do about Wedding Receptions. With weddings every week-end, they were a real problem. The commitment of time was enormous if you went to the reception. I decided that I would attend receptions if one or other of the bridal couple were the children of church members whom we knew well – the kind of people who would have expected me to be at the wedding anyway. Otherwise I generally declined.

However, I also had to deal with the Babes in the Wood situation, where it was clear that no one in the bridal party had a clue how to manage the reception, which was being held in – for example – the Co-operative Hall somewhere, and they appeared to be completely dependent on the minister to manage the reception, just as he had managed the wedding. These kind of premises would not at that time have had any kind of competent Master of Ceremonies in attendance, and there was a reasonable expectation that the event would be chaotic. I remember making copies of a sheet which could be handed out to couples which gave some indication of who among their families might be expected to make a short speech and on what topic. This covered things like the bride's father; the best man; the toast to the bridesmaids; the reading of the telegrams; the cutting of the cake; grace at the start of the meal, etc. In weddings where this information was desperately needed, I felt that I was obliged to attend in order to make sure that the whole event ran smoothly, and I always did. I often did this with no recognition of my role at all. No one even said thank you. Weddings were truly the most utterly and literally thankless part of my whole job.

Wedding Reception Stories

In most of the weddings where I was needed at the reception I made the main speech myself, and this included stories I had heard at conferences, from ministers like Jim Currie of Pollock, who were famous for their Burns Suppers and wedding receptions. I built up a collection of stories which were suitable, and cashed in on the fact that no one present had ever heard me tell them before. Some of these stories lasted well, and were still in use in Kirriemuir until I retired. I include only a few here:

'I do hope you've all had enough to eat. Especially any of you who will be going on to a Scottish bed and breakfast.

You know Jimmy Shand, the famous Scottish dance band leader, did a lot of travelling at the height of his success. He was once in a pretty poor B & B. After a particularly miserable breakfast on his first morning, he drew attention to the dry bread on the second day and said to the grim faced landlady:

"Could I have a drop of honey on my bread today?"

The honey, when it came, was vanishingly small and Jimmy Shand looked at the landlady and said:

"Ah! I see you keep a bee!"'

The next one is a Jim Currie story:

'I'm relieved when everything goes well at the ceremony. When you've done them as long as I have you know the opportunities for disaster are almost unlimited.'

I admit I wasn't in danger from the classic one – forgetting the bride's name. Jim Currie did that with a bridegroom. Thinking fast on his feet he invented a special new question: 'In what name have you come here today?'

The young man was a bit surprised, because it hadn't been in the rehearsal, but he rose to the occasion nobly:

'I have come here today in the name of the Lord Jesus Christ'!

I think Jim was also responsible for the following:

'Did you notice we've given up the bit about "with all my worldly goods I thee endow." Too many Scottish bridegrooms were fainting away before they could say the words.'

In practice many ministers omitted this passage, as it used to give rise to too many *sotto voce* comments among the congregation. Another of Jim's variations on this theme was as follows:

'Nowadays this subject is all taken for granted. A bit like when Donald passed away. It was known that he had a bit of money put by, and Sandy, an old friend, was curious, so he went to visit the widow.

"Now, Janet! Tell me. What did he leave?" "Everything", said Janet.'

This last story appeared in the local press in the 1990s:

'To make her wedding a little bit special, a Dundee bride requested something other than the usual wedding march for her stately procession up the aisle. She had been captivated by the ballad "Everything I Do, I Do for You", sung by Canadian Bryan Adams, and decided that was the tune for her big day. The song, which topped the charts for ages in the middle of last year, was used as the theme for the film *Prince of Thieves*, a story about the legendary Robin Hood.

Somewhere between the request being made, and being explained to the organist, something went terribly wrong. And so she marched, blushing, up the aisle to the strains of:

"Robin Hood, Robin Hood, Riding through the Glen".

By all accounts it brought the house down.'

Primal Therapy

Although treatment for my own breakdown was now concluded, I was continuing to study with Frank Lake, with a view to equipping myself to offer support to others who were experiencing anxiety. By the time we were encountering him in the late spring of 1970 his mind was full of new images and ideas and methods, and he had realised that LSD was no longer the only pathway to early experiences it had once been, and that relaxation and fantasy journeys were opening up a territory that anyone could use.

In group sessions with people he was training to become tutors in CTA, and also in working with individual clients, Dr Lake would ask people to go through a procedure of relaxation, usually in a seat or on a cushion on the floor. After suitable preparation the people concerned would be asked to try to identify with some imaginary situation. 'Rose bushes' and 'abandoned shops' were favourite themes. These conducted explorations were loaded for people's underlying anxieties. Considering what kind of rose bush you might be could turn out to be a powerful tool for self exploration.

It was but a short step from applying the breathing and relaxation techniques, which with fantasy journeys were such a powerful prelude to a training session in counselling, from applying them to therapy with an individual client. This person could be invited to imagine such things as the close approach to them of a long departed mother, or the loneliness and desolation experienced during her absence.

The experiences which clients entered into, and then reported on and shared with the attentive and insightful counsellor, were evidently every bit as much in touch with early events in their experience as those which had been unlocked by LSD. These techniques did not have the accompanying dangers of the administering of a highly dangerous drug; and it seems likely that this movement out of the medical experimentation realm was greeted with relief by many, and the new possibilities welcomed with open arms, without apparently much thought that these procedures could encapsulate their own and very grave dangers.

It seemed that now anyone could do Primal Therapy: it just took a bit of patience and commitment to stay with a troubled client for long periods at a time, and the following of a few simple rules. It seems unlikely that Frank ever set these rules down in any one place as a kind of code of guidance. If you wanted to practice counselling with the CTA Model you had to compile them as you went along.

I vividly remember the period of weeks and months when I realised that the skills and expertise I had been seeking long before in the Glasgow seminars were now available for use, and could even be backed up by a script that said: 'I myself have been there!' In anticipation of getting involved with people in trouble, whom I would previously have fended off, and of being prepared to offer them real help to work things out, I began to sketch out some ground rules and then I stuck to them.

By 1971 CTA in Scotland had two new tutors as Margaret and I took our share in running seminars in Glenrothes. By the same time my parish was producing a number of people whose presenting problems meant that my offer to take them on as subjects for Primal Counselling was readily accepted; and with my interest in certain areas of anxiety, being well known among CTA tutors in Scotland, I began to get people coming to see me by referral from other workers in the field.

I homed in on problems I found particularly fascinating, and where I felt instinctively that I might be of use. I experienced a considerable amount of success during the years from 1972 to 1975, with a variety of clients. Now I think back to those Glenrothes years. The case notes I kept have all been burnt long ago. Only my memories connect me with those days. As I write this I think 'What harm could there be in livening up this passage of reminiscences by recording the exciting moments when I was able to be present, and assist, as these people came to terms with the havoc their own early experiences had wreaked upon them?' However, the answer is that even if they are couched in the most general terms, references to the kinds of traumas people experience are always a breach of confidence; so all such recollections will remain where they belong, in my own private memory.

My willingness to take on counselling clients at this level quickly generated more, and by 1974 and 1975 I was seeing far too many people with serious problems to be able to keep a balance between my counselling work and my normal parish responsibilities, and the strain of conducting Primal Therapy was beginning to take its toll on me.

Jura

It was in April 1975 that I received a very unexpected telephone call from Jura. The person on the end of the phone was one of the church elders, Alick Keith, from Keils. Alick was the local postman and we knew him quite well from our summer visits. He had been commissioned to speak to us about the church. He said that we would know that the charge was now vacant and seeking its next minister. The Kirk Session, and the members of the congregation in general were all aware that we owned a house on Jura, and that presumably we had bought it because we had deep feelings for the island. Mr Keith and his fellow elders felt sure that if I were to apply for the charge, such an application would be given most serious consideration. We thanked Mr Keith for his good wishes and said we would give the matter much thought, and we certainly did.

My commitment to stay at St Columba's for what I considered a reasonable period for one ministry, or indeed at least ten years, was now under a great deal of strain. I was continually prey to the feeling that in the eyes of the congregation I did not measure up to their previous minister. Even in the AGM, which had just happened in March 1970 after I had been the minister for almost five years, one of my leading elders stood up in the body of the meeting and addressed me as Mr Levison. It may have seemed funny to the members, but it wasn't funny to me.

There was now a new and major conflict in my life. I was beginning to be torn between the ministry and my Clinical Theology counselling. Clients and their sessions were taking up more and more of my time.

I went to see Dr Lake and his colleagues, and it was agreed that if and when I was settled in the remote island parish of Jura, they would be able to direct certain clients to visit the island to spend some days in therapy there with Margaret and me. This possibility would fit the situation where people were having regular weekly sessions with a local counsellor, but where they and their therapist felt that they would benefit from a short and intensive approach along primal therapy lines, on which they would be able usefully to build when they resumed normal life and weekly sessions. This after all was the role which the clinic in Nottingham had been filling with many of the people who came to it for a few days at quite lengthy intervals.

On the basis of this discussion, and for other reasons, by the beginning of May we had made up our minds to go to Jura, and I sent an application for the charge to the Interim Moderator.

This seems the point to say that I had the highest regard and admiration for my predecessor, David Levison, whom I liked very much on the few occasions when we met. It certainly was not in any way his fault that he imprinted the Kirk Session of St Columba's so firmly with his ideas and enthusiasms that I was unable to make any impression on many things which were difficult for me. It is perhaps unfair to characterise my second ministry as being conducted in 'someone else's country' but, rightly or wrongly, the impression remains.

I have often tried to think out whether I made a wise decision in leaving Glenrothes when I did. I certainly laboured long under a deep sense of shame for having let the people of St Columba's down, for they had a quite reasonable expectation that I would give more years than I did to their parish and its ministry. Many people told me they thought I was doing the wrong thing. In fact, I think the decision was taken in haste. I was just feeling a bit down and depressed about my ministry, and going through a time when I felt I had lost direction.

For better or for worse, after deciding to go into the ministry in the first place the decision to go to Jura in 1975 was probably the biggest decision of my life.

Chapter Eight: A Far Western Country – The Isle of Jura

My induction to the parish of Jura took place on Wednesday, 31st July 1975. The induction service was conducted by the Moderator of the Presbytery of Argyle, Rev. Harry Donaldson, the minister of Ardrishaig. The Interim Moderator was a minister from Islay. There were some ministers there from the Presbytery. I want to speak about some of the important people in the island and the church, but perhaps I should first just say a bit about the island.

Moving to live on Jura was the biggest culture shock of my life. Buxtehude, London, Easterhouse, Glenrothes: all of them pale into insignificance compared to Jura. We already knew the island well, but that was only from summer holidays. Living there all the year round was a completely different affair.

Jura is an island, but it's far too big to appear to anyone on it to be an island. It's more than eight miles across, and it takes several hours even to walk across it. The island is long and cigar shaped, and lies north-east to south-west. It is largely composed of moor, with great areas of wet bog on the low ground, and bare rock and scree in the uplands. It has hardly any decent farmland, and what little there is is restricted to small patches along the east coast.

Jura has only one road: The Long Road, as I always called it. This starts at the Islay ferry, and runs down round the bottom of the island before setting off on its long journey up the eastern side of the island. The island's population all live somewhere along this road, with the main centre at Small Isles Bay, where the village is called Craighouse. Some houses are hard to reach, and many can only be gained by their own tracks and paths. Only the communities of Keils, Knockrome, Ardfernal and Inverlussa have spur roads to serve the houses there.

In the years we lived on Jura the settled population was a little over two hundred people. There were many regular summer visitors, many of whom had family ties with the island.

Employment on the island was easy to describe. There were the workers and staff of the Jura Distillery. The six estates employed gamekeepers and estate managers and farmers. Some of the native islanders were also registered crofters who took either their whole livelihood from crofting or used it to supplement some other income. There were some individual jobs – for example there was a lobster fisherman, and one or two scallop divers. There was a fish farm. There was periodic employment in forestry. There were people engaged in service, such as the doctor, the minister, the district nurse. There were two schoolteachers. There was a hotel manager and staff, a shopkeeper and staff, the postman and the bus driver. It was not hard to list all the men, women and children of the island's population, and during sleepless nights it was our common practice to count them off like sheep in order to get to sleep.

The island had a small group of children of all ages, and also a group of elderly and aged. About thirty of the native people spoke Gaelic at the time we went. The native people of Jura are called Diurachs in the Gaelic.

The Kirk Session

To return to my induction. The Kirk Session was present at the service and it was there that I met most of the elders for the first time.

There was Dougie Buie. Dougie bore one of the ancient names of Jura, for the Buies appear in medieval documents. He was related to the other Buies of Knockrome, but only through his mother. Dougie was a perfect example of the traditional Hebridean islander who has many different roles. He was by trade a joiner. He drove the island's bus. He was the telephone linesman, the Trinity House Lights inspector, and the local undertaker. Dougie was the Kirk Session Clerk, and was a good and loyal one for many years.

Dan Macdougall was the retired blacksmith, and lived in the house called Frisco in the community of Caigenhouse with his wife Effie Lindsay, who had been for many years the island's telephone exchange operator. Dan was a fine Gaelic scholar, and was prepared to give lessons to incomers who wished to study it. He was a fine elder, a good Christian, and intensely loyal to the minister.

Robert Shaw of Lagg was the retired builder of the island. When he first came to the island there were very few houses which had a second storey. Most of them were single storey croft houses. By the time he retired he had added a second storey to many of the dwellings. Many stories were told of him and his wife and the fine house he built in Lagg.

Neil McInnes of Gatehouse was factor and head keeper at the Tarbert estate, which belonged to the Astor family. Neil McInnes was married to Lily McKechnie. Both he and his wife belonged to large families, important in the life of Jura. Neil was a remarkable man. He was a great hillsman and the finest shot I have ever seen. We developed a close relationship.

The session of 1975 included two men who had arrived to work on the island, having been elders in their previous churches. Bob Prentice worked in the distillery, and was a man of considerable goodwill. David Lunn worked for the Jura Forest Estate as factor and gillie. He and his wife lived in the keeper's house at the Forest.

Two elders were absent from my induction. Alick Keith of Keils, who had first contacted me, was postman for the south of the island. He was on his rounds during the service. He and his wife Mary worked a croft at Keils (Mary was our district nurse). Sandy Buie was a full time crofter at Knockrome. Sandy became a close friend, with many skills and many stories to tell. He carved splendid walking sticks, which were always much in demand. He and his wife Nan were the hosts of the monthly services of worship I conducted at Knockrome. He was on his croft at the time of the induction service.

These men remained the backbone of the session for some years. In due course I ordained Jack Paton, a splendid gentleman who became my much valued Session Clerk when Dougie Buie retired.

Our Family on Jura

Family life on Jura was a new and different experience. The children both attended Small Isles Primary School in the village of Craighouse. Margaret went back to speech therapy, both on Jura itself, and across the ferry on Islay. I worked hard to make the manse watertight and to install some kind of heating system that worked. There was more than half an acre of complete wilderness inside the garden wall, and that had to be tamed and made to be pleasant and productive. The parish had got itself a minister who spent most of his time as a tradesman or labourer. I took lessons from everyone, and soon became competent at slating, re-wiring, plumbing and joinery. I used to say that the only secrets I never mastered were those of the plasterer.

Worship in Jura

I conducted my first service on Sunday, 3rd August 1975. The biggest shock awaiting me was in the matter of the hymns. An elder from Islay had played the harmonium at my induction, but I hadn't really noticed at the time. It became clear that there was no one on Jura able to play the hymns on Sundays. There was only one answer. The minister would have to play himself! The church harmonium had in fact quite a sweet tone and was not hard to manage. The only practical problem was that it took a good deal of muscular energy to pedal it, and I found that although I could give a good lead in singing the opening verses of a hymn, I would tend to run out of breath by about the fourth or fifth verse. For the first time in my ministry I employed the strategy of omitting verses three and five.

The harmonium had arrived in the church in the 1920s. It had been employed in the Round Kirk in Bowmore until then. One day a somewhat drunk Irish itinerant linen seller accosted a finely turned out gentleman on the main street in Bowmore, and pressed into his hand a ticket he held in the great Irish sweepstake. He was apparently making a gesture of support for the church. The man who had this encounter was the bank manager and an elder of the said church. The ticket won a considerable sum, and the recipient used it to purchase an organ for the Round Kirk. The harmonium was surplus to requirements, but the minister of the Round Kirk was friendly with Mr Robertson of Jura and offered to give it to him. It was rowed across the Sound of Islay, and Dan Macdougall and his father brought it up from the ferry on their cart. The harmonium's two pedals were made of a lattice of iron work, and worked into the design were the words 'Mouse Proof'. I didn't find playing the music in Jura was a problem, although I had to adapt my conduct of worship to the fact that I was tied to the harmonium for the hymns. I conducted the service from behind the table, which was only a pace away from the music. The only unavoidable pause came after the sermon when I couldn't reach the harmonium without a pause.

The weekly routine of playing and preaching was a bit stressful, and I came to look forward to the tourist season as there was always a good chance that I would find a real organist in the congregation, who would be willing to play. Inspired musicians came every summer, and when they were at the organ there would suddenly be amazing and exciting music.

After August was over and the summer visitors were no longer there to swell the numbers in church, the worshipping congregation settled down to its winter routine. In 1975 the Communion Roll of Jura was sixty-eight members and two adherents. Quite a number of people on the roll were infirm and unable to attend, and several lived in remote parts of the island, served by my monthly house services. The normal winter attendance at Sunday worship in the parish church was between twenty and thirty. The average would be about twenty-five. There was a small remote loyalty effect. People were conscious of the fact that they would be missed if they weren't there, and this resulted in about half the members coming regularly.

The Christian Year

I made it clear to the session that I wanted to hold a Watchnight Service late on Christmas Eve, and there was no objection, and indeed the service proved very popular. It became a complete sell-out as far as the little church was concerned.

My enthusiasm for Lent and Easter was equally unknown on Jura, although I was able to get across only a little of my interest in these festivals. I instituted a small service on Good Friday evening, and preached with enthusiasm on Palm Sunday and Easter Day, but otherwise I made no changes.

Harvest Festival was on the other hand a strong tradition in the church on Jura. It was the custom for one of the crofters to make up two sheaves of oats from a corner which was left standing in the field for this purpose. The distribution to the elderly and housebound was also traditional here, but the idea of selling the goods and sending the money abroad was welcome, and the harvest sale became a happy tradition from my very first season.

Remembrance Day was celebrated in traditional fashion in the Kirk, and I was asked to stand in front of the War Memorial, which was on the inside wall of the church, and read out a list of dead of the First World War. Little did I know on these occasions that many years later Margaret and I would investigate the death of her cousin Neil Whittle at the Battle of Roeux in 1917, and find that Private Donald Darroch of Jura had died there on the same day.

Funerals on Jura

With such a small population, deaths did not occur very frequently, and often many weeks could go by without there being a funeral on the island. I had only about forty funerals during my twelve years on Jura, and as the minister there, I conducted only about three and four funerals per year. Each one was a notable event, and was attended by the entire island population. Everything stopped for a funeral. The distillery closed, and even newly appointed mashmen-stillmen who insisted that they had never even heard of the deceased were expected to attend.

Funerals taking place at the northern community of Inverlussa would have a service in the house and the coffin would be carried to Inverlussa graveyard. The carrying was done with military precision, as if rehearsed, although it never was! Other funerals took place in the parish church and the great majority then went to the ancient cemetery of Kilearnadil.

A eulogy was expected; nay rather, it was more or less compulsory. The life should be summed up in a good deal of detail. This needed me to take the time to sit and ask the necessary questions to support the impressions I had formed personally of the deceased. In the early years of my tenure the undertaker and gravediggers of Islay were not involved in Jura. Dougie Buie was the undertaker, and laid out and coffined the body. The coffin would travel on the back of a long-wheelbase Land Rover. The grave would be dug by local men under Dougie's direction, and the grave was filled in and re-turfed after the committal while the assembled congregation stood silently watching. A dram of whisky was served after the interment, accompanied by cheese and oatcake. This custom was the source of one of my favourite island stories concerning myself and Dougie Buie. The first death had occurred and he had come to see me about the arrangements. There seemed little room for manoeuvre in the conduct of the service, although the church itself made the getting in and out of the coffin a very difficult business, especially as tradition said that it couldn't go out by the same door by which it had come in. This involved an awkward procedure to get the coffin round a sharp corner and out by the vestry door.

To return to Dougie Buie:

'Could I ask you a personal question, Minister?' he said.

'Certainly, Dougie!'

'You would not! Please God! Oh you surely could not be! You're not teetotal are you?'

'You can set your mind at rest about that, Dougie', I replied, 'I'm not teetotal; in fact I fine enjoy a dram. I'm not given to excess, you understand!'

'Oh! That's such a relief. Mr Macdonald was teetotal and it caused a lot of difficulty at funerals. He simply wouldn't stand by while the dram was given out. He just walked away. The people didn't like it. We would have given the poor man a mineral water, but he just wouldn't stay.'

Dougie seemed comforted to think that I wouldn't cause any difficulty on this score.

The church service held no terrors for me, but I was a bit apprehensive about the business in the graveyard. The committal went well, and then we had the long stand while the grave was filled in and the turf re-laid. This was a time of quiet thought, and a great contrast to the rush to get away from the cemetery in mainland funerals. Never on Jura did you have the backward glimpse from the car as it moved off, which showed the gravediggers shovelling the first sod into the hole.

The Land Rover came into place quite quietly, and in due course a small tray was brought to me to take my whisky and oatcake. I had my eye on Dougie, whose expression indicated that all was well. After a few minutes chat, I was aware that the young man with the tray was in front of me again. A single small glass stood in the middle of the tray. I looked towards Dougie again, and was rewarded with a frown and a slight shake of the head. I declined the second dram. A long time later, the company began to disperse and finally there was only myself and Dougie Buie left. I asked him for his thoughts on the service, and he was full of praise for the way I had conducted it. 'As if you had been doing them here for years,' he said.

I ran through the business of the whisky, and he confirmed that it was in order for me to take the dram, as I had. I said that I had not expected to be offered another one.

'Oh! It is the custom to offer a second glass to the minister.'

'But you indicated that I ought not to take it,' I said.

'Oh! Quite. You don't take the second one.' Dougie was firm.

'Tell me, Dougie, what would have happened if I had taken the second dram?'

'Oh. It would be all round the island by now that the minister takes an awful bucket!' was the reply.

I became accustomed to my local funerals, and after one or two I started to say a short grace before the dram was served. This seemed to be quite acceptable.

After a couple of years the Local Authority took responsibility for the upkeep of the cemeteries on Jura, and at about the same time the graves started to be dug by the Islay Council workmen, and the undertaker from Islay started to come over on the ferry with a hearse. The Jura folk still stood to watch while they filled in afterwards.

There was always room for the unexpected at funerals and sometimes for episodes which were profoundly moving. I think the occasion of the following story was the funeral of Miss Betsy McKechnie, who was well over ninety at the time of her death. After the committal was over and the dram had been taken, people were standing about the cemetery quietly chatting, as was the custom. Dan Macdougall approached me, and stood by me in companionable silence. After a pause he spoke, in the Gaelic.

'Ged's fada an dail, thig a cuireadh!' he said, and as he stood his eyes filled with tears, and shortly he moved away.

After a pause I went after him. I had not been able to translate the saying, but knew that it must have deep significance for him, so I asked him to repeat it, and then to tell me about the circumstances. He said that he had been at a funeral in this same graveyard when he himself was a child. I think he was in the company of his own grandfather who was an old man at the time, and they were present at the funeral of a resident who had died at almost a hundred years of age. The date of the funeral I am speaking of would be about 1980, and Dan would have been in his mid seventies at the time, so the saying he was recalling would have been uttered about 1910, and the resident who was being buried could have been born about 1810. I was confronted with a great vista of time past.

A couple of days later I went to Dan and Effie's house in the evening, and, once settled, asked for a translation of the saying, which I had scribbled down phonetically after the funeral.

The key words were *fada*, *dail* and *cuireadh*, which turned out to mean *long*; *delay* or *wait*; and *invitation*. So:

'Though long be the wait, still comes the invitation.'

This seemed to me then to be a saying to treasure, and I have done so.

Some Characters of Jura

Willie and Bella Cameron lived at Strone Farmhouse. Willie was from Glasgow and came to Jura to work as the gardener for Jura House. Bella came from Islay, and hated Jura and everything it stood for. Bella was obsessed with cats and had well over thirty. Willie looked frail, but was actually very tough. He fell into a flooded ditch on the way home one night and lay there till morning, but despite an experience which might have killed a lesser man he was back at work the next day. However, he became ill, I think with emphysema, and had to go into Islay Hospital. Hearing that Bella was on her own, I made several attempts to visit her, but was unable to persuade her to open the door to me. The doctor tried to prepare the way by saying I was coming, and urged me to shout that I was the minister through the letter box. This was ultimately successful and I was admitted. Bella would by then have been about seventy, and was short, stocky, wrinkled and far from beautiful. The house stank of cats, which were all over the place. I asked after Willie, and was told that he had had it coming to him. His illness was a judgement on him because he had been kidnapping her cats, smuggling them out of the house and taking them to the far west coast of the island where he would leave them to fend for themselves. Bella's conversation was as eccentric as everything else about her, and as I was making an evening visit, and it was by now dark, I decided I would leave. This did not suit her, and she kept positioning herself between me and the door, and blocking my exit. I finally managed to get out, and crossed over to my car.

Bella came out and stood at her doorstep to wave me off. She called a farewell:

'My, but you're a fine young minister!' she cried.

I let in the clutch and moved off, to hear her parting shot carried on the still air as the car rolled down her path: 'You're too good for Jura!'

In due course Bella also had to be admitted to Islay Hospital. She and Willie were in female and male wards which were remote from each other, and when I visited them they would each ask how the other was. Both were well able to be about and to go to visit each other in the opposite wards, but neither would give the other the satisfaction of doing so. I carried messages between them until Willie died. Bella followed a month or so later.

An important family with a considerable influence on the island were the McKechnies of the north end. The patriarch of this dynasty was Calum McKechnie, who was quite seriously ill when I took up my office in Jura, and who was being looked after by one of his daughters, Lily McInnes at Gatehouse. Calum had a brother and sister living at Inverlussa. Lily was one of a large family, and as the news went out that the old man was gravely ill, family members began to arrive to be close when the time came for him to die. I was paying almost daily visits to Gatehouse, and each time I went there would be more family members. Some of the daughters were married to Rankin men. On one visit, when I had lost count of McKechnies, I approached a small elderly man with fair hair and said:

'And you'll be another McKechnie then?'

He drew himself up to his full height.

'Indeed I am not!' he said, 'Alistair Shaw is the name!'

I had made a serious mistake. In due course Calum did die and I had my first Ardlussa funeral. Over the following years his brother Angus McKechnie became one of my closest friends. He was universally known as Uncle Angus on the island, and he was a wise and genial companion. He prided himself on the strength of his handshake, and he shook my hand for the first time as he took my leave after his brother's funeral. I wear a signet ring on my right hand, and the old man's grip crushed the ring into my fingers, and left a bruise which lasted for days. The experience was agonising, and ever after I would slip my ring on to my other hand in anticipation of Uncle Angus' handshake. To this day, so many years later, I still do this when standing waiting to shake hands with any company of people.

Uncle Angus was a great source of stories about the north end of the island, and the fine photographs of his own forebears which are part of the collection of photos on display in the parish church all came from him. It became a custom over the years for people of the island to go up to Inverlussa to celebrate the Gaelic New Year in Uncle Angus' house. It was not a night to try to use the Long Road, and the company would remain, drinking, talking and sleeping by turns for several days. Uncle Angus died in 1986, and at New Year, 1987 the island's worthies did their best to set a new record for the New Year in his house. It apparently lasted almost six days!

Dan Macdougall and Archie Black were both very literate in the Gaelic tongue, and when it became evident that there were a number of incomers, such as myself, who were keen to learn the language it was agreed that the two men would conduct classes jointly. The classes assembled with about eight or so learners keen to make progress. Unfortunately our two teachers didn't quite see the subject in the same light, and no sooner had one of them set forth a passage, with spelling and translation and comment, then the other would take issue with some aspect of his interpretation. The learners would be forgotten as the two men became involved in deep and learned debate about the point in question. We made little progress, and the venture soon came to an end. I got all my help from then on from Katie Darroch, who would listen to my attempts to read passages aloud from the Scriptures. She taught me the Lord's Prayer and the 23rd Psalm, and several other famous passages, and I became sufficiently adept to be able to include a suitable passage at island funerals where the Gaelic language seemed to be much desired. I never became a fluent speaker, although I learned to exchange greetings and to make suitable comments on the weather. I heard two old residents speaking about my attempts one day:

'Oh the poor man does his best', they said, 'but everything that he says has the blas Sassunach'. That means the taste, or the flavour, of English. I think that is termed 'being damned with faint praise.'

Katie Darroch and Her Stories

Katie Darroch was full of stories. I copied many of them down, and some have found their way into the pages of my book on Jura. She was the first person I heard telling the story of the Witches of Knockrome. She was certainly still close to the ancient superstitions of the island, and when speaking of her distant relatives, she would occasionally slip into the first person singular, and seem to be speaking of herself. Katie was the resident who, as a little girl, had known Dunacha Sha, whose story will emerge in connection with American emigration. She remembered that he had lost a leg, and when greeted in the Gaelic would reply that he was fine, but wallowing about like a seal in Lowlandman's Bay.

Katie loved to teach me sayings in the Gaelic, and two of her proverbs I have always treasured. I can still remember the Gaelic for them to this day.

One was about the unlucky things that could happen in the New Year.

'I saw a foal with its backside towards me,
Chunnaic mi searrach 'sa chuile rium,
And I saw a snail on a bare slab,
Is seilcheag air leac lom,
And I heard the cuckoo without having eaten a morsel of bread,
Cuthag gun mirium bhreim,
And I knew the year would be a sorrowful one for me.
Dh'aithnith mi nach soirbhicheadh a' bhliadhna rium.'

Katie would usually finish these sayings off by telling about an old man who lived in Ardfernal and was terribly superstitious, so much so that he would go to sleep in the spring with a morsel of oatcake under his pillow and put it into his mouth on awaking so that he wouldn't run the risk of hearing the cuckoo on an empty stomach.

Katie's favourite saying had a typical Gaelic joke in the last line.

'There are three things that have no flavour,
Tha tri rudan gun blas,
Egg without salt,
Ugh gun salann,
Tea without sugar,
Ti gun suicar,
And a kiss without whiskers.
Agus pog gun fheusagan.'

Katie was an enchanting companion, and a giant of her generation the like of whom I will certainly never meet again.

'*Gus am bris an la*' as it says on Jura tombstones. 'Till the day breaks.'

The Blacks of Keils

Archie Black lived alone in the Black family house in Keils. This was a fine dwelling, and the only one in the township with a second storey on it. I had sadly missed the day of Archie's older brother, Donald Black, as he had died by the time I took up my office. Everyone who spoke about him would tell you their favourite one of his stories. He had a keen wit, and could make fun of any situation, although the tales often have a sting in them. I managed to get five of these stories into my Jura book.

Archie Black was not a churchgoer, but treated me always most cordially and would happily talk at length if we met. He made it clear that I was welcome in his house. His was the only house on Jura with no running water and no electricity. The hydro-electric man had approached his brother Donald at the time that power was being brought to Keils.

'Now, Mr Black, you'll surely be letting us put water in your house?'

'Putting it in, is it?', replied Donald, 'It's all I can do to keep it out.'

I remember a number of sessions in Archie Black's house, late on a winter's night, with the Tilley lamp flickering. On one occasion I had just encountered the collection of Jura tales I will later refer to as The

Robertson Fada stories. The collection came from early in the century, and many of them were familiar to me. It was those which I hadn't heard myself, and which I thought might have become lost over the years, that particularly interested me and several of these concerned Keils. I had chatted to Archie about one in particular concerning an enclosure high above the township, known to the people of Keils as the Long Rig. (A rig is a high ridge, in the Scots dialect.) He said he knew no stories about it, and that it was a useless piece of ground, but that I would be welcome to come and see him and discuss it further. Once we were well settled, I read him the story. It concerned a sailor who had landed in Small Isles Bay, and was asking a local man about the said enclosed area high on the hill above the church. He was seeking confirmation that it was called 'goirtean fada' – 'the long enclosure' – and the Jura man, having twice insisted that it was so, blurted out a whole long sentence in the Gaelic:

'*Is e, agus chunnaic mise an t-Iomaire sin g'un rachadh tu gu do ghluinnean air am fuil dhaoine.*'

This translated means: 'It is, and I've seen that rig so that you could go to your knees in men's blood.'

I read the story aloud to Archie, in my best Gaelic, and as I came to the punch line he broke in with a loud shout in English:

'Knee deep!' he cried, and again: 'Knee deep!'

Then he recovered his composure and pulled himself together and chided himself for being a silly old fool. 'I suppose there must have been a battle up there long ago,' he said, 'I think the old men spoke about it, when I was a child.'

It remains one of the most memorable moments of my twelve years on Jura, and another of the most privileged ones.

The Evil Eye

One of my favourite stories brings together the two Sandys of Knockrome and the people of Ardmenish. Sandy Buie and Sandy Darroch were very different men, but they had worked together in adjacent crofts all their lives and were evidently very close. One day the manse phone rang and it was Sandy Buie.

'Have you heard that one of Sandy Darroch's highland cows has had twin calves?'

I said that I hadn't heard, and was asked if I would like to see them. I said that I would be up right away, and left at once. Sandy Buie was waiting for me, and conducted me into the nearby byre where the mother cow and the calves were. New-born highland calves are most attractive creatures, and the fact that there were the two of them increased my excitement. I said how fine they appeared to be, probably not once, but several times, and I also gave it as my opinion that the mother cow was as fine an animal as I had seen. I heard a slight clearing of a throat and looked up to see Sandy Buie standing looking at me with a face like thunder. He made a slight movement of his head which indicated that we should go outside at once, and when we were in the open air together he turned on me.

'Minister, minister! What on earth do you think you are doing, man?'

I protested, 'I'm sorry. What have I done? I haven't done anything.'

'We never praise a man's beasts the way you were doing in there. Did you not see you were making Sandy most anxious. We never praise a man's stock like that, it's a sure way for them to get the Evil Eye.'

'But what should I have said?' I asked in considerable confusion.

'Och! They're fine enough beasts' would have been more than sufficient.'

I thought a lot about it later, and concluded that it was a bit like the way somebody can be apprehensive if they hear a friend boasting that he's been driving for years and never had an accident. That kind of statement can well provoke the saying: 'Touch wood! Touch wood.'

There was a sequel. A few days later I was visiting the croft house of Ardmenish where Neil Shaw and his sister Morag lived. I put the question to Neil:

'Now you're a man of the kirk,' I said, 'Would you be worried if I were to go into your byre and saw one of your beasts and began to heap praise on it – that it might get the Evil Eye?'

Neil said: 'Oh, Minister, you're asking the wrong person there, I'll have to get the expert through.'

And he called for his sister, Morag, who came bustling in from the kitchen.

'Now tell Morag what you've been telling me, and ask her your question.'

I said exactly the same thing to Morag, ending with: 'Would you be worried it would get the Evil Eye?'

Morag looked hard straight at me:

'Not a bit, Minister', she said, 'You don't have it'. And went back to the kitchen.

The House at Lagg and Other Tales

I was engaged in my first round of house visits in Jura some months after my induction, and I was confronted with visiting the houses on the main road up the island. Neil McInnes had told me that I would get a warm welcome at Lagg at the house which sat on the road, looking out over the bay. The resident was a single man called Jock Mollison, and he was employed as a gillie gamekeeper on the Tarbert Estate. 'Jock will be happy to see you,' he said. 'He's not one for attending the church, but he has no ill-will for it either.'

So armed and forewarned I paid my visit and was warmly welcomed in by a short man with a cheery grin, and a slight stutter in his speech. He told me he was divorced from his wife. He had several grown-up children, one of whom was his son Johnny, who was working away from home at the time. He offered me a cup of tea, and was not put out when I asked if I could have coffee. In due course he arrived back with the Nescafe. While he was in the kitchen making it, I was taking my ease in the parlour. He had mentioned that the house was very ancient, and had been one of the Change Houses of Jura. In other words it had been an inn, where travellers would get a change of horses. Lagg was at the end of the cattle drove road from Islay, and had been the site of many wild goings on when the cattle were loaded on the ferry for the crossing to the mainland in the last century. As I sat thinking over what Jock had said, I became conscious that I was hearing someone else in the house. Jock was in the kitchen, but this other person was in the room above my head. Later, I re-examined my memory for exactly what it had been that had made me so confident of this human presence. There had been the sound of a footfall on bare wood. There had been the creaking of a bed spring.

This was the Lord High Commissioner's splendid red helicopter – the subject of my sally while speaking to the Duke.

Myself and Frankie Vaughan at the entrance to the church hall at Lochwood in July, 1968, after he addressed a meeting of youngsters in the hall.

Frankie Vaughan. He is speaking to a crowd of young people, many of them associated with the Drummie Gang. I can be seen standing behind him and giving my support.

Plate 10

Jura parish church, with some visitors.

Kilearnadil Cemetery: the ancient graveyard at Keils.

Jura Manse, with my trusty David Brown tractor.

Our milk cows in the glebe front field.

Some of our assorted hens.

Pip and Docken, two of our calves.

Sheba, our great dane, with Jet.

The minister at work on his peat bank.

Plate 12

St Andrew's, Kirriemuir – my last parish church.

I was very fond of the fine chancel.

Folk having fun at At Andrew's.

I have no record of the donkeys in my earlier churches, but this was the Kirriemuir one.

Margaret and I off to North Carolina in 1986. A happy day!

There had been the undoubted sound of someone clearing their throat. When Jock came back I said to him:

'I thought you said you were alone here, Jock. So who else is in the house?'

'Oh, it's himself you'll have been hearing. He's often about when I have visitors.'

He explained that he shared the house with another resident, who had apparently been at Lagg for a very long time, at least to judge from the fact that many earlier residents had reported his presence.

'He never causes me any trouble, so I just leave him alone,' he said.

'I'm not sure that I'm ready to accept what you're saying,' I said.

'Oh, you can go up and have a look if you like. Go on then. Turn left at the landing, there's only the two rooms.'

Nothing loth I got up and went out to the little hallway and started up the stairs. I must have turned the wrong way at the wee landing, for when I opened the door at the top of the next three steps I found myself in what was evidently Jock's own bedroom. There was an unmade bed, and a general state of untidiness. I turned round and went down the steps to the landing and up those on the other side. I tapped on the door before going in. It was the spare room. It was sparsely furnished with a single bed, made up, and a rug on the floor. There was a small table with a basin and jug pourer on it, and a small chest of drawers in front of the window. A bare bulb hung from the central flex.

I went back downstairs.

'Oh, you mustn't be too surprised,' Jock said, 'he doesn't actually let you see him. Indeed, if there's someone staying here he seems to make himself scarce, but he often fools me. A few months ago I was expecting Johnny back from England on the afternoon boat. I came back in from the stalking, and got washed. I heard him moving about, and knew he was home so I made some tea and a sandwich and took it up to him on a tray. He phoned later to say that he'd missed the ferry and wouldn't be home till the next day.'

I asked Jock what he did with the tea and sandwich?

'Och, I left it there for him, in case he fancied it, but he never touched it.'

There was a widely held belief among the old folk of Jura that there had once been a monastic priory at Lagg, in the middle ages, but that the monks had been dispossessed and the building knocked down. Some of the dressed stone had been re-used in the construction of the Change House. The long-term resident was believed to be a member of the priestly community who was reluctant to leave, and remained behind near the site until he died – hence his attachment to Jock's house.

There were other houses on Jura with curious stories and odd atmospheres, and one of the most compelling, strangely enough, was the one we had bought – our own Corran House. We found one of the two upstairs bedrooms to be cold and hostile, while the other, with an identical setting and structure was perfectly pleasant. Our children wouldn't sleep in the cold one, and visitors also quickly expressed a preference. The house had strange stories attached, and by all accounts some of the inhabitants had been most odd. There was a tale of a young man who took a girl from Knockrome to a dance down in Craighouse, and let her slip off his horse as they crossed the Corran River on their way home. The girl was drowned, and the boy told no one. When the family were roused and found her body on the shingle spit, they drove the offending family from the island. When I heard the story I always thought of the Kennedys and Mary Jo Kopechne and Chappaquiddick. Sandy Buie was always reluctant to tell this story:

'It reflected no honour on the folk of Knockrome. We were hasty and less than just,' he would say.

As in the case of the Evil Eye, the stories associated with these goings on were all simply accepted as a normal part of life on the island. One other tale fits neatly into the same category.

It would have been about 1980 that Angus McDonald of Ardfin was much about the manse as he had a lease of grazing for some of his cattle. One bright sunny day he came knocking at the back door for some minor matter. We stood in the sunshine and passed the time of day.

'Ah yes!' Angus said, 'It was on just such a day as this that I stood here chatting with your predecessor, Mr McDonald, poor man. As we stood, we saw Angus McKay of Feolin Farm, over there, come through the gate in the upper field and make his way across the grass towards Keils. We both watched him, and I said how pleased I was to see him back on the island and obviously able to be getting about, when the last I had heard was that he was gravely ill in a Glasgow hospital. The minister was happy to agree with me, and we spoke of other things. It was later that day that the minister contacted me just to say that Angus had died in Glasgow the night before. Of course it was nice that he was just able to pay a last visit to his own place.'

Clinical Theology in Jura

The project of having a clinic in the manse, which had been our main reason for leaving Glenrothes, all had to be put on hold while we worked to get the old manse to the point at which it was in a good enough state for clients to be comfortable, and for our counselling work to go on under reasonable conditions.

By the end of our first two years the manse restoration was largely complete, and our project to accept residential clients for Clinical Theology therapy got under way. Our first clients arrived in 1977 and our counselling work quickly became a steady commitment which we tried to limit to one week in each calendar month. This was a busy and very absorbing project from 1977 to 1980. We were almost completely dependent on people being referred to us by counsellors in Scotland and England. The people who came were usually having regular sessions with a counsellor, who had decided that a period of intensive Primal Therapy might assist them in achieving a breakthrough. Such people would arrive at the beginning of the week at the same time that Lyn and Donald would be leaving to go to school, and by the time the children came home for the week-end the clients would have gone away again. The therapy was even more demanding and intensive than it had been in Glenrothes. In particular I found the recording and note-keeping took a great deal of time.

It has been my practice in these pages to maintain complete confidentiality concerning the people Margaret and I supported over the years through Clinical Theology, and the work in Jura falls into the same category, so no names or case notes appear here. Some clients came a number of times, and went on to become close friends. Some of these people came back to spend a relaxed time with us in better health and in good company. I destroyed all personal notes on such clients many years ago, so by now only they know who they are. I cannot even remember many of their names so many years later, but the total number was very considerable indeed.

By 1980 when Frank Lake himself came to visit us, he was becoming very ill. He would die in 1982, and his hand was no longer firmly on the tiller of the Clinical Theology ship. We had thought that our Jura project was going to have the support of the entire Clinical Theology organisation, but it became clear once Dr Lake had become unwell that he had, as so often in other situations, played the cards very close to his chest. Once he was no longer in charge of the organisation, no one really knew that our facility existed, and the flow of clients gradually slowed down and finally simply ceased. By the end of 1981, six and a half years after we arrived in Jura, our counselling work had more or less come to an end.

We were now living in a manse which was fully repaired and in working order. The manse garden was becoming productive, and with my small island community being the only thing that needed my attention, I was beginning to look around for new projects and new worlds to conquer.

The Glebe

Jura manse sat in the midst of farm land which during our first years there supported a number of cows. There was a local grazing tenant. This land was called 'the glebe', and was administered from Edinburgh. After some negotiation I became the tenant in 1981, with a view to farming my own glebe as many previous ministers had done. There was much to do. I put the skills recently used on the manse to work restoring the farm buildings, and emerged with a barn, a byre and stable and a dairy with water and electricity. I managed to borrow some capital from my aunt and my cousin. The plan was that I would keep some Friesian cows to milk. I could supply unpasteurised milk on the island, as well as butter and buttermilk. The cows could be served by the township bull and I could put the calves to market. I could make hay on my land to feed the animals, and also have oats and potatoes as crops. We could keep chickens as a sideline.

I went shopping in Islay and bought a tractor, a plough, harrows, a buckrake, a mower and a potato ridger. I bought an electric milking machine and all the equipment for a small dairy.

I bought a seven year old Friesian we called Bramble and a five year old Ayrshire called Sorrel. Both of these were in calf. I bought twelve point of lay chickens: Suffolks, Rhode Island Reds and Minorcas.

I started off with a great deal of local help and advice, learning how to manage, feed and milk my cows, and getting lessons in ploughing my fields. I was fortunate to have willing and capable people to try to keep me right, and most things began to work out as planned. There was a ready sale for fresh milk, which was not available on Jura, and people came to collect it daily, or sent milk cans via the local bus. Apparently as long as I didn't bottle or distribute, I was not considered a milk producer and could avoid pasteurisation.

Some of my experiences will bear examining in some more detail.

By the time the cattle came I had already planted half an acre of oats and half an acre of main crop potatoes in the field below the garden. Alick Keith taught me how to broadcast oat seed by hand. When he did it you couldn't see any thick or thin places when the corn came up, but my field had thick patches and bare patches all over the place. I sowed two hundredweight of Astor seed oats.

I spread fertiliser all over my potato field. I was recommended to plant Maris Piper main crop potatoes, and I bought fifteen hundredweight, which cost me £105. After I had ploughed my potato field and finished harrowing it I hitched on my brand new ridger, and I went up and down the potato field. When I had finished it looked quite splendid with its evenly alternate hills and valleys. I had even managed to get them looking straight! I was going to sow my seed potatoes by hand. There was no alternative, and so I filled a bucket and set off down a row, dropping one potato every foot or so and trapping it in position with a toe. It took a long time and was back-breaking work. I had been told by my teacher what the next job would be.

I was told that it was called 'splitting the field', and would consist of going to and fro with the tattie ridger behind the tractor. This time the ploughshares of the ridger would run down the middle of the ridges and split them so that they would fall outwards on either side and cover the rows of seed potatoes. It sounded simple and logical, and I started in high spirits.

I had only gone a few yards when I realised that all was not well. I looked back, and found my ridger was not running in the middle of the ridges at all, but had slipped sideways and was running along the middle of the furrows and splitting the seed potatoes in them neatly in two. I picked up the ridger and got out as best I could. You always leave complete carnage behind when you have to scramble out of the field, but I started again, this time more slowly, and watching behind me all the time. There was no help for it, my bonnie ridger would not stay on top of the hills I had made, and immediately slipped down into the valleys again. I struggled out again and parked the tractor. I knew that I needed help, and I went and got it.

'My God, Minister!', said big Alan, 'What on earth did you think you were doing? We never ridge the field up like that when we're planting the tatties. You don't make ridges like that until they're well up and you're ridging them up to control the weeds. You'll never split a field that's ridged like that! We only just kiss the field at this stage, to make wee shallow grooves, just enough to show where we're dropping the potatoes, then you can make the ridger cover them all right.'

I hadn't known.

The story came to mind of the minister long ago, confronting his congregation in an Aberdeenshire kirk.

'And the Lord God in his infinite wisdom and mercy will send ye all to Hell. And there in Hell you will complain to the Lord above and you will say:

"Lord, Lord, We didna ken! We didna ken."

And then the Lord God in his infinite mercy will say to ye:

"Aye weel! Ye ken noo!"

Well – I did indeed 'know now'.

I was in trouble. I asked what I was to do.

'Oh! There's only the one thing to do. You'll have to pick them all up and start again.'

If it took me a long time to drop the potatoes it took me four times as long to pick them all up again. Bucket by bucket I was at it for several days. The word got round the island what I was doing, and a variety of folk stopped on the road and leaned on the wall to wish me well. Various comments were passed.

'That doesn't look like much of a crop you're getting there!'

'I thought it was planting time, not lifting time. '

And so on. Years later I heard that wagers were placed in the pub as to whether I'd stick to it, and whether there would be any potato crop taken off the minister's field. Well, those who had no expectations of me lost their bet, for I was far too proud to be defeated. Once all the potatoes were lifted again I harrowed the entire field flat. I had been advised to plant at right angles to my first attempt. I also got a stabiliser fitted to give me more control over the wandering ridger. This time I made my planting furrows very shallow, with the mere kiss which had been mentioned, and this time I was able to split the field successfully. Later, when the tattie shaws were well up I was able to employ my ridger as it was meant to be used and created a satisfactory field of banked up ridges, scraping out the weeds.

I managed to harvest my first crop of potatoes and cut my first oats. I sold the ware potatoes (i.e. those selected for table use), and fed the rest to the cattle; and I tied the oats in stooks and fed them to the cattle on the stalk.

I made four acres of hay the traditional way, by mowing and hand raking. The summer of 1982 was fine and dry all through the harvest season and the hay was got in without any soakings.

By October it was time for the cows to come in for the winter. Now my planning of a milking parlour and calf shed began to pay off. The new seasonal task of mucking out began with the milk cows, and with calf straw. The business of morning milking in midwinter was a strangely pleasurable one. Although the weather was cold, I was eager to get up early and go out to my byre. The place was warm from the presence of the cows, and it seemed to be a friendly place to go into and to begin to start milking.

By the end of the winter I lost patience with Sorrel's bad temper. She never really stopped being difficult to milk, and even after many months she still kicked me at every opportunity. In February 1983 I sold her and bought Poplar, an Islay Friesian, and Alder, another Friesian, who was bred in Ayrshire. They both calved, and we then had four calves: Pip and Docken and Hazel and Sage.

Red Water

In the summer of 1983 Alder was the source of another of my most memorable experiences. I took her in to milk one morning, and she spread her back legs to pass water, as they do, only on this morning the urine that flooded out was bright red. I ran into the house and called the vet, who was at this time a pleasant young lady called Miss Blackadder.

'Oh dear,' she said, 'I'm afraid your cow has got Red Water fever. I'll come over right away.'

It turned out that Alder had a disease acquired from ticks in the pasture. A plasmodium parasite enters the bloodstream and attacks the blood cells, which break down and are passed out as urine – hence Red Water. There was an injection, which didn't take effect, followed by another. I learned that island cattle build up an immunity to Red Water but my mainland cow didn't have it. No one warned me of this. I was told: 'Oh, the minister is a well-educated man, and had probably taken measures to protect his pedigreed cow. It wasn't our place to become involved.'

The morning after the injections Alder was lying flat out in the stackyard and barely alive. I called the vet again.

She knew of only one last chance. It seemed likely that the parasite was no longer alive, but that so much of the cow's red blood had been destroyed that she would not recover. Only a blood transfusion might save her.

'Wait a moment,' I said, 'I'm fond of my cows, but I'm not giving them my blood.'

'Not your blood!', said the vet. 'Blood from another one of your cows. I'll be right over. Organise a strong man to be there.'

I phoned Willie Macdonald, and he was at the manse by the time the vet arrived.

We brought in Bramble. We roped her legs and knocked her down beside Alder. The blood had to be taken out of the donor cow and stored temporarily in sterile bags from which it would be run into Alder. The bags had crystals inside to stop the blood congealing. The only size of bag available to the vet had been human transfusion bags holding one pint. The appropriate amount of blood for a cow transfusion is a gallon and a half – twelve bags. The vet drew some blood off Bramble, and once some bags had been filled we started to run their contents into Alder. I acted as an upright human transfusion stand, holding the bags high enough up to get the blood to flow down. After a little while it began to rain and the vet became anxious that the rain would chill the blood. Margaret ran inside for the big black ministerial umbrella, which I held up in my free hand. I found myself standing there in my stackyard between two horizontal cows with a blood sack raised high from one hand and my umbrella in the other, and wondering if I could have imagined being part of this scene when I was deciding to become a minister in the church of Scotland in the 1950s. I concluded that it was unlikely.

Once the procedure was completed Willie, who had been a tower of strength throughout, untied Bramble, who scrambled up and simply went about her business. After about ten minutes Alder was making attempts to stand as well, and well within half an hour she was up and walking and drinking water. She made a complete recovery and was back on stream producing milk twenty-four hours later.

In September 1983, I bought Bracken, a seven year old Ayrshire who had a Charolais cross calf we called Barley. I was now at my planned maximum of four milking cows.

In 1983 I produced another very good potato crop which I grew on the little field next to the garden wall, known locally as 'the dial' (perhaps from a former sundial); and I took another hay crop from the big field, but the weather was much more unsettled and I got some experience of what it is like to get hay in in wet weather in the western isles.

During the first two years of the glebe venture our chickens performed quite satisfactorily, producing eggs for our own use and for sale, and the occasional chicken for the table.

We had no way to predict that the glebe project would fail. In due course, however, the cows I had taken to be served by the bull did not produce calves. Their lack of success in this matter was put down amongst the native crofters to the fact that I was a beginner, and may not have known when to take the cows, and the fact that I was also the parish minister may not have helped. Too late the vet did tests and found my fields were very low in copper – hence the infertility. My cows went dry, and I sold up. I carried forward into the future my debt to my aunt and cousin, and a further loan I had had from the Highlands and Islands Development Board. I was finally able to repay all my creditors, my inheritance from my father putting an end to the affair.

I made no further effort to work my glebe lands. I sub-let the grazing on the glebe, and in 1987 I held a public roup of all my farm and garden equipment. I felt sad about the way the venture came to an end. I tell myself that at least I didn't simply quit, at the first sign of trouble, but had to be more or less closed down before I gave it all up. Nowadays, when I look back on my farming days, I find much more to give me pleasure than to make me sad.

Shooting

We arrived on Jura with a family which included a very large Great Dane, and a Siamese cat. We saw at once that the land around the house was carrying a huge population of rabbits, so I applied for a firearms certificate and bought myself a rifle with a telescopic sight, and at once began to shoot rabbits for the animals. By the time we arrived in Jura in 1975 I hadn't fired a rifle since the army, but it turned out to be a bit like riding a bicycle and I had, after all, been very well taught in the Seaforth Highlanders. Indeed, at the time of all that training I had been a very good marksman. I found that I had no trouble in killing rabbits, and seldom missed anything I had decided to hit. With an eye on our fragile economy I soon became aware that there were a lot of red deer coming into our glebe fields in winter nights, and that it should be possible for me to shoot these as marauders.

The first red deer I shot myself was up in rough ground above the fields, known as the Black Park. The beast was a fairly big hind. It came very close to me, and stood still. I shot it through the heart. I had already discovered that I am a true carnivore. I can appreciate the beauty and splendour of a wild animal right up to the moment when I kill it. None of what then needs to be done causes me to feel squeamish. With this first hind, I was in new territory, but I knew from general conversation that I had to open a blood vessel in its throat, and then cut its stomach open and leave the contents of its abdomen on the ground, as what is termed 'the gralloch'. I then dragged the rest of the beast down to the manse, and stood looking at it wondering what to do next. It happened that the head keeper of one of the estates turned up at the manse just as I was trying to decide what to do next.

He gave me my first basic lesson, and showed me exactly what to do. He fashioned the wooden spreader which holds the animal's back legs apart. He told me to throw a rope over a joist in the barn, and using the car, to pull the beast up to hang from the joist before tying off the rope to a convenient peg. He showed me how to skin the animal. He did this with his bare fist. Keepers all seemed to be able to do this, but I never could. Once the skin was off, and the main internal organs like the liver and lungs had been removed, he took off the hooves and the head of the animal and asked me for an ordinary hand-saw. He sawed right down the middle of the beast. It had to be central to remove the spinal cord which should not be cooked or eaten.

As far as butchering the animal was concerned, he asked me if there was such a thing as a black magic marker in the manse. I was sure there was, and Margaret fetched one from the study. My teacher drew all the principal cuts of venison on the bare flesh of the skinned animal with a few deft strokes of the marker, and left me all set up to butcher it myself. With my instructions clear on the beast and a sharp carving knife I had the carcase divided into joints ready for the deep freeze in a very short time, and after that instruction I was never again unsure of what I was doing with a red deer carcase.

That hind was the first of many deer, and we were seldom without venison in the freezer during our years on Jura. I never killed for anything other than our own table. I found all the beasts I shot on my glebe land, and one very fine stag inside the manse garden. I had gone out one morning early in the year to get some brussels sprouts, and was greeted by the extraordinary sight of two rows of bare stalks sticking up out of the ground. The sprouts themselves had been neatly nipped off as in the manner of eating corn on the cob. A neighbour told me it had been a stag, and that he would be back. There was certainly some fine green broccoli still standing in the next row. Margaret and I lay in wait for him the following night. I slid the lower sash of the study window up, and took my position with the rifle resting on the window ledge. Margaret stationed herself by the switch inside the front door which controlled our outside light. When I heard a distinct munching sound I signalled to Margaret, and the light came on. He was a splendid beast, boasting ten points, and he stood stock still in the light with his head up. He was only about twenty yards away, and I shot him once through the heart. He never moved. I always felt a bit guilty about him, as I felt it was very unfair to take advantage of him like that, apart from probably breaking all kinds of laws. Still, he had converted all my sprouts into excellent meat, and the venison was superb.

One big stag I shot in my front field. He was just beside the top of the manse drive. Although I was sure that I heard the solid impact of the bullet, he went off like the wind, and I thought I must have missed him. He bolted straight across the field towards the neighbouring farm land, but was brought up short by our ditch and boundary fence. He went down on the ground at that point and was stone dead when I got up to him. Once he was skinned and I was butchering the carcase I was able to see that my bullet had entered his chest and gone through first one lung and then the heart and then the second lung, and was lodged against a rib on the exit side. The animal must have had an immediate and explosive decompression of his heart, and was in fact dead from the moment the bullet hit him. He still ran about a hundred yards at full tilt, which I have always thought remarkable.

The manse lands lie on the frontier between two estates. To the north, and up the island, lay Jura Forest estate, where the head keeper was my good friend. To the south and towards the village lay Jura Estate, with its head keeper, a much younger man, with whom I was also on very good terms. It seemed that there was always somebody who had heard me shooting on the glebe, and the fact that I had got a deer seemed to get quickly known. I would meet my neighbour from The Forest in the village the next day.

'There's word that you got a decent beast last night, Mr Youngson?'

'Yes indeed! Not bad.' I would reply.

'It wouldn't have been a twelve point, would it?'

'Now, you know better than to ask that. I wouldn't take a royal stag. He was a big eight pointer.'

'Indeed, and do you mind telling me where he would have been coming from?'

'Well, you know, he was coming in from the south, and he would have been moving up towards the Forest.'

'Just so. Good morning.'

And the meeting was over.

Later on I would encounter my friend from the Jura Estate, and exactly the same conversation would take place with him, only I would tell him:

'Oh, he was coming down the island. He came in from Feolin fields and would have been heading towards you.'

'Just so. Good morning.'

The underlying thrust of both conversations was twofold. Good royals, or twelve point stags, were uncommon on Jura, as there was not sufficient good grazing for them to become as heavy as they can on the mainland. The keepers were jealous of the few good heads there were and wanted to be able to present them to their lairds or the paying guests in the stalking season.

The question of the direction the beasts were moving was a matter of who had been fattening them up. Every keeper hated the idea that a stag had been feeding well and growing strong on the pasture of his estate, only to wander on to someone else's land and get himself shot. I was always wise to suggest that he was moving towards the keeper's land but hadn't reached it, and to hope that the two keepers didn't get talking to each other.

Geronimo

It was in 1979 that I encountered Geronimo. Angus had bought a young Hereford bull calf called Geronimo to run with cows on the hill. Angus was in the glebe one day, and told me that he was about to lose Geronimo. The beast was in Alick Keith's cattle shed, and he was waiting for the vet to look at it. The animal was seriously injured as a result of some kind of freak accident. It had been running on the hills above Keils and had been seen that morning badly hurt. No one knew how the damage had occurred, but it was plainly mortal. The animal seemed to have been sliced open just below the lower jaw with the effect that all the soft tissue below the jawbone was hanging loosely down giving the appearance of a second mouth. Could it have fallen downhill and struck a high tensile wire? Could it simply have fallen on a bare rock face with such force that its massive weight had torn the jaw? No one could say. What was obvious was that Geronimo could not eat, and would swiftly starve. I asked what Angus was going to do? He made it clear that there was nothing to do but dig a deep hole. He would get the vet to slaughter the beast, he had no time to do anything else. I was astonished by his news, but not surprised. Angus' earlier unruffled acceptance of the death of a cow and calf on the glebe had seemed remarkable to me, and now here he was showing the same attitude towards Geronimo. I knew that he had spent £600 on the bullock, and was now facing losing it all.

I asked Angus about the animal. Had it sired calves? Would the meat be fit for human consumption? He said no to the first and to the second that it would be superb. I asked if it would be a practical proposition for me to buy it and butcher it for my own use?

'Yes. But it would be a big undertaking.'

We went to meet the vet. There was nothing he could do with Geronimo. He had not treated it, and said he would not do so as antibiotics would render it unfit for human eating. Yes! The meat could be eaten, all except the tongue which would have to be discarded. The vet would not destroy the beast, as it was mobile and could be humanely put down where it was going to be of use. The vet left. I paid Angus a good sum for Geronimo (several hundred pounds, in fact), and I led him away from Keils by the rope through his nose ring. Back at the manse I tethered the bull, and contacted Ian Cameron who came round with his shotgun. He was loaded with SSG cartridges which each contained only four large balls, instead of the usual large number of tiny ones I associated with shotgun cartridges. He fired point-blank at the bull's head and hit him just above the eyes. The bull blinked and shook his head, but was otherwise unharmed. The shield of bone at that point must have been so thick that the shot couldn't penetrate. Ian reloaded and shot again – this time a little lower between the eyes – and the bullock sank down, stone dead. Ian bled the carcase and went off to get on with his day's work, leaving me confronted by this mountain of beef.

I first dug a mighty deep hole as near to the stackyard as I could get it, then I set to work to skin the beast. I didn't know that I could have sold the hide for a good sum if I had kept it all in one piece, but I skinned it in sections. I went into the beast's abdomen and was confronted by all its different stomachs. Each one made a huge load for the wheelbarrow, and they filled my first hole completely. I had to dig several more holes. One took the head, the lungs and the heart. I sawed my way down the mid-line, and across the body behind the fore legs and in front of the hind quarters. I got the fore-quarters into the barn, but I couldn't get a whole hind quarter into the barrow. I telephoned back to Glasgow and spoke to Mr McFadyen, who had been our butcher while we were there, and had become a good friend. He gave me some simple and basic instruction about how to cut up the carcase. He said that normally the carcase should be hung, but under the circumstances I would have to forego that. As the meat was to be frozen, it would tend to mature in the freeze. It took me two days to cut up the bull and I had to borrow deep-freeze space from several people on the island. I kept a record of how much meat came from Geronimo.

It went like this: Roast 138 lb; Steak 40 lb; Mince 64 lb; Stew 40 lb; Dog meat 55 lb; Offal 14 lb.

I made a handsome return on my investment, but I doubt very much whether I would have tackled the job if I had known in advance what it would entail. I certainly have never done anything like it since, and I can say with honesty that I will never forget Geronimo. We ate the meat over a period of about a year, and it was absolutely superb.

One Sycamore too Many

Once the wood stove was up and running, and we were depending on it to heat the water, it was up to me to keep it continually supplied with wood. I bought a heavy-duty chain saw, and began to work my way through the old sycamore trees around the manse. One of them was a giant, and definitely more than I could handle alone. Danny and Eddie Moran were brothers and both worked in the distillery. They made up part of the Roman Catholic population, and were both good friends. Eddie had been a forester had worked in the Jura woodlands. I approached him to see if he would help with the big tree. I offered him a price, and we considered the problem. The main weight of the old tree seemed to be on the side facing the manse, and it was important to persuade it to fall the other way. Eddie put the necessary preliminary cuts into the trunk, and we put the tractor into the middle of the field and put a stout rope from the top of the tree to the tractor. When all was ready Eddie took out the last bit of the big trunk and the tree started to move. Despite all our preparations, it fell towards the manse, easily dragging the tractor across the field. Only the lightest branches actually reached the house, but they did a lot of damage to the gutters and downpipes on the low roof. The tree completely blocked the way in and out of the manse, and there was nothing for it but to saw it up sufficiently to clear the drive. Eddie and I worked together taking it in turns to either use the chain saw or to pull the cut branches clear. On one of my shifts cutting down through the branches, I was not particularly thinking of where Eddie was, and just caught sight of a shock of black hair somewhere below my descending saw blade. I wrenched the blade upwards, but thought that it might just have touched the dark mass below it. Eddie, for it was he who had been beneath the saw, and pulling at a branch, stood up:

'Did that thing touch me?' he asked, and put his hand up to his head. Blood was spurting out of a shallow cut in the top of his scalp.

'Only just', I replied as I helped him into the house. The young man was as white as a sheet as he sat in the manse, and with good reason. The saw would have cut his head off quite effortlessly had it travelled down a few inches more. I had to call the doctor, who left his car on the other side of the felled tree and came in to put in a couple of stitches in Eddie's head. The cut was little more than a scratch, but scalp wounds always bleed copiously. Eddie never held the episode against me, and we remained good friends.

A few nights later the hotel bar was full, and a discussion was going on about the latest outbreak of violence in Northern Ireland. Dougie Buie spoke up:

'Och,' he said, 'They should send them over here. We've got a minister here who takes a chain saw to Catholics.'

The Minister's Water

It was in the spring of 1976 that I learned about the Minister's Water. This was the name of the bay at the bottom of the drive. There had long been a right for the minister to net it for salmon. The method was called gill netting, and Alec McIsaac, an elderly resident, offered to teach me. He had the boat and the net. The net was about forty yards long and six feet deep. The rope which ran through it along the surface of the water had plastic floats spaced about a yard apart. A heavy line with lead weights on it was threaded through the bottom edge of the net. This kept the net hanging vertical in the water. One end of the top rope was tied to a mooring ring on a heavy rock on the shore. The bulk of the net was arranged in the stern of the boat so that as you rowed away from the shore the net would stream out over the stern. It would then deploy itself downwards and hang like a curtain in the water. Once you had rowed out to the end of the net you threw a heavy weight out of the boat. Sea trout came into Small Isles Bay following the scent of fresh water from the various streams which ran into it. The minister's water depended for its success on the water flowing in from the minister's burn, one of the main streams running into the bay. The trout would meet the burn water and turn along the shore towards Corran Beach and its river. As they made their way along, just offshore, they would encounter the net. The fish pushed their noses into the mesh and the strands of the net slid along the sides of the head and caught around the gill covers.

The net was set in the evening, and was visited in the early morning. If there were fish in the net, one or more of the floats would be sunk below the level of the water. Alec and I caught quite a few fish in the summer of 1976, but he was unable to continue after that. When he died he left me his boat and net, and I carried on by myself. It was hugely absorbing and exciting, and it was wonderful to have a supply of splendid fish in the freezer. However, it was not simple. You could find there had been a storm, and the net was weighed down with tangles of seaweed and rocks. It would have to be taken up to the house and hung out between the trees to dry. It took hours of work to clean the seaweed and stones out, before it was fit to be set. There was also the matter of what got caught. Not only sea trout got into the net. There were frequent catches of grey mullet and dogfish. There were big jellyfish. There was competition too. Seals came close inshore and ripped the fish out. It was also possible to find a fish head in the net, neatly severed from its body. This was the work of an otter, which simply took the body and left the head.

On one unforgettable occasion I found the net had caught a fishing party of the west coast cormorants called shags. I spent a long time disentangling the dead birds and rescuing those that were still alive. It was a trying experience, and I have never forgotten it. Indeed I used the incident as the basis of a sermon called 'The Birds in the Net' on the theme of setting things free.

The average sea trout in the net would be about five or six pounds, but there were occasionally fish heavier than twelve pounds. My biggest recorded fish was fifteen and a half pounds in weight. The biggest ones always get away, and it was the case with me. The morning of the big fish remains in my memory. More floats were sunk by this fish than I had ever seen before. When I reached the affected portion I could see this huge fish hanging vertically down the side of the net. It appeared to stretch from where its teeth were entangled in the mesh right down to the bottom of the net, which would have made it at least five feet long. The approved method of dealing with this situation was to get some distance away from the fish and try to bring the bottom line of the net upwards to form a bag in which the fish could lie. The moment I touched the bottom line the fish's teeth tore out of the net and its body slid down the net and could be clearly seen lying flat upon the sand. The water at the spot was about six feet deep. I couldn't bear just to leave this huge fish lying there. It appeared to be dead. I stripped in the boat, and put my spectacles on a thwart. I am a strong swimmer and an experienced skin diver. I slid over the side and swam strongly down to the bottom. At my first attempt I got my hands round the body of the big fish. At the touch of my hands it revived instantly and with a huge explosion of irresistible power, it left at once. The fish would have had to be at least twenty pounds in weight; but it got away.

My colleague Ian Cameron had a similar experience. One morning at the net I heard a remote loud noise, and could see at the distant Jura Forest pier that Ian was standing up in his boat. When I had finished with my own net I took the car along to see him. His story was similar to mine. A huge fish entangled in his net had broken free and floated on the surface. Tortured just as I was, Ian Cameron seized an oar and tried to brain the fish with it. It was the sound of the oar striking the water that I had heard. The fish however, regained consciousness and swam away. We compared notes and agreed that it may very well have been the same fish.

During the years that I operated my sea trout net I kept a little book with a record of the catches. The book has gone, but the best year remains. It records the four weeks in 1978 when the fish were running, and the weights caught were as follows:

1st week 16 lb; 2nd week 12½ lb; 3rd week 19¾ lb; 4th week 26¼ lb:

Total for the period 74½ lb.

There is one footnote to be added to this story. It is that at some point in the 1970s it became illegal to catch fish with a gill net, not only in the UK but also throughout the European Community. Fisheries Protection vessels patrolled the coasts of the mainland and the Hebrides confiscating and destroying nets. It seems likely that the local boat knew perfectly well that the minister of Jura was netting his own bay, but deliberately left me alone for fear of causing embarrassment to the island's church members. I was not really aware that this was the legal position, but I doubt if I would have stopped netting anyway, as I was certainly having too much fun.

The Peat Bank

It was my first spring in Jura, and on a Saturday in March Sandy Buie of Knockrome unexpectedly arrived at the manse back door. He had been down in the village on his tractor and was on his way home. I invited him in and asked him how I could help.

'Well, Mr Youngson,' he said, 'it's the first of April on Monday, and the first of April is the day on Jura when we start cutting the peats.'

'Oh, indeed' I said, to keep things going.

'The minister of Jura has always cut his own peats on the island.'

I could see immediately which way the wind was blowing, and I had no intention of becoming involved in the business of peat cutting, so I began to mount my defence.

'That's interesting, Mr Buie, but I understand that a peat bank is required before one can cut any peats.'

'Indeed! A peat bank has been arranged' came the reply.

I was not finished yet though.

'Is it not necessary to be equipped with a variety of peat cutting tools, which I of course don't have?' I asked.

'The tools will be provided' came the reply.

I gave it one last attempt. 'That's all very interesting,' I said, 'But I wouldn't have the foggiest idea how to go about cutting peats.'

'No! But you will be instructed' said Sandy Buie, thus putting an end to the matter.

I arranged to be up at the peat fields on the Monday morning at seven o'clock sharp, for my first lesson. The peat bank which had been arranged was in fact part of Sandy Buie's own bank, and situated above Knockrome village in an area of moorland later to become well known as Cul a Bhaile – 'the back of the township'. There on the Monday morning I had my first lesson. I found out that there were in fact three tools. There was a huge spade with a great triangular shaped blade and a broad horizontal handle. This was intended for splitting the surface of the turf and was employed with a vertical up and down movement, making cuts through the turf.

After the vertical cuts had been put in you moved on to 'stripping the bank'. In this operation you used your second spade. The crescent shaped blade had been ground to a razor sharp edge. The long, square-sectioned shaft had a broad T-shaped handle. You took your stance down on the lower surface from which the old peats had already been removed, and you presented the tip of the stripper to the face of the bank. The tip of the spade had to be positioned just five inches below the top surface of the turf. With the tip of the blade in the proper position you thrust it forward on a horizontal path into the bank. You kept it lined up with your hands, but the impulsion came from the front of the thigh above your leading leg. I remember well when I applied my spade in this position for the first time, and thrust forward. The blade went in about an inch and stopped dead. I looked helplessly up at Sandy.

'Och! You've hit a root', he said; 'Here, let me do it.'

The old man took the spade and thrust it forward, and it went in like a knife into butter. I took the spade back and tried again with the same lack of result.

'Another root!', said Sandy. But I'm afraid it wasn't a root at all. It was the fact that I wasn't strong enough to push the spade in. Sandy had been doing this for years and had muscles like steel. I persisted, and finally managed to force the spade in as far as the first downward line. When the turf was loose you put down the spade and lifted the turf and laid it down neatly on the bank behind your feet. You had to make up the moor, and leave it the way you found it. It was no good leaving it a mess. The grass had to start to grow again, and cattle could get their feet caught and trip themselves up if you didn't do it right.

'In the old days the Factor came to inspect the bank after you were finished, and if it wasn't tidy he would fine you,' Sandy told me.

Once the turves had been taken off I now had an area of freshly exposed peat ready for the actual cutting. The actual cutter, with its horn handle, was thrust down into the peat and cut two sides of a square. If properly employed it could be twisted back a little at the end of each stroke and the newly cut peat would come up on to the top of the bank, stuck to the face of the cutter. This was the theory, but in practice the new peat fell off the spade and landed on the bottom of the bank, where it would often break and have to be picked up and put on the top of the bank by hand.

The newly cut peats were laid out on the uncut moor beside the cutting, in neat parallel lines. If they weren't laid neatly there wouldn't be room for them. If the weather was fine and dry they would be ready for 'lifting' within a week or ten days. If it was wet, it could take much longer. The tradition on Jura about the way you lifted the peats was for 'cnocan' – the same name as with hay – pronounced krochkan, and meaning 'little hills'. These were made by standing four peats on end leaning in towards each other. Four more were stood leaning against the first four in the gaps between. On top of this little stack two or more of the short corners were sat to keep the rain off. The bringing in depended very much on the weather. In a dry season you could hope to have the bank clear and the peats home by the beginning of June. In a very wet one they could stay out much longer. The business of getting a tractor to the bank could be tricky, and many a tractor got bogged down getting the peats home.

I persisted practising my technique and I came to enjoy my peat cutting. There was simply nothing like working up on the bank in the spring sunshine with the magnificent view of the Sound of Jura and Skervuile Lighthouse and the hills of Knapdale beyond. Fine stags might be grazing nearby and there was even an occasional visiting eagle. Sandy Buie always got his peats cut far quicker than I did.

This was not just a matter of years of practice, but from the fact that he kept at it steadily for hours at a time.

One morning we were cutting on our respective banks. It would have been about my third season, and I saw him coming across for a look as he had done many times before. He stood a while and then spoke:

'Aye', he said, 'You're coming on!'

That was praise indeed, but the high spot came some seasons later.

I was working on the bank and noticed Sandy put down his spade and straighten up and begin to walk across the intervening hundred yards or so. He arrived, but did not speak. He got his pipe going. I asked if there was anything I could do for him.

'No,' he said, 'I just felt like a crack!'

I was suddenly too full to speak. The idea that this wonderful old highland gentleman, with all his wisdom and experience, should be happy enough to come to see me just for a crack conferred on me the greatest sense of my human dignity and stature that I could ever remember. I don't suppose I ever managed to tell him, and he's long dead now, but still when I think of him it is for that moment above all others that I give thanks.

Family Affairs

Once life had settled down in Jura we could see everyone's role taking shape. Margaret continued to work both in Islay and Jura, and of course was also my partner in counselling.

Lyn and Donald started school at Small Isles Primary. Lyn went on to Bowmore High School in 1978, and into digs during the week. Donald went to the High School in 1981. He had a difficult time there as there was a lot of tension between the pupils of Islay and Jura, and he had the misfortune to come from Jura. When he reached sixteen, he announced that he was not going to stay on at school, and he left and went off to the Fishing Course at Lewes Castle in Lewis, and in due course to an apprenticeship on a fishing vessel in Stornoway. None of this was any surprise to us as Donald had been fascinated by fishing boats ever since we went to Jura, and was forever down at the village pier watching what was going on. Lyn had shown a great facility for drawing and painting from an early age, and again it came as no surprise when she went in for Art. In 1983 she left school and went off to Dundee to Duncan of Jordanstone College of Art, where she lived in student accommodation.

The Presbytery

The Presbytery of South Argyll held its meetings in Tarbert Parish Church on the first Wednesday of the month. The Presbytery meeting took place in the evening, which meant for me an overnight stay in Tarbert eight times a year. I usually spent the night in the Tarbert Hotel, where I became quite well known.

It was on my first visit to the Presbytery, and consequently my first night at the Tarbert, that an encounter took place which became one of my favourite stories. I had been served my evening meal in the dining room, and afterwards I made my way into the bar. I had been alone at my meal, and there was only one other customer in the bar. He was an elderly man perched on a bar stool, and wearing the kind of thick knitted blue sweater I associated with the fishing boat fraternity.

The barman knew who I was and greeted me warmly. He asked me what I would have. I said that I was going to have to get to know something about whisky now that I had come to the islands, and asked him which of the famous local whiskies he would recommend.

'Oh, in that case, I would suggest your very first Laphroaig, Sir,' he said.

The man along the bar turned towards me, smiled, and spoke:

'And you'll be from the tropics, Sir?' he asked.

It was a strange question, and I looked towards the barman, uncertain if I should be taking him seriously. The barman was smiling, and nodded a kind of reassurance. It was evidently safe to go on with the conversation.

'No!' I replied. 'Not from the tropics.'

'Not from the tropics! Then how is that you are having the malaria?'

Another smile from the barman, encouraged me.

'No. I don't suffer from malaria, either,' I said.

'Not from the tropics, and not having the malaria. Then, sir, How is it that you are having to take your quinine?'

I was puzzled, but the barman pushed the glass towards me.

'Now you are ready for your drink, Sir,' he said.

I lifted the glass and tasted the Laphroaig, and as I swallowed it I got the sudden sharp medicinal aftertaste, not unlike TCP; this was the 'quinine'. I immediately realised that I had been the victim of a beautifully crafted set up, which I could now enjoy. The gentleman had his proper reward, as I asked him:

'Thank you, Sir. What will you have?'

He had a whisky. It was my first encounter with the most famous of the many Islay Malts. I gradually acquired a working knowledge of most of them. It was a very pleasant learning curve.

Church Work in Islay

There was plainly no reason why the minister of Jura should not help with vacancies in Islay. I was Interim Moderator twice in Port Charlotte between 1975 and 1980. These roles were always hard to manage from my base on Jura because of the problems with ferries and bad weather. There were more funerals in Islay than I had in Jura, and these required a crossing to Islay. I encountered some of Islay's curious superstitions in connection with some of these. One funeral service I conducted in the church in Port Charlotte was going to the nearby ancient cemetery of Octomore. Imagine my amazement when the cortège emerged from the church and turned the opposite direction from the nearby cemetery. We drove many miles through remote country roads to arrive at the graveyard from the opposite direction. The short and direct route was debarred for the cortège because that was the road that had been used in bringing the deceased's body to the church, and it could not be travelled again.

There was a well-known family who had lived at a lonely croft house in the middle of the moor. The croft was called Moine Mhor. There had been several brothers and sisters living together. They had apparently all been hard working and responsible in their youth, but one had brought strong drink into the house and they had all succumbed to alcoholism, one after the other. The family's burial plot was at the remote and beautiful graveyard of Ardnave, and at the committal of one of the brothers who had died during the time of the minister who had been Interim Moderator for Jura when I arrived, an altercation took place over the distribution of the cords on the coffin. Shouting occurred and blows were exchanged, and the minister's hat was knocked off and fell into the open grave to land on top of the coffin. All this I was told by a trusted old friend in Bowmore, who did his best to warn me of what might take place when I was asked to conduct another funeral for this family.

I think the man whose funeral I was being asked to conduct would have been the third last of the family, leaving only one elderly man and one old woman. The Islay undertaker took me out along the moorland road, and stopped short of the near derelict croft.

'If you're going to say a few words, you'd best say them out here, Mr Youngson. You can't possibly be going inside.'

I replied that I had had some interesting ministries before coming to Jura and I certainly wasn't going to be stopped going anywhere on Islay, and I made my way to the house and went in. It was in a poor state, but I had seen worse in Glasgow. The surviving family members were sunk in dejection and had evidently taken whisky. I said a short service and we went off to Ardnave. It seemed as if the remaining family members would have liked to have created some kind of brawl as in the old days, but they were much too weakened and enfeebled with age. The committal passed without anything untoward taking place. It was a sad event for more reasons than one.

Old Kilchoman Manse

While I was Interim Moderator at Port Charlotte I had a call from a family who had come from England and set up a business. They had bought a fine old house beside the ancient church and graveyard of Kilchoman, on the remote north-west coast of the island. It was in this cemetery that the great Kilchoman Cross stood. The church was in ruins. The house turned out to be the former manse of Kilchoman church, which had been sold by the Church of Scotland when they acquired the new manse in Port Charlotte. The family were experiencing some kind of distress connected with the house, and were most anxious for me to visit the place to give advice. I was perfectly happy to go.

I arrived during the day and both husband and wife made me most welcome. The three children were at school. The story was a strange one. They spoke of the presence of someone or something in the house. This presence manifested itself during the hours of darkness, usually late in the evening, or in the middle of the night. Nothing had actually been seen or heard, so I wanted to know what it was that betrayed this presence. The couple told me that they would wake up and suddenly experience a feeling of deep sadness. The feeling could be so intense that they would simply hang on to each other, and one or both of them would find themselves sobbing uncontrollably for some minutes. Then the feelings would pass and they would be able to rest and sleep. The children had started coming to their parents bedroom late at night, and they expressed in their own way a quite identical set of feelings. They would be very upset and reluctant to go back to their own rooms. The family felt that the house had experienced some kind of great disaster or sad happening, and they were quite clear that if this misery could not be dealt with, they would be unable to stay.

My own first concern was to try to make sure that I wasn't the victim of some kind of hoax, although I felt that the couple were pretty transparent, and that their concern seemed quite genuine. I also couldn't see how my involvement could be turned to their advantage in any way. They told me that they had asked the solicitors who had handled the sale of the property if there were any stories associated with it, but had been met with a complete stone wall.

I went to see my old friend in Bowmore. He was reluctant to speak about the house. It was clear to me that there was much he could tell me if he decided to do so, and he asked time to think it over. Finally he appeared to make up his mind and began to tell the story. The house had a sad history. It had been sold by the kirk as long ago as the 1920s. The last minister before it was sold was a serving Chaplain in the First World War, and had seen action on the Somme. He had served throughout the war and returned to his parish in Islay. He was known to have suffered from bouts of depression. One summer day he encouraged his wife to take the children out into the garden, and while they were playing on the lawn they heard a shot. The minister had put a shotgun inside his mouth, and had blown his brains out. There was blood apparently on the high ceiling above his head. The wife and children left Islay and the manse was sold. The shotgun went into auction and was sold and was now in the possession of an elder in Portnahaven church. The house had changed hands very many times during the ensuing fifty years, although for obvious reasons everyone involved tried hard to conceal what had caused it to be sold and re-sold so frequently. Many stories had circulated in the island, all amounting to more or less the same thing. People had been unable to settle in this house because something about it made them feel profoundly unhappy. My family were by no means the first, but only the latest in a long line. I met the Portnahaven elder, and he confirmed the whole story.

I telephoned to say that I had some news, and I planned to come across to Islay and spend the night in the house as their guest. They were immediately agreeable, and we arranged for my visit. I suggested that they should arrange for a friend to take charge of the children for that night, and that was agreed. On the appointed day I was entertained to supper. My hosts were suitably impressed with my research, and we chatted at length about it all. I told them that I proposed to occupy their spare room, and keep some kind of vigil throughout the hours of darkness. If there were any manifestations such as they had described I would perform my 'office' in an act of prayer and exorcism, and involve them if it seemed appropriate. I went to my guest room at about ten thirty and changed into pyjamas and dressing gown. After about an hour I became drowsy, and lay down. Having been asleep for a time, I found I was suddenly wide awake, and very cold, and I felt an almost irresistible desire to make a loud noise. The sound I wanted to express was a deep howling, and the emotion behind it was one of utter black despair. I rose and took my bible and went along the passage to my hosts' bedroom. I found them seated on their bed, in tears, and it was evident to me that they were undergoing an experience similar to my own.

I had written what I thought would be a suitable prayer, and I had the passage from Matthew chapter 16, verses 18 and 19 ready to read. This is the age old passage about the 'keys of the kingdom', and about 'binding and loosing'. I had been taught that if the problem concerned some kind of entity which for some reason had become attached to a place inappropriately, and for some reason could not go away, a command that it be loosed from that place and go to its own proper place, wherever that might be, could be issued in the name of God the Father, the Son and the Holy Spirit. This command would have sufficient authority to break the bad connection.

I still have a copy of the words I used there on that occasion:

'In the powerful presence of God I address you ... You who are not. You are not of us and have no part with us here. You have lingered long in this place but you have no business here, and our God will not permit you to remain. It is his plan that there is a proper place for you: and to that place you must go.

In the strong name of the Trinity – Father, Son and Holy Spirit – I command you to be loosed from this place: and to go now to your own place, there to be obedient to the Father's disposal.'

As I started saying this passage there was a feeling of great protest and resistance, but once I had finished I had a strong sense of a significant change in the atmosphere, and it seemed appropriate to suggest to the family that we might all now go back to bed. I slept well for the rest of the night, and my host and hostess told me that they had done so as well. I left after breakfast.

I later had a good letter from them, saying that there had been no further bad experiences, and enclosing a gift of money, which I put into the church funds. About a year later the house changed hands. Strangely, the folk who bought it became active members of the church at Port Charlotte, and my good friends, and I was later invited to stay overnight at their new house.

I slept in the same room I had occupied earlier, and had no bad experiences. The new family in due course learned of the history of the house, but it apparently no longer had an occupant – sad, or otherwise. The episode seemed to be closed.

Rowing the Sound

Before I leave the topic of my Interim Moderatorships, I want to mention the problems they caused me in getting to and from Islay. Quite a number of meetings which required my presence took place on Sundays, and there was no Jura ferry which could get me to Port Charlotte in time for worship. Archie Campbell, the ferry pilot at Port Askaig, was happy to help, and we established a successful procedure for any Sunday when I simply had to get there. I would drive down to Feolin Ferry. Archie would come across in his Longliner, and take me to Port Askaig, where a car would be waiting to take me over to Port Charlotte. On an important Sunday during the vacancy which led to the new minister's appointment, I got to the jetty as usual, and Archie was already there. When I was settled in the boat he began to pull the starter on the big outboard motor, but it didn't fire. It had become flooded. I got out and went a short walk so that he could express himself freely at the motor, but nothing was of any use.

'Well, Peter,' said Archie, 'We have the two choices. You can either abandon all plans to cross today, or we can row the Sound together.'

In view of the importance of the service I really wanted to get across, but I hadn't thought of rowing.

'Can we really do that?' I asked Archie.

'Oh, it's a fine quiet day with hardly any wind, and its just about slack water as far as the tide is concerned. It won't take us long.'

I got in, and we took one long oar each. It was perfectly straightforward, and we made good time. I think we would have made the crossing in about fifteen minutes.

Now in the Pier House at that time lived Neil MacMillan and his wife Morag. They were committed Christians, and Neil was an elder in the local congregation. Neil and Morag had become good friends of mine over the years, and many was the cup of tea I had had in the Pier House while waiting for the ferry to cross on a bad day.

Neil was standing at his front room window and watching what was going on.

'Come and see this, Morag! Now isn't that a terrible thing. The minister of Jura having to row across the Sound to come to help us with the kirk in Islay.'

Morag answered her husband at once:

'Don't you go wasting any sympathy on Mr Youngson, Neil. Mr Youngson will be having the time of his life. He'll be getting a children's address out of this. He'll be getting a sermon point out of it, and he'll be telling his grandchildren for ever about the Sunday he rowed across the

Sound of Islay to get to the kirk. Don't you waste any sympathy on Mr Youngson at all.'

It was Neil himself who recounted this story to me later, and said to me:

'I dare say Morag would be right enough. She is a wise woman, is Morag.'

She certainly was that, and, as it happens, she was correct in every detail.

The Grey Lady

Tarbert, where Presbytery met, was linked with the old parish of Kilberry. Kilberry House, in the parish, was the home of Marion Campbell. She was an interesting person, and a keen amateur archaeologist who had done fieldwork in Jura, and whose records of sites were often the basis for later excavations by the Royal Commission on Ancient Monuments. I was often asked to her house, and spent several nights there. She lived with a lovely and gentle companion of many long years called Mary Sandeman. She was the daughter of Dr Sandeman, the GP for many years in Jura.

It was through my contacts with Marion Campbell that I heard of the Grey Lady of Kilberry House. She was an apparition who was apparently frequently seen. She was supposed to be the shade of a former laird's wife of the 17th century. The story went that the young laird had gone to Edinburgh in search of a wife, and brought his bonnie young bride back to Kilberry. There she found that he had been previously married, and had had six children by his first wife, who had died in childbirth. His new bride inherited the house and estate and the family, and in due time died young, worn out by her tasks. She would now be seen wearing a grey dress and often carrying a duster. An overnight guest apparently said at breakfast: 'I didn't know you had a housemaid in the place? My, but she's a real treasure that one. She was standing at the foot of my bed when I woke up.'

There was of course no housemaid. Mary Sandeman told me of the encounter she had recently had with the Lady.

'We had been in Glasgow,' she said, 'and we decided to invest in a proper modern vacuum cleaner. You know? With all the attachments. We had brought it home, and I was trying it out on the long stair carpet when I felt somebody watching me. I looked round, and there she was. She was standing with one arm round her chest holding the other elbow. The other hand was up along her cheek with a finger beside her eyes. She had her head tilted to one side. I knew exactly what she was thinking. She was thinking: 'My goodness! I could have done with something like that!'

The American Connection

It is sometimes hard to recognise important turning points at the moment they are happening. It was so on the day in 1982 when I went to answer the manse doorbell. I opened the door and found myself confronted by a man and a woman who were perfect caricatures of American tourists. The man wore a stetson and had several cameras hung round his neck. His wife had blue rinsed hair and sun glasses with projecting 'wings'.

The man spoke:

'Are you the minister?' he said.

I replied that I was.

'Thank God,' he said, 'we want you to tell us who we are!'

I was so startled that I think I made a foolish reply like:

'Oh! I'm sorry, don't you know who you are?'

I invited the couple in, and they told me their story. They explained that since Alex Haley's novel *Roots* had appeared on television in the USA in 1978, there had been a growth in interest among citizens who wanted to trace their ancestry. The gentleman now in my manse was called Buie, and had established by research in the States that he was descended from people who had originally emigrated to North Carolina from the island of Jura. I knew a little about this movement from Donald Budge's book, which told about the movement of Jura people to North Carolina in the 18th century. I said that I was delighted to meet my visitors and asked how I could help. They wanted to know if they could look at my early church records in the hope of finding information about their ancestors. It emerged that the records they wanted to see were from a couple of hundred years earlier. I explained that although I did have some modern records, the old records such as they were seeking were all lodged in Edinburgh.

'In Edinboro'! My gosh, we just bin to Edinboro'!'

I felt I was not being much help, but they asked if there was anyone living on the island of Jura who bore the name of Buie. I replied that there were two such families, and asked if they would like to meet them. They were overjoyed. Dougie Buie turned out to be off the island on that day, but I phoned Knockrome and spoke to Sandy Buie. I explained the situation briefly and asked if I could bring the visitors up to meet him. He was quite accommodating, so I asked them to follow me in their hired car and drove up to Knockrome. Sandy came out to the doorstep when he heard the cars, and took a few steps forward. My American couple got out of their car and Mr Buie moved forward to Sandy. When he reached him, he enveloped him in what I can only call a bear hug, and exclaimed:

'Well, Hi! Cousin!'

Sandy was no doubt a little confused, but never less than a perfect gentleman, he took them into his house and introduced them to Nan. They took a number of photographs and in due course left for the ferry. After they had gone Sandy came to me:

'Well now, Minister,' he said, 'what on earth was all that about?'

In the course of the next months I had several similar visits from people concerned about their ancestry. I felt somewhat inadequate, since I certainly couldn't advance their researches in any way.

I began to make regular trips to Edinburgh, where I sat in the Records Office and copied out the Statutory Registers of Births, Marriages and Deaths, together with the 19th century Census records. I typed up all these handwritten copies and lodged them in the front room in the manse so that they could be consulted by anyone trying to trace their ancestry. This was a successful approach, and resulted in many satisfied visitors. I also became involved in the story, and in other aspects of the population of the island during the 1800s, about which I had previously known very little. Word of the support I had provided was carried back to North Carolina, so that a number of later visitors arrived with more information, and sometimes knowing in advance that I could help them.

Tom Shaw, a teacher from Fayetteville, brought a party of friends and relatives. He had good records showing an ancestor who had lived at

Cnocbreac, a ruined township beyond Inver, and Donald Darroch took his group in to visit the ruins. His family had treasured as heirlooms letters from one Duncan Shaw of Jura. He turned out to be Dunacha Sha of Ardfernal, who had lived into the 20th century and was remembered by old residents like Katie Darroch. The letters proved invaluable in establishing bridges between the North Carolina descendants and the original emigrants. Other visitors continued to arrive. The American dimension had become part of our life.

Invitation to North Carolina

In 1985 Tom Shaw suggested that we might visit the USA. The idea would be that the present minister of Jura would visit the churches where many of the descendants of the first emigrants worshipped, and preach in their pulpits. I would also give talks, and show slides about the island of Jura in the past and present, to groups of people with an interest in their Scottish ancestry. I already knew a good deal about the area known as The Valley of the Scots, near Fayetteville in North Carolina, and we had read a lot about how the early colonists had moved up the Cape Fear River and settled the sandy country there. There was even a town called Buie's Creek. We were worried about the cost, as we had always had very little spare cash, but Tom Shaw assured us that there would be plenty of money coming from pulpit supply fees and payments for lectures and talks. In any case, we would be given hospitality everywhere and wouldn't be laying out cash on hotels and food. It seemed as though four weeks might be long enough to cover the needs of North Carolina. However, some of our contacts had come from a second wave of emigrants who had moved south and west. Don Macdougald was in this group and he undertook to arrange a second month centred around the south-east coast of Georgia. We thought that if we worked hard for two months we could justify a third month of holiday, and we decided to drive right across to the Pacific Coast in a rented car, and fly home from California. That would let us continue to follow the emigrants' trail as far as the Buies of Texas, and go on to visit with family members in Los Angeles.

We Go to the United States

We decided to undertake this adventure in 1986 and get leave of absence from Presbytery for April, May and June. We put in a lot of work on planning and preparation and finally took off from Heathrow to Baltimore on 31st March. Margaret kept a detailed diary of the next three months, which I have transcribed and of which copies exist amongst my records. We also have many slides and photos, and since our return I have given talks about the trip to a variety of groups in various parts of Scotland.

We also have to bear in mind that we were able to return to the USA on three further occasions, in 1989, 1992 and 2002, so our memories of the places and the people have been reinforced by these later visits. We still think fondly of our many friends in the USA, although we think it is now unlikely that we will ever go back again.

Writing about Jura

On my arrival in Jura I had researched the date of the Bicentenary of the church, and I had written a little souvenir book for that occasion. I came to feel that there was a need for something else which would be useful to visitors and I wrote a Motorist's Guide to the island. This little book ran to only forty-eight pages and followed the road from Feolin Ferry to Kinuachdrach. I decided to entitle it The Long Road, and I tried to pack on to the pages all I had learned about the people and places the road passed, and deal with twenty numbered places all the way up to the north end. Small addenda dealt with the little spur roads to Keils, Knockrome and Ardfernal, and Inverlussa. I added a collection of twenty-one stories of Jura. Some of these had been published already, and the rest I collected myself. The book proved very popular indeed. My original copy comes from about 1982. The book has seen a number of new editions and is still going strong. I no longer expect to take any share of the small profits, but retain the copyright. The main changes over the years are that the last miles from Lealt to Kinuachdrach are now blocked by a padlocked chain, and have to be walked, and that the famous Crossman bridge over the Lussa has been replaced.

During the years when I was recording the archives for the use of American researchers I became aware that there was much more that could be done. A notable minister of Jura in the 1960s had been Rev. Donald Budge of Skye. He had written and published his own account of Jura.

His book was a fascinating source of scholarship about the island, but it was becoming very dated, and it very much reflected his own interests. John Mercer was a palaeontologist and writer who had also written about the island. His book also had strengths, but was limited by its need to deal with Gigha and Colonsay as well. Before his tragic death he was enthusiastic that I might write about Jura, and encouraged me to make use of his work. I began to think of re-writing 'Budge', and got encouragement to do so from both Mr and Mrs Budge, while they were alive.

I spent a good deal of time working with the extraordinary archive called The Campbell of Jura Papers, and I began to accumulate a considerable amount of material. It was as if my many interests were bringing records and resources together for a substantial book about Jura, and I began to think seriously about writing it. I discussed the possibility with Hugh Andrew, the Director of Birlinn, the Edinburgh publisher, who was very positive and enthusiastic. When I came to leave Jura in 1987, I took every scrap of research material with me. I was determined that away from the island itself, I would find time to write the definitive book about Jura, and I fully expected to devote myself to the task during the first year or two after I moved away. It would be more than ten years before I would actually start. It was perhaps as well that I did not know that at the time.

The incumbent of Jura before Donald Budge had been one Donald John Robertson. He had been the minister for forty-four years, and had died in 1947. During the 1980s an American student made contact with me from the States. He had been researching Jura and had found that there appeared to be some original writings by a Rev. Robertson lodged in the National Library of Scotland. When next in Edinburgh I followed this lead, and found to my great excitement two exercise books full of stories of Jura in Gaelic and English, which had evidently never seen the light of day. Although the author had been a minister in Jura, and was called Robertson, he was not my Donald John Robertson but one Charles Moncrieff Robertson, who had been the minister of the United Free Kirk from 1908 to 1914. Old residents remembered him well. The Church of Scotland minister had been a short man, but Charles Robertson was well over six feet tall. The two men were known on the island as 'Robertson beag' and 'Robertson fada' or Wee Robertson and Long Robertson. Robertson fada turned out to have been a notable Gaelic scholar and collected folklore wherever his appointments took him. Some of his stories I knew already, but many were quite new to me. I wrote a little book about him and set out many of the tales, with responsible English translations prepared by my colleague Rev. Roddy McLeod of Cumlodden. I left Jura before this work could be published, but I am proud to say I was able to get it in print shortly afterwards. "Ancient Hebridean Tales of Jura" was attractively illustrated by my daughter Lyn, and has sold steadily in the more than fifteen years since it was published. It has evidently filled a need for many readers.

The End of It All

The end came quickly, and was prompted by only one thing. This was the state of health of my mother and father in Perth. Since about 1983 there had been occasional small emergencies which seemed to require my urgent presence. It was not at all easy to get from Jura to Perth in a hurry, and my parents were plainly not coping without support. In July 1986 my mother had her eightieth birthday, and was in generally very poor health. She was up out of bed less, and becoming less alert. In September of that year, my father was eighty-two, and appeared really very fit, although he was subject to an increasing number of angina attacks, and had decided that he should no longer continue to drive his car. It was plainly out of the question to think that they should both come to live in Jura. It began to seem to us both that the only course of action left was to look for a parish somewhere within a reasonable distance of Perth, so that we could offer reasonable support and a measure of actual presence and help.

In 1987 I began to look for another parish. It immediately became clear that great city churches were looking for ministers no older than their mid-forties. I applied to several, but was considered too old.

It was plainly not going to be so easy to find a suitable charge. Kirriemuir, St Andrew's was advertised, and I applied. A colleague minister in mainland Argyll had been in Kirriemuir, and said that he had been very happy there and wished that he had never left. It seemed strange that although I had been born and brought up in Aberdeen, I had hardly ever heard of Kirriemuir, and certainly had never visited it.

I knew that J.M. Barrie had come from Kirriemuir, but that was about all. I discovered that Kirriemuir was a small town in the county of Angus. It lay near Forfar, well inland from Arbroath, and north of Dundee. The vacant church had a large congregation, and its manse stood immediately opposite the church. There were two churches in the town. The previous minister had been more than twenty years in the charge. Kirriemuir seemed to be about the right distance from Perth and my parents.

I applied to Kirriemuir, and it was arranged that I should go to Forfar and preach for the Vacancy Committee in St Margaret's Parish Church on Sunday, 27th September. The conduct of worship seemed to go well, and the interview with the committee was a very relaxed and happy one. On 6th October 1987 I received a letter from the Clerk of the Vacancy Committee asking me to become sole nominee for the vacancy.

I accepted the invitation and went to preach in St Andrew's, Kirriemuir, on Sunday, 15th November 1987, to a big congregation. The vote was in favour, and a date was set for my induction on 14th January 1988.

Farewell to Jura

We had told the Kirk Session of Jura in the late summer that I had decided to look for a charge on the mainland and that we would be leaving the island as and when a suitable call was offered us and closed with. The news went round the island, and great interest was shown in every stage of our proposed move.

We also made it very clear that there was only one reason why we should move, and that we didn't want to. That reason was the problem of giving support to my parents. The culture of Jura was intensely centred on the family, and while other reasons for leaving might have inspired confusion or hostility this, which was our true reason, was completely accepted. While people expressed their deeply felt regret that we were leaving after what had been a very interesting twelve years, no one in any way held it against us that we were going, or felt that we were letting the island down.

A Farewell Social was held for us in the Jura Hotel on Tuesday, 29th December, when presentations were made and speeches were given. I have the text of my speech on that occasion also.

I preached my Farewell Sermon in the pulpit of Jura Kirk on Sunday 3rd January 1988, and we left Jura on Wednesday 6th January for Kirriemuir.

Chapter Nine: A Strangely Familiar Country – Kirriemuir

We arrived in Kirriemuir at the beginning of January 1988. Our first impression was that we liked the friendly appearance of the red sandstone used in most of the older buildings. We had been apprehensive about leaving the beautiful isolation of Jura, but were soon comforted by the wild country of the Angus Glens which was within easy reach. We had anticipated that we would miss the sea, and it did indeed turn out to be so, but we found we could get to fine sandy beaches at Arbroath, Lunan Bay and Montrose in about forty minutes, which wasn't too bad.

It turned out that the manse was in the midst of a small area in the southern part of the town, much associated with the past history of its churches. My own church – St Andrew's, standing on the other side of the road from the house – had been built in 1903, when it was the Free Kirk, and was the survivor of a complicated site. Nearby stood the cottage called Window at Thrums. This had long connections with J.M. Barrie, and his later residence on the nearby street corner. I soon developed the habit of taking visitors and visiting parties of children to stand at the entrance to Manse Lane, and giving a short talk about the buildings which could be seen from that stance, with suitable historical references.

The Moderator of Angus Presbytery in 1988 shared the induction service with Robert Ramsay, who preached the sermon. Robert later became a good friend. The tea and social was held in the Church Hall.

Worship

My memory of my first Sunday in St Andrew's is clear. As I went into the church building the cold air hit me like a slap in the face. I would later learn that St Andrew's had a nickname. It was called The Cauld Kirk o' Kirrie. The heating system was archaic, and depended on free-standing radiators just like the ones I remember from the classrooms in Gordon's College. They were installed when the church was built at the beginning of the century. The boiler was antiquated and almost continually breaking down. The system was so inefficient that the heating had to be put on several days before the week-end in the hope of getting the church warm enough for Sunday worship. It never was. After a year or two we ripped it all out and replaced it with a very fine system with overhead radiant heaters and heated tubes beneath the pews. The church was no longer hostile or uncomfortable.

The early congregation probably amounted to about sixty or seventy attenders, so there were about a thousand absentees, if you based attendance on the number of names on the roll. I had thought that mere curiosity would bring them out on that first Sunday in January, but there was no sign of that. The number of people attending the morning service at St Andrew's grew steadily during the first months of 1988. I liked to tell myself that it may have had something to do with the word getting round that the worship was lively and interesting, but it was more likely due to the rise of temperature in the church as the weather got warmer. By the time Easter came we were seeing about a hundred and twenty-five folk in the kirk on a Sunday morning.

I stuck with the kind of service I was used to, and quickly fell into my favourite Sunday technique of preaching a series of sermons on a connected theme from week to week. This seemed quite popular in Kirriemuir, but revealed a situation I had never encountered before. I began to be aware that I was seeing a different group of people in church every Sunday. One day a departing family commented on how much they had enjoyed the sermon. They said:

'It's such a pity that we'll miss next week's one, but it isn't our Sunday for coming.'

They belonged to the people who worshipped very regularly, but fortnightly. It seemed that there were people who wanted to support the church but did not want to appear to be overly religious, so didn't want to go every single week. They came every other week, and since they were perfectly content with this arrangement, there seemed nothing to be done about it.

Old Favourites

I fell back on many old favourites in Kirriemuir. I held services throughout Holy Week, with 'hand washing' at an informal communion on the Thursday, and special Good Friday worship, led by the choir. I revisited an old high spot when the children of Southmuir Primary came to church for their Easter end-of-term service in 1989, and I managed to arrange for a live donkey, as many years before in Lochwood. Seven children were dressed up as disciples, and a young lad was able to ride round the church as Jesus, to the great delight of the school. There were lively stories, enthusiastic singing, and the school band. A memorable event!

Christmas at the church was traditional, with a Children's Gift Service on the Sunday before, which resulted in great sacks of toys being taken in to a charity distribution point in Dundee. I introduced a Watchnight Service which was immediately very well attended and remained so throughout my time. The local pubs were very responsible and didn't turn out their drunks, and we never had any trouble during this service, which became a happy time for me.

I formed a Youth Fellowship of a traditional pattern, which met every Sunday evening in the manse. It was a great success in the early years, and one summer I took its members on a retreat to the Island of Jura, which everyone enjoyed. I set up a weekly vestry hour in the church, and this was well used. I started a weekly bible study and prayer group on a Wednesday evening.

Healing Services

Once we were back in a normal mainland church setting, it seemed reasonable to resume our interest in healing through laying on of hands.

This had been an important part of my ministry in Glenrothes, and one of the few areas in which Margaret and I could work together in the church. In the summer of 1988 I announced that such services would take place on a monthly basis on Sunday evenings.

I think there were between twenty and thirty people at the first Healing Service in Kirriemuir, and that we laid hands on about half a dozen folk. The services ran monthly, apart from the summer. We held seventy-nine such services until the end of 1996. The attendances never got larger than about thirty-five people, and we were never required to lay hands on more than could be fitted into a reasonable length of service. A small number of other members took part in laying on of hands. People came from a considerable distance, and several came regularly from Montrose and Arbroath.

Looking back on these services from a distance of more than ten years since they finished, I can recall that they contained many times when I was more confident about what I was doing in the ministry, and about what I believed in, than at any other time during my years as a parish minister.

Funerals

It very soon became apparent to me that I had never so far been in what might be thought of as a typical Church of Scotland parish, as far as bereavement was concerned. I really had very few funerals in any of my previous charges. It was quickly evident that Kirriemuir would be a different experience.

I conducted my first church service in Kirriemuir on Sunday, 17th January, and had my first funeral to take the next day, on Monday the 18th. I had another on the 21st and a third on the 29th. During my first year at St Andrew's I had thirty-two funerals, which was probably more than I had done in the previous fifteen years or so. During my eight years in Kirriemuir I conducted two hundred and forty funerals.

Cremation services for funerals involved a journey to Dundee. I would travel in the front seat of the principal family car, and I normally slid the glass panel behind me to its closed position so that the driver and I could converse in comfort. I got to know a number of regular drivers very well.

One spoke with a broad Angus accent, and on an early funeral, while we were pursuing the hearse down the dual carriageway to Dundee, he said:

'My, Mr Youngson, but Jim's going at a fell awful rate the day!'

I didn't really understand the phrase, but later found that I had just heard the famous Angus adjective 'fell', meaning 'very' – as in 'It's fell cauld', meaning 'It's very cold.'

In this case he meant 'very fast': 'a fell awful rate today.'

I found it exciting to hear the local Angus dialect during my first months. One's ear is sharpened at such time to hear things which are unfamiliar. There were also local sayings which were new to me. It was frequently hard for me to understand what was said to me. One day I was driving to Forfar and saw a young man hitching a lift on the main road. I slowed down and opened the window.

The hitchhiker spoke to me:

'Are ye far far far?' he said. (This meant: 'Are you for Forfar?')

I told him to get in and took him to Forfar, but I took a long time to work out that he had been asking me if that was where I was going.

One day in late January I was raking up rubbish at the front of the garden near Glamis Road. There had been a heavy snowfall, but most of it had melted in the previous days. A passer-by stopped to chat on the pavement. We both noticed a thin line of unmelted snow lying close to the wall.

'Aye!', he said: 'Waitin' for mair'.

This was completely new to me, although I was brought up not far to the north in Aberdeen. The idea that the last lingering line of snow was 'waiting for more' was a sheer delight.

Back to Making Music

During my years in Jura the thing I had missed most was making music – both my solo singing and working with a good choir. I knew that Kirriemuir would not be considered a cultural centre for classical music, but I was determined to do what I could.

The first problem I had was with the old pipe organ. The organ console occupied a dominant place in the middle of the chancel. It was very hard to work around, and after something of a fight I was able to have the console moved out of the centre of the church and into the left transept, and the action electrified. With the front two pews removed, and some blue carpet, the front of the church was transformed, and would clearly be most suitable for musical performances.

Immediately I arrived I started to recruit a church choir to sing in four part harmony, and with an evening practice once a week it made rapid progress. It led the praise every Sunday and began to produce fine oratorios for special occasions. For these we were able to borrow keen singers from our neighbouring church. During the years up to 1996 the St Andrew's choir gave performances of *Amahl and the Night Visitors*; Handel's *Messiah*; Bach's *St Matthew Passion*; Stainer's *Crucifixion*; parts of the *Requiems* of Brahms and Verdi; and many other notable works.

St Andrew's choir gave me more satisfaction than any group of musicians I had ever worked with and I will always be grateful to the members for their loyalty to me, and for their considerable musical achievement.

I myself found opportunities for resuming my career as a solo bass-baritone singer during these years. I concentrated on German Lieder and gave many performances of Schubert songs. I also sang as a guest soloist in Forfar and Arbroath. To be able to make music again in the company of other fine musicians was one of the high spots in my life in the 1990s.

The Open Door

The Vacancy Committee had heard my concern about 'the open door' and had given assurances, which were accepted in good faith by the Kirk Session, so the church stood open every day. I helped with the routine of this myself as the manse stood directly opposite the church door. I took enormous satisfaction from the fact that you could go into St Andrew's during the day. It is a very beautiful church with a truly peaceful atmosphere. I was particularly moved and impressed by the behaviour of the community in the days following the massacre at Dunblane, when the building was in continual use, and from my vantage point at my study desk I could see small groups of pupils from Webster's High School going into their church to spend a short quiet time together.

Family Matters

Our daughter Lyn and our son Donald had left home while we were still in Jura, and neither of them ever lived with us in Kirriemuir. Lyn graduated from Duncan of Jordanstone in 1987 and on 7th May 1994 I had the joy of conducting her wedding to our son-in-law Richard Ovenden. On 5th June 1995 our first grandchild was born when Lyn gave birth to Caitlin Margaret, and on 29th October 1998 her sister Anna Elizabeth was born. The family now live in Oxford where in 2003 Richard was appointed Keeper of Special Collections and Western Manuscripts in the Bodleian Library, and where he has recently been promoted to Associate Director. I and everyone in the family are very proud of him.

After his training period in Stornoway Donald joined the fishing fleet at Carradale on the Kintyre peninsula in 1986. He and his boat and his crew were closely involved in the tragic sinking of his vessel's sister ship, the *Antares,* by an American submarine, and shortly afterwards he left the fleet. In 1990 he went to work on oil rigs until 1995 when he went to Hong Kong to live, and to work in the bar trade. He is now married to Janicel Goran Busto, from the Philippines, and they have a little boy, Jamie, and a daughter, Hannah, who were born in 2002 and 2005.

My Parents' Deaths

In February 1991 my father had a heart attack and he died on the 16th. My mother was very frail by then, and came to live near us in a nursing home in Forfar. She survived my father by only three months and died of a chest infection on 22nd June. My father was cremated, as had been his wish, but I buried my mother in Kirriemuir cemetery and inscribed my father's name on the stone.

My father's estate was considerable, and my inheritance also included the money produced by the sale of the house in Perth. Suddenly we had enough money to plan for our retirement. My father left me stern advice about how to invest his legacy. Most particularly he said I should not spend it. I am happy to report that we disregarded his instructions, and had a wonderful time spending almost all of it. For the first time in our lives we were able to think about travelling abroad and we did.

Correen – Our Retirement House

By 1993 my mother's and father's estates had been settled, and we were able to think about buying a house for ourselves. After exploring all the options for a place to live in retirement we decided to stay in Kirriemuir. We had come to realise that we probably felt more at home in Kirriemuir than anywhere else we had lived.

In August 1993 our lawyer told us about a bungalow he thought would suit us. We went to see Correen, and liked it at once. We made an offer which was accepted.

By the mid-1990s Margaret had been suffering from arthritis for a number of years, and her knees had become continuously painful and were limiting her movement. We decided to ask permission from the church to give up living in the church manse, and take up residence in Correen, where there are no stairs.

This meant enlarging the bungalow, which we had always known would be too small for us. We added a study, a sun lounge and an en suite shower room. We installed central heating. The existing garden was cleared and a new low maintenance layout established. A qualified personal friend drew up the plans for the conversion. We got planning permission in July 1995. I had decided that with my experience of building and restoration at the manse in Jura, I would do as much of the conversion work as possible myself. By March 1996 the modernisation of Correen was complete. It had taken eight months. We moved in right away, and I continued to use the church vestry as my office.

My Ministry Comes to an End

When I came back from Jura I was surprised to discover that every Presbytery now had a plan for the future of its various churches. In the plan for Angus, my kirk was to be linked with the nearby rural parish of Oathlaw and Tannadice. The readjustment could take place only when one of the ministers moved, and in 1996 Tannadice suffered the loss of its minister. I felt it was unfair that the members of Tannadice should have an unknown minister settled upon them as a result of this move, and rather than have that happen I decided I would retire early from St.

Andrew's to allow the linking to take place. I was of course recompensed by the church for any loss of earnings involved in this procedure, which is termed demission. Despite the fact that this all took place with the best motives on all sides, I still felt that events had somehow manipulated me out of my parish, and I felt quite unhappy about it all.

The week-end following the Presbytery Meeting at which I intimated my decision, I conducted my final service at St Andrew's, Kirriemuir, which would be the last time I would conduct worship as the ordained minister of a church of my own. On 10th November 1996 I gave a short speech after the close of worship, summing up my feelings after eight years as the minister and expressing my thanks to everyone who had supported me, together with my wife, Margaret.

Chapter Ten: Completely Unexpected Far Countries

I called this book 'Many a Far Country' for reasons which seemed obvious to me at the time. However, it will have been clear that apart from my army service in Germany, and certainly since our marriage in 1956, Margaret and I had no experience of really far countries. We had lived in London, Aberdeen, Glasgow, Glenrothes, Jura and Kirriemuir. Until we moved to Jura in 1975, our annual holidays were spent in the Hebridean islands of Islay and Jura. With two growing children, and an assortment of dogs and cats, the possibility of exploring any countries beyond Scotland never really arose, and certainly never featured in any plans we might have had.

I suppose, with our previous lack of experience of travel, it was all the more extraordinary that we decided to embark on our American adventure in 1986. There is no doubt that it changed Margaret and me for ever. In our time in the USA we were honoured guests, but we found the countless church services and lectures and the continual changes of hospitality homes very wearing. However, the times we spent on our own exploring wildlife parks like the Okefenokee Swamp were experiences that drew us closer than we had perhaps ever been. The final month of our trip when we drove our hired car from the east coast to the west was something we never forgot. Not only did we have an opportunity to see the vastness of the USA, but we were immensely impressed by the National Parks we visited, like Mesa Verde, the Grand Canyon, the Organ

Pipe Cactus Reserve and the Sequoias. We ended our trip in Los Angeles and San Francisco.

Although we had no reason to anticipate any major changes in our life style in the future, or any change in our finances, we returned from the United States with a real taste for visiting foreign countries, which would in fact never go away.

Paris and a Return to the USA

In April 1989 we decided that it was time we saw Paris, and we made a short visit. April in Paris was for ever memorable for the extremely low temperatures we experienced there. We had not expected to find snow lying on the steps of the Eiffel Tower. However the art galleries, the famous sights, and the wonderful food were everything we had hoped for.

Later in the same year I was invited to be chaplain to the famous Highland Games of Lumberton in North Carolina. This was an expenses paid trip, and let us meet again all our friends from 1986. We felt immediately at home, and found a lot to enjoy. The photos of Margaret and me standing in front of the manse in Kirriemuir – with me in full Highland Dress and Margaret in her long tartan skirt – remain one of the most joyful images of our later life together.

All these travels awakened an appetite in us, and with the children long away from home, and the remoteness of Jura no longer the barrier it had been to travel, we could now very much please ourselves in what we did.

Our First Adventure in France

In 1990 we decided that our brief visit to Paris had merely whetted our appetite for France, and we drove all the way from Kirriemuir to Bordeaux. We visited the famous vineyards of the Medoc. We stayed in Cahors and saw the magnificent painted caves of Pech Merle. We toured the valleys of the Lot and Célé, going to Sarlat and Rocamadour. The high point was our visit to Lascaux II. This is the modern replica of the original caves with their amazing prehistoric wall paintings.

P.Y. had always said that the D.Y. Cameron etching of my old enemy the Devil of the staircase was a gargoyle on a French cathedral he called

Poitiers-Tours. We stopped on our French journey to see several famous cathedrals, but the Devil didn't put in an appearance.

We were saddened by the deaths of my father and mother in 1991. However, although this closed one chapter in my life, it opened another. Margaret and I chose to ignore completely my father's advice that we should invest all of his capital, and spend as little as possible. We decided that we would spend as much as we felt we ought to. I have already mentioned our retirement home, in which we both were immediately very happy. We also improved the quality of our life by buying some modern appliances and a better car, but the main change we experienced was the new sense of freedom we had to engage in further travels abroad.

Florence and Rome

We had always longed to see the great Italian Renaissance art works, and in 1991 we spent a week in Florence and another in Rome. In Florence we loved the Fra Angelico paintings at the Museo San Marco, with their individual cells. Michelangelo's statue of David was a joy to behold, and the Uffizi Gallery had wonders like Botticelli's 'Primavera'.

By this time we had done the research on our D.Y. Cameron etching that we should have done before going to all those French cathedrals. We now knew he wasn't a gargoyle at all, but a bronze by Giambologna, and that he lived in the Bargello museum in Florence. He was famously called 'The Little Imp of Florence'. There was no sign of him where he was reputed to be in the Bargello, but with the help of the museum staff and a lady called Beatrice Strozzi we were sent to the Vecchio to see Signor Sottanei. He took us specially to see the Imp in a part of the gallery that was being restored. This was a wonderful gesture as the floor was all temporary boards. We had finally found the model for our D.Y. Cameron etching and I took lots of photos.

We hired a car and drove all over the wonderful countryside around Florence, visiting San Gimignano, with its weird towers. We brought home two little porcelain angels from the Ponte Vecchio, from a man who offered to take me out truffle hunting with him. Sadly, time ran out before we could go!

We went on to spend a week in Rome. We saw all the famous sights. We visited the Sistine Chapel. There was absolutely no one there when we first got inside, and we were able to take our time as the other visitors gradually arrived. Near the Roman Forum we had the unpleasant experience of being importuned by Gipsy Children.

From Rome we went to Pompeii. This was a coach trip, and took all day, going through fine country with views of Vesuvius and Naples. Pompeii was marvellous and the guide was excellent. The whole tour was very exciting. This was one of our magic visits.

Our first visit to Italy was absolutely wonderful. We saw everything we had hoped to see and much, much more. It was also a bit exhausting, and we walked much further than we would have liked. The people were friendly and the food was magnificent. We both resolved to go back!

France again and a Third Visit to the States

In 1992 we went back to France. This time we flew to Bordeaux and hired a car. We drove up the superb valleys to the Spanish border, and saw many beautiful alpine flowers, and spectacular butterflies. We had decided that Lyn, our daughter, should be asked to accompany us, and the three of us had a happy time together. We had been told that a small narrow valley high in the Pyrenees had Griffon Vultures breeding successfully. This we felt we had to see. We stopped overlooking a cliff and a deep broad ravine. As I scanned the valley with my binoculars, Lyn grabbed my elbow.

'Look Dad,' she said, 'It's the gang!'

I looked where she pointed, and there they were – all five of them, flying in tight formation, wing tip to wing tip. They looked quite menacing, but also faintly absurd, with overtones of the Disney film of 'The Jungle Book'. It was a moment never to be forgotten.

Later in 1992 we made a third visit to the States. This time we could afford a simple holiday. We drove from Washington to the Outer Banks to see the Wright Brothers Centre at Kitty Hawk. We visited many friends, and then went south to the Bayous, and up the Natchez Trace to Memphis, from where we flew home. The hired car showed 3,000 miles at the end of the journey: another trip full of wonderful experiences.

The Holy Land and Norway

In January 1993 we went to the Holy Land as part of an introductory tour. We saw all the famous locations associated with the historical Jesus of Nazareth, but were profoundly disappointed by the experience. Sadly we found that the places we had had such high hopes for, like Bethlehem, the Sea of Galilee, Capernaum, Cana in Galilee, and perhaps most of all Jerusalem, had all been so exploited by Jesus' various groups of followers down the ages that it was hard to find any trace of him at all. The sites that had no connection with Jesus, such as the Port of Joppa and Qumran and the Dead Sea Scrolls, seemed to us to be splendid. We thought seriously about going back to Palestine on our own. We thought that we might manage to make a more realistic contact with Jesus' life and country on our own, but we never managed to organise it.

In April 1993 we took the car by ship to Bergen in Norway, and did a long driving tour, seeing fabulous fjords and high mountains. On the spectacular Stardalen road Margaret saw an avalanche. I was facing the wrong way when she shouted, and by the time I had turned around it was all over. I had missed it! It became, and then always remained, 'Margaret's avalanche.' We saw many famous places such as Alesund, the Trollswegen, and the Romdalshorn. The high Hardangervidda road was just open, and gave us an extraordinary experience of the great snow fields of Norway's interior. We enjoyed our visit, but felt no great inclination to return.

The Road to Bukittinggi

Late in 1993 I spotted an advertisement in a magazine. A travel company were offering a journey to the Hill Stations of the Malay Peninsula and the Island of Sumatra. The trip was entitled 'The Road to Bukittinggi'. It was for nineteen days and the cost was £1600 per person from Heathrow. I knew from my reading that Bukittinggi was very close to the parts of the Sumatran Jungle where the biggest flower in the world, the Giant Rafflesia, grows. Inquiries revealed that during the stopover at Bukittinggi it would be possible to hire a guide to go into the jungle and look for this plant. I had known about Rafflesia since I read about it in

Arthur Mee's *Children's Encyclopedia*, when I was a little boy being ill in bed. I knew what it looked like and what it smelt like, and I knew a good deal about Sir Thomas Raffles, who had discovered it and named it and also, incidentally, founded Singapore.

Margaret said that I persistently left this advertisement lying about in conspicuous places, and brought it out again if she tidied it away. She finally worked out that I was desperate to go, and although she was horrified by the prospect of spending all that time on a coach with twenty other travellers, she generously agreed that we would sign up for the trip.

We flew to Kuala Lumpur early in February 1994. The coach was soon climbing into the highlands with hairpin bends. There were forests all round and wonderful views. We stayed at Fraser's Hill, and I went off to do a bird walk led by Duria, who was a born-again Christian, and a member of the RSPB! I saw twenty-eight new kinds of bird including the Great Hornbill.

Later, on the long road to Cameron Highlands, we saw rubber tapping and bamboo basket weaving, and visited an Orang Asli village. These people are the aboriginal natives of this part of Malaysia and a few small colonies hang on in the jungle. They were delightful, and we were allowed to try blowing darts at a target from a blowpipe.

The tour took us to a tea plantation, and ultimately to Penang from where we flew to Sumatra. We visited many exciting places. I bought a flute and Margaret bought some batik cloth. At our hotel at Parapat we laid out all our changed currency, now rupiahs, on our bed, and found we were millionaires!

Later at Lake Toba I bought a fabulous carved stick to use in telling church children's addresses. Unfortunately the theme of the carving turned out to be a story unsuitable for children. One morning I found a huge rhinoceros beetle which had been attracted to the hotel lights. We crossed the Equator at Bonjol at 6.30 pm just before dusk. We took photos and bought T shirts.

We went on to Bukittinggi. We were now in West Sumatra, the home of the Minankabau people who live in beautiful houses with tall buffalo horn roofs. In due course I engaged my jungle guide and set off to see Rafflesia. The guide was splendid and produced buds and dead Rafflesia flowers, and then finally a giant bud just about to open. Second best –

but what a second best! I was over the moon! Our flights home were without incident, although very long.

There were some drawbacks to our Far East trip. We often felt not very well. The food was uniformly poor and expensive. Nevertheless, I enjoyed myself enormously, and saw many things I could never have previously dreamed I would ever see, and of which I still have the most vivid memories now, fourteen years later. Margaret said she had some good times too, but the whole thing for her was overshadowed by simply hating the business of a coach trip, about which she simply said: 'Never again!'

Siena and Assisi

In May 1995 we went back to Italy. This time we chose to visit Siena and Assisi. We loved the churches and galleries of Siena, and saw famous paintings by Duccio and Simone Martini. We walked round the streets a good deal and learned about the 'contradas', the territorial ancient clans of Siena. At the end of our first week we went on to Assisi. We visited all the famous religious sights, and drove in alpine meadows near Mount Sabasio. We saw lots of alpine flowers. This description doesn't sound very exciting, but we took a great deal of quiet pleasure from the quite ordinary places we saw, especially the many small towns which were off the main tourist trail. We still had the same strong feelings about Italy and contemplated a further visit in the future.

The West Coast of Ireland

In May 1996 we decided to spend a fortnight in Ireland. We went first to Dublin where I wanted to see the Book of Kells. There was of course only one double page open to view, but it was still inspiring for me.

After Dublin we drove to the west coast and Killarney. We drove round the Ring of Kerry and the Dingle peninsula. Leaving Killarney we went to Limerick, and the famous Burren. Almost at once we got into limestone clints and grikes, an amazing landscape!

We toured Galway and Sligo, finding lots of literary sites and some wonderful sea shells on the west coast beaches. Back home the car showed 2,200 miles. Ireland was great fun, and we had a happy time.

Further Travel

I see that this travelogue has now gone on for some pages, and I am beginning to lose confidence in it. Reading it may be a bit like looking at someone else's holiday photos. I will summarise our travels in the years after 1996 which are the years of my retirement. We visited Malta in 1998. We found the archaeology interesting, but were horrified by the widespread slaughter of migrating wild birds.

In 2001 we went to Amsterdam, and enjoyed the city and its famous paintings. Vermeer and Rembrandt made a deep impression.

In 2003 we went back to Italy, this time to stay in Verona and Padua. We felt we got less mileage out of this trip, although we had a very happy time together.

The Somme and our English Cathedrals

Two other projects engaged our interest during the past few years. The first came from researching the circumstances in which three of Margaret's relatives – two uncles and a Scottish cousin – were killed in the battles of the Somme. We went twice to the battlefields, and at the end we felt we had done something to bring recognition of their sacrifice to our own generation, and to record it for our successors.

We also spent a good deal of time since the millennium visiting the cathedrals of England. We were never completely confident that we hadn't missed one or two, but we actually set foot in almost fifty, and found it a most exciting project. Every cathedral we visited was quite unique, and many made deep impressions on us: not only because of their architecture – stained glass, spires and the like – but because of the extraordinary range of different kinds of welcome we were given as we made our visits.

As I look back over the past twenty years, I am amazed at the variety of countries we managed to see, and my mind is filled with wonderful memories of the times Margaret and I spent in visiting them.

Chapter Eleven: My Final Far Countries – Retirement

After the dust had settled on my resignation from St Andrew's, I remember thinking: 'Everything has fallen apart! I've made the worst decision of my life, and I've lost my church! What on earth am I going to do now?' I suppose I was bound to suffer some kind of reaction. After all I had been an ordained minister of the Church of Scotland for thirty-five years, and suddenly I didn't have a church.

It all brought back something which had happened ten years earlier, while we were in Jura. The congregation had worked out my milestones, and had calculated that I was going to have been twenty-five years in the ministry in May 1986. They decided to hold a Semi-Jubilee Social for Margaret and myself. I told my mother and father in Perth about this event although they were by that time not fit to make the journey to be with us. On the day itself I had a phone call from my parents' own minister, with whom they were very good friends.

'I hear it's going to be your Semi-Jubilee tonight in Jura', he said. 'I wondered if it would be a happy idea for me to go and spend the same period of time with your mother and father this evening.'

I told the minister that I thought it was an inspired thought, and that I would take it very kindly if he did as he suggested.

The party on Jura was splendid and was enjoyed by the whole island as well as by Margaret and me. The following day, my father's minister telephoned me to report on his own visit which, he told me, had gone very well. I was very pleased, and grateful, and said so. He had more to report, however.

He said: 'Your father said a curious thing.'

My heart sank somewhat, but I asked him please to go on.

'Well, I said: "Now, Mr Youngson, you must be very proud of Peter. Twenty-five years completed in the Ministry of the Church of Scotland."

"Oh well," he said, "Perhaps he's found something he's going to stick at."'

Five years later in 1991, when my father was eighty-six and suddenly died, I was still sticking at it, which I hope had given him some satisfaction. The story reminded me forcibly of the days when he used to come home and announce that he had made an appointment for me to start as a street sweeper in Aberdeen. The three years from my departure from Jura until his death had been very satisfactory for both of us, in that we had been able to finally get a bit closer than we had been during all those earlier years.

Strangely enough, the two topics we seemed to be able to discuss in safety were the same ones which are usually banned from discussion in public houses – politics and religion.

My father was a lifelong dyed-in-the-wool Tory, and I had always been fairly left-wing. It sounded like a recipe for conflict, but I think we both knew it wasn't a life-or-death topic. When Margaret Thatcher was returned to power, my father would telephone me early in the morning of the result to gloat. When Tony Blair finally got into No.10, I was on the point of phoning my father early in the morning, when it suddenly came to me that he been dead for several years by that time. I shed more than a few tears.

We could discuss the church on a similar basis, because my father felt that it was going to the dogs, and I had a good deal of sympathy with his many complaints, which centred on modern versions of the scriptures and new hymns he didn't know.

To return to 1996: life suddenly centred on Margaret, as it had finally been decided that she should have two artificial knee joints. She was admitted to Stracathro Hospital on 25th November, and when I went to the hospital that night she had had both knees replaced in a procedure which had lasted about six hours. She looked pretty poorly, but was much livelier the next morning. She was up and walking within a couple of days, and with splendid physiotherapy, she came home on the ninth day after surgery. Physiotherapy continued for a number of weeks, and her new knees functioned well from the very start. It was plainly a new lease of life for her to be without pain, and we were able to begin to go for short walks together, which was a great joy.

My First Locums

I suppose I was still smarting from the loss of my parish at the beginning of 1997, but I had decided to look forward, and planned to take on some locums.

I had already decided that this was the year when I would start to work seriously on my notes about Jura, with a view to publishing a major book on the island. The fact that I had never been able to find enough time to tackle this project since I left the island in 1987 now made me very determined to give the project a much higher priority.

My willingness to do locums was taken up quickly. In February 1997 Margaret and I went to Caithness to look after Canisbay linked with Keiss for a month, and I followed that with with an appointment at the big church of St Margaret's in Forfar, where I stayed for a whole year. This was an interesting time, which involved me in more bereavement work than I had ever experienced before. I conducted almost one hundred funerals in the year.

In January 1999 I took on the churches of Newtonmore and Laggan for nine months while their minister was ill. During this appointment in Speyside we commuted from Kirriemuir for two days each week, and I was determined to use this period to get my book on Jura really on the move. I made a habit of going into my study first thing on Wednesday morning each week, and working steadily for most of Thursday and Friday. On Saturdays I did my preparation for Sunday. This approach worked very well and I began to see completed chapters of the book mounting up. In April I managed to spend some time in Register House in Edinburgh, confirming archive records for Jura – especially in connection with the Campbell of Jura Papers. The locum at Newtonmore lasted until August, and by the time it came to an end I felt that I had broken the back of the book project and, although there was still obviously a great deal to do, I could see the end in sight.

Early in 2000 I was asked to do another locum, this time in Rothesay, at a church called Trinity. This started in May, and we stayed for two months. I tried to treat this locum like all the others, and restrict my parish work to Sundays and two week-days, although it was not always possible. I had brought all my Jura book material to Rothesay, and I managed to spend at least two days a week working on the book.

The Jura Book

By New Year 2000 I felt I was really making a lot of progress with my book on Jura, and just as I was pushing on to complete it, a letter arrived from the Director of Birlinn, the Edinburgh publisher, reminding me of an earlier discussion about a Jura book, and inquiring about progress.

I replied in May sending a summary of my approach to the book and a variety of general comments. I enclosed several completed chapters.

I waited anxiously for a response to this letter. To my great surprise, a letter arrived within a week, making a firm commitment to publish the book, and looking at publication in 2001.

I was immensely excited to receive this letter. I did in fact push on with the text, and my diary has an entry for Tuesday, 20th October 2000: 'Jura Book Finished'. I took the completed text to Edinburgh, and on 2nd November a Memorandum of Agreement (my contract with my publisher) was drawn up for signing.

My book turned out to be much too long, but I was allowed to make all the necessary cuts myself. My original draft had many long appendices, and all of these simply were not included. They contained population studies, such as the Baptismal Register, the 1841 Census, and graveyard records, together with my extensive lists of all the major groups of wildlife: flowers, birds, insects, fungi etc. I had prepared these lists myself, and in due course I produced my own copies, and consigned all of them to the Jura Historical Society at its premises on the island. They now reside in the Society's archives, where they can be consulted on Jura itself.

Jura – Island of Deer was published in hardback by Birlinn, and went on sale at £30.00 per copy. It was launched in Islay and in Jura Hall in July

2001. My good friend Angus Ewart set up an opportunity for it also to be launched in Kirriemuir in his Art Shop on 24th July. It was immensely exciting to see the book actually in print and on sale and I did author's signings at all the launches.

Despite many ups and downs in its progress to publication, the book emerged into bookshops very much as I had first envisaged it.

In my book I tried to deal with as many aspects of the island of Jura as I could think of, and I am sure that it is the most comprehensive account of the island ever to have been published, as I tried hard to avoid the limits imposed by the personal enthusiasms of earlier writers.

I was of course worried that the arrival of the book would be completely ignored by the world at large, and that my work would disappear without trace. This did not happen.

The reviews of my book on Jura were uniformly splendid and very encouraging. I am proud to set out some phrases taken from them here:

'Throughout this account of Jura, Youngson is the perfect guide. Forget dry learning and canyons of lists. Youngson is at his happiest when he is putting humanity back in the picture. This is a good book, encyclopaedic and entertaining, and deserves a wide readership to match its virtues.'

'The author of this delightfully old-fashioned book stands in that long tradition of scholarly parsons who have totally absorbed themselves in the life of a rural parish, and whose enthusiasm for local history, topography, flora and fauna is every bit as fervent and as contagious as their desire to save souls.'

One reviewer called the book 'a labour of love'.

USA reviewers did me proud, and on our visit to Red Springs in 2002 the copies of the book vanished like snow! I was immensely pleased to receive a lot of personal letters from friends and family who had got a copy of the book. I treasure a large collection of these.

In due course Birlinn let me know that the hardback issue of the book had virtually sold out. This meant that 1250 copies of the book were out in the wider world. This is a source of great satisfaction to me.

The paperback version was published in September 2003. The run of this issue was also 1250 copies. The paperback apparently sold well, although I believe that at this time of writing copies are still available.

In June 2002 we did another locum in Caithness, at Dunbeath, Latheron and Berriedale. This lasted for six weeks.

Back in Angus I was almost at once asked to do another locum at Carmyllie, Colliston and Arbirlot. I was appointed from Sunday, 11th August 2002, and stayed until February 2003.

After I finished this appointment I decided to do no more locums.

In the spring of 2004 I found myself approaching my seventieth birthday, and this seemed like a reasonable time to retire from preaching and other ministerial duties. I put it about that I was no longer available for pulpit supply or helping colleagues out with funerals.

I write these words in 2008, and I have taken on no ministerial duties since the end of 2003. Although in this matter I definitely jumped before I was pushed, I have very seldom had feelings of regret about it.

On 14th May 2004 I celebrated my 70th birthday, and as I write these words I am now past seventy-four. My mind is still full of memories of the things that have happened to me in the 'Many Far Countries' I have visited over the years, some of which I have set down here. I have no ambitions to visit any more Far Countries, and hope to pass my remaining years here in Kirriemuir.

I had always hoped that I would be able to share such time as was left for me with my beloved wife, Margaret, but I have to record that that is no longer part of my future.

Margaret was diagnosed with ovarian cancer in March 2008. We were encouraged to believe that her tumour would respond to chemotherapy, and she did in fact start having treatment for it. Margaret was apparently responding very well. We were at this point in the procedure very happy together, and were both immensely optimistic about a shared future, for possibly a few more years. Unfortunately, Margaret had an unexpected heart attack in Ninewells Hospital on 12th June, 2008, while waiting for her routine treatment, and died in a very few minutes.

I am now experiencing something which as a Parish Minister I had to deal with professionally over many years – namely the death of my closest companion and intimate friend of more than fifty-two years. I am glad that, as I look back over the many bereavements I have tried to help people with, I don't think I have ever offered trite comments or shallow advice. I think I have probably restricted myself to trying to create and conduct helpful funerals, and to assuring the bereaved that I would be 'thinking of them.'

As I face up to living out my remaining years without my beloved Margaret, I am grateful for the enormous help and insight I have received from my daughter Lyn; my son Donald, and the members of both their families: also for the loyal and constructive support I have had from an exceptional circle of close friends.

This little book is dedicated to Margaret, and although she is mentioned by name in its pages only seldom, in all the chapters which relate to my life after she and I met in 1955, she is actually present in my heart on every single page.